THE

OXFORD BOOK OF

APHORISMS

JOHN GROSS is a writer and reviewer, and has been theatre critic of the *Sunday Telegraph* since 1989. He was editor of the *Times Literary Supplement* from 1974 to 1981 and on the staff of the *New York Times* from 1983 to 1988. His books include *Shylock: A Legend and its Legacy* (1992) and the memoir *A Double Thread* (2001). He is the editor of the *Oxford Book of Essays* (1991, 2002), *The Oxford Book of Comic Verse* (1994, 2002), *The New Oxford Book of English Prose* (1999), and *After Shakespeare: an Anthology*, published in 2002 to rave reviews.

THE
OXFORD BOOK OF
APHORISMS

CHOSEN BY
JOHN GROSS

OXFORD
UNIVERSITY PRESS

*This book has been printed digitally and produced in a standard specification
in order to ensure its continuing availability*

OXFORD
UNIVERSITY PRESS

Great Clarendon Street, Oxford OX2 6DP

Oxford University Press is a department of the University of Oxford.
It furthers the University's objective of excellence in research, scholarship,
and education by publishing worldwide in

Oxford New York

Auckland   Cape Town   Dar es Salaam   Hong Kong   Karachi
Kuala Lumpur   Madrid   Melbourne   Mexico City   Nairobi
New Delhi   Shanghai   Taipei   Toronto
With offices in

Argentina   Austria   Brazil   Chile   Czech Republic   France   Greece
Guatemala   Hungary   Italy   Japan   South Korea   Poland   Portugal
Singapore   Switzerland   Thailand   Turkey   Ukraine   Vietnam

Oxford is a registered trade mark of Oxford University Press
in the UK and in certain other countries

Published in the United States
by Oxford University Press Inc., New York

Introduction and compilation © John Gross 1983

ISBN 978-0-19-280456-3

Contents

❀

Introduction	vii
Aphorists & Aphorisms I	1
Nature	3
Religion	10
Mankind	20
Life	28
Desires & Longings	33
Fears, Hopes, Passions	38
Design & Chance	44
Individuals	50
The Sense of Identity	54
Self-Love	59
Self-Knowledge	67
Self-Doubt	72
One Among Many	77
Fame & Reputation	86
The Arts of Success	90
Action & Achievement	96
Money & Rank	101
The Social Fabric	106
Politics	115
Rulers	126
Friends & Foes	133
Sympathies & Antipathies	140
Men, Women, Marriage	146
Love, Jealousy, Libido	153
Happiness & Sorrow	166
Good & Evil	174

Vices & Virtues   184
The Moralist   195
Praise & Blame   201
Conversation & Manners   208
Secrets   214
True & False   218
Illusion & Reality   225
Thinking & Reasoning   229
Wisdom & Folly   240
Intelligence & Insight   247
Beliefs & Opinions   253
Knowledge & Ignorance   263
Learning & Teaching   267
Memories, Dreams, Expectations   272
The Human Comedy   276
Language   280
The Written Word   285
Artists & Authors   291
The Arts   297
Criticism, Judgement, Taste   305
Great & Small   312
History & the Passing Generations   319
In Sickness & In Health   326
Pleasures & Penalties   329
The Family   334
Young & Old   338
Time & Transience   346
Observations & Oddities   351
Death   355
The Afterlife   362
Aphorists & Aphorisms II   364
Acknowledgements   367
Index   375

Introduction

❀

THE earliest aphorisms – the first to go by that name, at least – were a collection of brief medical teachings and sayings by Hippocrates, and when the term was revived in the Renaissance it initially looked back to its scientific origins. In the words of the *Oxford English Dictionary*, it signified 'a concise statement of a principle in any science'. Soon, however, it came to denote the formulation of a moral or philosophical principle as well, and gradually this took over as its accepted everyday meaning. By the early eighteenth century the shift was so complete that it was possible for the physician and versifier Sir Richard Blackmore to feel safe in loftily dismissing the *Aphorisms* of Hippocrates as nothing more than 'a book of jests', of worldly-wise commonplaces – a blunder which enabled Dr Johnson, in the *Lives of the Poets*, to make short work of Blackmore's scholarly pretensions and his 'supercilious derision of transmitted knowledge'.

Johnson himself defined an aphorism, in what was by then its current sense, as 'a maxim; a precept contracted in a short sentence; an unconnected position'. 'A maxim' is also one of the definitions in the *OED* (along with 'a short pithy statement containing a truth of general import'); and if we go on to recall that the most famous of all collections of aphorisms, La Rochefoucauld's, is entitled *Maximes*, we can hardly avoid concluding that 'maxim' is as close as we are likely to get to a synonym. Yet although the two words certainly overlap, they are far from interchangeable. An *Oxford Book of Maxims* would not, I think, sound particularly inviting: all too often a maxim suggests a tag, a stock response, something waiting to be trotted out in the spirit of Polonius. Aphorisms tend to be distinctly more subversive; indeed, it is often a maxim that they set out to subvert. And they are less cut and dried, more speculative and glancing. One need only think of the labels under which many of them first saw the light – observations, reflections, *pensées*, 'discoveries', 'detached thoughts'. Still others began life in an even more fragmentary way, as notebook jottings or random flashes of insight.

Without losing ourselves in a wilderness of definitions, we can all agree that the most obvious characteristic of an aphorism, apart from its brevity, is that it is a generalization. It offers a comment on some recurrent aspect of life, couched in terms which are meant to be permanently and universally applicable. But the same could be said of proverbs; and aphorisms, unlike proverbs, have authors. The third distinguishing mark of the aphorism, in fact, is that it is a form of literature, and often a highly idiosyncratic or self-conscious form at that. It bears the stamp and style of the mind which created it; its message is universal, but scarcely impersonal; it may embody a twist of thought strong enough to retain its force in translation, but it also depends for its full effect on verbal artistry, on a subtle or concentrated perfection of phrasing which can sometimes approach poetry in its intensity. (At the same time one should add that compression is not necessarily the supreme stylistic virtue in an aphorism, and that the finest examples are not always the most terse. A good aphorism – and here too it differs from a proverb, which has to slip off the tongue – may well need to expand beyond the confines of a single sentence.)

An aphorism, finally, has to be able to stand by itself; as Johnson said, it is an 'unconnected' proposition. Yet in practice many aphorisms are also retorts and ripostes, shafts aimed at the champions of an established viewpoint or a shallower morality. They tease and prod the lazy assumptions lodged in the reader's mind; they warn us how insidiously our vices can pass themselves off as virtues; they harp shamelessly on the imperfections and contradictions which we would rather ignore. There are times when the very form of the aphorism seems to lend itself to a disenchanted view of human nature. Anxious to distance himself from the platitude, the aphorist is drawn towards the unsettling paradox. Compelled to exercise his wit in a narrow compass, he takes pleasure in the cynical thrust, the *mauvaise pensée* – and naturally we respond. As a notable connoisseur of aphorisms, Logan Pearsall Smith, once wrote, 'a malicious thought, a *cattivo pensiero*, as the Italians call it, we are apt to find – such is our fallen nature – more amusing than a charitable one'. But then we reach a point at which cynicism palls. A reaction sets in: after simple truth has been miscalled simplicity for long enough it begins to look rather more interesting than it did, and for that matter rather less simple. And this too is the aphorist's province: to renovate old truths, and refine on rough estimates.

Anyone hoping to represent the whole range of aphoristic literature is in fact liable to come up with as many contrasts as parallels, as many discords as variations. The aphorists quarrel among themselves: Blake denounces Bacon for purveying 'Good Advice for Satan's Kingdom' in his essays, Vauvenargues rebukes La Rochefoucauld for libelling our common humanity. The greatest of them tend to be inwardly divided, too, haunted by irreconcilable conclusions and torn between rival impulses. And there are of course as many different kinds of aphorism as aphorist: aphorisms which cut and aphorisms which glow, classic aphorisms and romantic aphorisms, aphorisms which deflate and aphorisms (rather fewer) which console. It is true that most minor practitioners of the art remain of the world, worldly, and that in its decadence the wit of the salon tradition can easily degenerate into the mere wisecrack. But the masters – the secular prophets, the Emersons and Nietzsches, no less than their religious precursors – are at least as likely to strike an oracular or metaphysical note, to probe into the mysterious depths of experience. And yet they in turn generally have their own fund of worldliness and urbanity.

For all this profusion, an anthologist who adopts too strict a definition of the aphorism runs the risk, as he goes on, of producing a certain deadening effect. When I began making the present selection I considered limiting myself to what might be called the aphorism pure and simple – the brief direct statement, A equals B. But it was soon borne in on me that to read a series of such pronouncements in unbroken succession would be to diminish their value, that one would eventually be left with a rat-tat-tat of 'one-liners'. (Wagner said that collections of aphorisms always reminded him of performing fleas – an unfair reaction, needless to say, prompted by hostility to Nietzsche, but one knows what he meant.) And in any case, few aphorists themselves have been willing to submit to such a self-denying ordinance. It seemed to make better sense, on reflection, to interpret the idea of aphoristic writing more loosely, and as a result I have included a fair number of slightly longer passages, some poetry, a few mock-aphorisms, a sprinkling of miscellaneous outbursts and oddities. Once or twice I have also broken the rule which says that aphorisms ought to deal with universals rather than particulars – but only, I hope, when the epigram in question readily lends itself to a more extended application.

Like many anthologists, I owe a considerable debt to previous anthologies. This is particularly true in the case of the minor French aphorists, where I have taken advantage both of older selections such as those by Solly (*A Cynic's Breviary*) and de Finod (*A Thousand Flashes of French Wit, Wisdom and Wickedness*), and two major contemporary dictionaries of *citations françaises*, those published by Robert and by Larousse. I am also indebted to the work of a contemporary English enthusiast, Denis Brearley's *From the French* (Leeds, 1973).

The dates following sources cited are generally those of publication.

but in a number of instances (usually when a work was first published posthumously) it has seemed to me more helpful to give the date or approximate date of composition. In the case of correspondence, journals, notebooks and so forth, the date (with a few obvious exceptions) is that of the individual letter or entry.

There is one gap in this anthology which I particularly regret. I had hoped to include a number of aphorisms by Wittgenstein, drawn principally from *Philosophical Investigations* (1953) and *Culture and Value* (1980), but unfortunately permission to do so was refused by his literary executors. I am grateful to Christopher Ricks, Pat Rogers and J. P. Stern for help in tracking down a number of quotations.

JOHN GROSS

Aphorists & Aphorisms

I

Everything has been said before, but since nobody listens we have to keep going back and beginning all over again.

> ANDRÉ GIDE, *Le traité du Narcisse*, 1891

Good things, when short, are twice as good.

> GRACIÁN, *The Art of Worldly Wisdom*, 1647

The most attractive sentences are not perhaps the wisest, but the surest and soundest.

> THOREAU, *Journal*, 1842

A new maxim is often a brilliant error.

> MALESHERBES, *Pensées et maximes*, mid-18th century

Summaries that contain most things are always shortest themselves.

> SAMUEL BUTLER (I), *Prose Observations*, 1660–80

It is my ambition to say in ten sentences what other men say in whole books – what other men do *not* say in whole books.

> NIETZSCHE, *Twilight of the Idols*, 1888

Men's maxims reveal their characters.

> VAUVENARGUES, *Reflections and Maxims*, 1746

The hunter for aphorisms on human nature has to fish in muddy water, and he is even condemned to find much of his own mind.

> F. H. BRADLEY, *Aphorisms*, 1930

Maximiste, pessimiste.

> JOSEPH ROUX, *Meditations of a Parish Priest*, 1886

There must be more malice than love in the hearts of all wits.

B. R. HAYDON, *Table Talk*, early 19th century

The malice of a good thing is the barb that makes it stick.

SHERIDAN, *The School for Scandal*, 1783

A perfectly healthy sentence is extremely rare.

THOREAU, *Journal*, 1841

There are things which don't deserve to be said briefly.

JEAN ROSTAND, *De la vanité*, 1925

For aphorisms, except they should be ridiculous, cannot be made but of the pith and heart of sciences; for discourse of illustration is cut off; recitals of examples are cut off; discourse of order and connexion is cut off; descriptions of practice are cut off. So there remaineth nothing to fill the aphorisms but some good quality of observation.

SIR FRANCIS BACON, *The Advancement of Learning*, 1605

Remarks are not literature.

GERTRUDE STEIN, *The Autobiography of Alice B. Toklas*, 1933

The only way to read a book of aphorisms without being bored is to open it at random and, having found something that interests you, close the book and meditate.

PRINCE DE LIGNE, *Mes écarts*, 1796

Nature

❁

The universe ought to be presumed too vast to have any character.

        C. S. PEIRCE, *Collected Papers*, VI, late 19th–early 20th century

All things come to their fulfilment as the one universal Nature directs; for there is no rival Nature, whether containing her from without, or itself contained within her, or even existing apart and detached from her.

        MARCUS AURELIUS, *Meditations*, 2nd century

My suspicion is that the universe is not only queerer than we suppose, but queerer than we *can* suppose.

        J. B. S. HALDANE, *Possible Worlds*, 1927

God could cause us considerable embarrassment by revealing all the secrets of nature to us: we should not know what to do for sheer apathy and boredom.

        GOETHE, cit. Riemer, *Memoirs*

But perhaps the universe is suspended on the tooth of some monster.

        CHEKHOV, *Notebooks*, 1892–1904

Everything in the universe goes by indirection. There are no straight lines.

        EMERSON, 'Works and Days', *Society and Solitude*, 1870

Anything that is deliberate, twisted, created as a trap and a mystery, must be discovered at last; everything that is done naturally remains mysterious.

        G. K. CHESTERTON, *Robert Browning*, 1903

Individuality seems to be Nature's whole aim – and she cares nothing for individuals.

        GOETHE, *Maxims and Reflections*, early 19th century

All the thoughts of a turtle are turtle.

EMERSON, *Journals*, 1855

Probably a crab would be filled with a sense of personal outrage if it could hear us class it without ado or apology as a crustacean, and thus dispose of it. 'I am no such thing,' it would say: 'I am MYSELF, MYSELF alone.'

WILLIAM JAMES, *Varieties of Religious Experience*, 1902

Just as foolish as it must look to a crab when it sees a man walk forward.

LICHTENBERG, *Aphorisms*, 1764–99

The endless variety in the world has not been created by law. It is not of the nature of uniformity to originate variation, nor of law to beget circumstance.

C. S. PEIRCE, *Collected Papers*, VI, late 19th–early 20th century

It may be that the stars of heaven appear fair and pure simply because they are so far away from us, and we know nothing of their private life.

HEINE, *The Romantic School*, 1833

The sun, we say, is the cause of heat, but the heat *is* the sun, here on this window-ledge.

MARK RUTHERFORD, *More Pages from a Journal*, 1910

A drop of water is not immortal; it can be resolved into oxygen and hydrogen. If, therefore, a drop of water were to maintain that it had a quality of aqueousness which would survive its dissolution we should be inclined to be sceptical.

BERTRAND RUSSELL, *What I Believe*, 1925

Water is H_2O, hydrogen two parts, oxygen one,
but there is also a third thing, that makes it water
and nobody knows what that is.

D. H. LAWRENCE, 'The Third Thing', *Pansies*, 1929

Even stones have a love, a love that seeks the ground.

MEISTER ECKHART (*c.* 1260–1327)

A grey rock, said Ruskin, is a good sitter. That is one type of behaviour. A darting dragon-fly is another type of behaviour. We call the one alive, the other not. But both are fundamentally balances of give and take of motion with their surround. To make 'life' a distinction between them is at root to treat them both artificially.

SIR CHARLES SHERRINGTON, *Man on his Nature*, 1940

Life is an offensive, directed against the repetitious mechanism of the Universe.

A. N. WHITEHEAD, *Adventures of Ideas*, 1933

In the beginning of the individual living creature is the beginning of life, every time and always, and life has no beginning apart from this.

D. H. LAWRENCE, *Psychoanalysis and the Unconscious*, 1921

The thing-in-itself, the will-to-live, exists whole and undivided in every being, even in the tiniest; it is present as completely as in all that ever were, are, and will be, taken together.

SCHOPENHAUER, 'On Ethics', *Parerga and Paralipomena*, 1851

Does the cell, moving freely in the pond or in our body, *seek* its food? Is there some modicum of mind in it? That is a question natural to ask. It is not decisively answerable.

SIR CHARLES SHERRINGTON, *Man on his Nature*, 1940

It is far from easy to determine whether Nature has proved to man a kind parent or a merciless stepmother.

PLINY THE ELDER, *Natural History*, 1st century

Nature! We are surrounded by her and locked in her clasp: powerless to leave her, and powerless to come closer to her. Without asking us or warning us she takes us up into the whirl of her dance, and hurries on with us until we are weary and fall from her arms.

GOETHE, *Maxims and Reflections*, early 19th century

A fountain breaks out in the wilderness, but that fountain cares not, whether any man may come to fetch water, or no; a fresh and fit gale blows upon the sea, but it cares not whether the mariners hoist sail or no; a rose blows in your garden, but it calls you not to smell it.

DONNE, sermon, *c.* 1620

Earth's nature is our nature. The situation creates the life which fits it. The dry land created the feet which walk it. Our situation has created the mind which deals with it. It is an earthly situation.

SIR CHARLES SHERRINGTON, *Man on his Nature*, 1940

. . . we receive but what we give,
And in our life alone does Nature live.

COLERIDGE, 'Dejection: An Ode', 1802

The principal task of civilization, its actual *raison d'être*, is to defend us against nature.

FREUD, *The Future of an Illusion*, 1927

Those whom we are so fond of referring to as the 'lower animals' reason very little. Now I beg you to observe that those beings rarely commit a *mistake*, while we — !

C. S. PEIRCE, *Collected Papers*, I, late 19th–early 20th century

The most accomplished monkey cannot draw a monkey, this too only man can do; just as it is also only man who regards his ability to do this as a distinct merit.

LICHTENBERG, *Aphorisms*, 1764–99

Whenever you observe an animal closely, you feel as if a human being sitting inside were making fun of you.

ELIAS CANETTI, *The Human Province*, 1978

In an aversion to animals the predominant feeling is fear of being recognized by them through contact. The horror that stirs deep in man is an obscure awareness that in him something lives so akin to the animal that it might be recognized.

WALTER BENJAMIN, *One-Way Street*, 1925–6

The wild deer, wand'ring here & there,
Keeps the Human Soul from Care.

> BLAKE, *Auguries of Innocence*, c. 1803

What differentiates man from other animals is perhaps feeling rather than reason. I have seen a cat reason more often than laugh or weep. Perhaps it laughs or weeps within itself – but then perhaps within itself a crab solves equations of the second degree.

> MIGUEL DE UNAMUNO, *The Tragic Sense of Life*, 1913

Bees are not as busy as we think they are. They just can't buzz any slower.

> KIN HUBBARD, *Abe Martin's Sayings*, 1915

How do you know but ev'ry Bird that cuts the airy way,
Is an immense world of delight, clos'd by your senses five?

> BLAKE, *The Marriage of Heaven and Hell*, 1790–3

It does not require much study of the pain-organs and their arrangements to show that the infliction of injury which they envisage and react to is in vast preponderance injury inflicted by other species of life.

> SIR CHARLES SHERRINGTON, *Man on his Nature*, 1940

What would become of the garden if the gardener treated all the weeds and slugs and birds and trespassers as he would like to be treated, if he were in their place?

> T. H. HUXLEY, *Evolution and Ethics*, 1893

A hen is only an egg's way of making another egg.

> SAMUEL BUTLER (II), *Life and Habit*, 1877

Every moment Nature starts on the longest journey, and every moment she reaches her goal.

> GOETHE, *Maxims and Reflections*, early 19th century

Even while a thing is in the act of coming into existence, some part of it has already ceased to be.

> MARCUS AURELIUS, *Meditations*, 2nd century

To create a little flower is the labour of ages.

> BLAKE, *The Marriage of Heaven and Hell*, 1790-3

Nature, often as she hugs the old, seems seldom or never to revert to a past once abandoned. Evolution can scrap but not revive.

> SIR CHARLES SHERRINGTON, *Man on his Nature*, 1940

Many grains of incense fall on the same altar: one sooner, another later – it makes no difference.

> MARCUS AURELIUS, *Meditations*, 2nd century

> The world of dew is
> A world of dew . . . and yet,
> And yet . . .

> KOBAYASHI ISSA, *c.* 1800 (trans. Geoffrey Bownas and Anthony Thwaite)

What do the baths bring to your mind? Oil, sweat, dirt, greasy water, and everything that is disgusting. Such, then, is life in all its parts, and such is every material thing in it.

> MARCUS AURELIUS, *Meditations*, 2nd century

I am not fond of expecting catastrophes, but there are cracks in the universe.

> SYDNEY SMITH

We should remark the grace and fascination that there is even in the incidentals of Nature's processes. When a loaf of bread, for instance, is in the oven, cracks appear in it here and there; and these flaws, though not intended in the baking, have a rightness of their own, and sharpen the appetite.

> MARCUS AURELIUS, *Meditations*, 2nd century

Is ditchwater dull? Naturalists with microscopes have told me that it teems with quiet fun.

> G. K. CHESTERTON, *The Spice of Life*, 1936

As to the foolery of 'indoor' and 'outdoor' nature, it's not worth the notice of an argument. What is good of each is good of both; nature is not two persons but one and the same.

JOHN CLARE, *Fragments*, 1825–37

Nature, to be commanded, must be obeyed.

SIR FRANCIS BACON, *Novum Organum*, 1620

All things are artificial, for nature is the art of God.

SIR THOMAS BROWNE, *Religio Medici*, 1642

Religion

❀

Our dream dashes itself against the great mystery like a wasp against a window pane. Less merciful than man, God never opens the window.

JULES RENARD, *Journal*, 1906

There are certain questions which are made unimportant by their very magnitude. For example, the question whether we are moving in Space this way or that; the existence of God, etc.

THOMAS HARDY in F. E. Hardy, *The Later Years of Thomas Hardy*, 1930

If God were not a necessary Being of Himself, He might almost seem to be made for the use and benefit of men.

JOHN TILLOTSON, *Sermons*, 1694

Probably no invention came more easily to man than Heaven.

LICHTENBERG, *Aphorisms*, 1764–99

That fear first created the gods is perhaps as true as anything so brief could be on so great a subject.

SANTAYANA, *The Life of Reason*, 1905–6

It is ridiculous to suppose that the great head of things, whatever it may be, pays any regard to human affairs.

PLINY THE ELDER, *Natural History*, 1st century

Heathen, *n*. A benighted creature who has the folly to worship something that he can see and feel.

AMBROSE BIERCE, *The Devil's Dictionary*, 1906

The Ethiopians say that their gods are snub-nosed and black, the Thracians that theirs have light blue eyes and red hair.

XENOPHANES, *Fragment 15*, 5th century BC

The religions we call false were once true.

EMERSON, 'Character', *Essays*, Second Series, 1844

It is the heart which perceives God and not the reason.

PASCAL, *Pensées*, 1670

Faith is under the left nipple.

MARTIN LUTHER

A man cannot become an atheist merely by wishing it.

NAPOLEON, *Maxims*, early 19th century

If God created us in his own image we have more than reciprocated.

VOLTAIRE, *Le Sottisier*, 18th century

Men are given to worshipping malevolent gods, and that which is not cruel seems to them not worth their adoration.

ANATOLE FRANCE, *Crainquebille*, 1901

God's merits are so transcendent that it is not surprising that his faults should be in reasonable proportion.

SAMUEL BUTLER (II), *Notebooks*, 1912

The God of the Christians is a father who is a great deal more concerned about his apples than he is about his children.

DIDEROT, *Addition aux Pensées philosophiques*, *c.*1762

Nobody has every been able to understand why God preferred Abel's sacrifice to that of Cain.

LEO SHESTOV, *All Things are Possible*, 1905

All that is truly amiable is God, or as it were a divided piece of him, that retains a reflex or shadow of himself.

SIR THOMAS BROWNE, *Religio Medici*, 1643

'Tis Socrates' opinion, and mine too, that it is best judged of heaven not to judge of it at all.

MONTAIGNE, 'Apology for Raimond de Sebonde', *Essays*, 1580–8

If I was a nightingale I would sing like a nightingale; if a swan, like a swan. But since I am a rational creature my role is to praise God.

EPICTETUS, *Discourses*, 2nd century

The sufferer alone is permitted to praise God in his works. But all men suffer.

FRANZ ROSENZWEIG, note, 1928

To lift up the hands in prayer gives God glory, but a man with a dungfork in his hand, a woman with a sloppail, gives him glory too. He is so great that all things give him glory if you mean they should.

GERARD MANLEY HOPKINS, Sermon: 'On the Principle or Foundation', 1881–2

I love to pray at sunrise – before the world becomes polluted with vanity and hatred.

THE KORETSER RABBI, 18th century

The smoke of the sacrifice rises to heaven,
Of a sweet savour, no doubt, to Somebody; but on the altar,
Lo, there is nothing remaining but ashes and dirt and ill odour.

CLOUGH, *Amours de Voyage*, 1858

God was satisfied with his own work, and that is fatal.

SAMUEL BUTLER (II), *Notebooks*, 1912

There can be no Creator, simply because his grief at the fate of his creation would be inconceivable and unendurable.

ELIAS CANETTI, *The Human Province*, 1978

I respect the idea of God too much to hold it responsible for a world as absurd as this one is.

GEORGES DUHAMEL, *Le Désert de Bièvres*, 1937

The impotence of God is infinite.

ANATOLE FRANCE, *Under the Rose*, 1925

God dwells wherever man lets him in.

MENDEL OF KOTZK, cit. Buber, *Tales of the Hasidim: The Later Masters*

They say God is everywhere, and yet we always think of Him as somewhat of a recluse.

EMILY DICKINSON

God, Who winds our sundials.

LICHTENBERG, *Aphorisms*, 1764–99

Heaven can do whatever it likes without anybody being able to interfere with it, especially when it is raining.

CERVANTES, *The Mayors of Daganco*, 1615

Live among men as if God beheld you; speak to God as if men were listening.

SENECA, *Epistles*, 1st century

There are few men who durst publish to the world the prayers they make to Almighty God.

MONTAIGNE, 'Of prayers', *Essays*, 1580–8

God is ashamed when the prosperous boast of his special favour.

RABINDRANATH TAGORE, *Stray Birds*, 1916

Man considers the actions, but God weighs the intentions.

THOMAS À KEMPIS, *The Imitation of Christ*, c. 1420

God wants the heart.

The Talmud

If there be a God, *since* there is a God, the human race is implicated in some terrible aboriginal calamity. It is out of joint with the purposes of its Creator.

J. H. NEWMAN, *Apologia pro Vita Sua*, 1864

It is harder for the men of this century to believe in the Devil than to love him.

BAUDELAIRE, *Projets de préface aux Fleurs du Mal*, c.1860

The only thing that stops God sending a second Flood is that the first one was useless.

CHAMFORT, *Characters and anecdotes*, 1771

If God were suddenly condemned to live the life which he has inflicted on men, He would kill Himself.

ALEXANDRE DUMAS *fils* (1824–95), *Pensées d'album*

The holiest attribute of a temple is that it is a place where men weep in common.

MIGUEL DE UNAMUNO, *The Tragic Sense of Life*, 1913

All religions correspond to the same human needs; all have a common denominator. What it is I dare not say.

HENRY DE MONTHERLANT, *Notebooks*, 1930–44

A man who has faith must be prepared not only to be a martyr, but to be a fool.

G. K. CHESTERTON, *Heretics*, 1905

The true way goes over a rope which is not stretched at any great height but just above the ground. It seems more designed to make men stumble than to be walked upon.

KAFKA, 'Aphorisms 1917–19', *The Great Wall of China*

If reason was bestowed on us by Heaven and the same can be said of faith, then Heaven has presented us with two incompatible and contradictory gifts.

DIDEROT, *Addition aux Pensées philosophiques*, c.1762

The most fundamental of divisions is that between the intellect, which can only do its work by saying continually 'thou fool', and the religious genius which makes all equal.

W. B. YEATS, *Estrangement*, 1936

All religions promise a reward for excellences of the will or heart, but none for excellences of the head or understanding.

SCHOPENHAUER, *The World as Will and Idea*, 1819

Wandering in a vast forest at night, I have only a faint light to guide me. A stranger appears and says to me: 'My friend, you should blow out your candle in order to find your way more clearly.' This stranger is a theologian.

DIDEROT, *Addition aux Pensées philosophiques*, *c.*1762

God's contempt for human minds is evidenced by miracles. He judges them unworthy of being drawn to Him by other means than those of stupefaction and the crudest modes of sensibility.

VALÉRY, *Tel Quel*, 1941–3

Every miracle can be explained – after the event. Not because the miracle is no miracle, but because explanation is explanation.

FRANZ ROSENZWEIG, *Judah ha-Levi*, 1927

It is absurd to try to make children's games reasonable and a great folly to try to purify religions.

RÉMY DE GOURMONT, *The Cultivation of Ideas*, 1900

From the moment that a religion solicits the aid of philosophy its ruin is inevitable.

HEINE, *Religion and Philosophy in Germany*, 1835

Great and terrible systems of divinity and philosophy lie round about us, which, if true, might drive a wise man mad – which read like professed exculpations of a contemplated insanity.

WALTER BAGEHOT, *Literary Studies*, 1879

Many a long dispute among divines may be thus abridged: It is so. It is not so. It is so. It is not so.

BENJAMIN FRANKLIN, *Poor Richard's Almanack*, 1743

The entertaining a single thought of a certain elevation makes all men of one religion. It is always some base alloy that creates the distinction of sects. Thought greets thought over the widest gulfs of time with unerring freemasonry.

THOREAU, *Journal*, 1852

No kingdom has ever had as many civil wars as the kingdom of Christ.

MONTESQUIEU, *Persian Letters*, 1721

Religion: a sixteenth-century term for nationalism.

attrib. SIR LEWIS NAMIER

To what excesses will men not go for the sake of a religion in which they believe so little and which they practise so imperfectly!

LA BRUYÈRE, 'Of Free-Thinkers', *Characters*, 1688

It were better to be of no church than to be bitter for any.

WILLIAM PENN, *Some Fruits of Solitude*, 1693

A religion, even if it calls itself the religion of love, must be hard and unloving to those who do not belong to it.

FREUD, *Group Psychology and the Analysis of the Ego*, 1921

Of all learned men, the clergy show the lowest development of professional ethics. Any pastor is free to cadge customers from the divines of rival sects, and to denounce the divines themselves as theological quacks.

H. L. MENCKEN, *Minority Report: Notebooks*, 1956

I like the silent church before the service begins, better than any preaching.

EMERSON, 'Self-Reliance', *Essays*, First Series, 1841

Religions are kept alive by heresies, which are really sudden explosions of faith.

GERALD BRENAN, *Thoughts in a Dry Season*, 1978

You have to be very religious to change your religion.

COMTESSE DIANE, *Maximes de la vie*, 1908

Is there any religion whose followers can be pointed to as distinctly more amiable and trustworthy than those of any other? If so, this should be enough.

SAMUEL BUTLER (II), *Notebooks*, 1912

If Morality was Christianity, Socrates was The Saviour.

> BLAKE, *Annotations to Dr. Thornton's 'New Translation of the Lord's Prayer'*, 1827

To become the founder of a new religion one must be psychologically infallible in one's knowledge of a certain average type of souls who have not yet *recognized* that they belong together.

> NIETZSCHE, *The Gay Science*, 1882–7

It is not enough for a religion to include everything. It must include everything and something over. That is, it must include everything and something as well. It must answer that deep and mysterious human demand for something as distinct from the demand for everything.

> G. K. CHESTERTON, *The Man who was Orthodox*, 1963

If Comtism had spread the world would have been converted, not by the Comtist philosophy, but by the Comtist calendar.

> G. K. CHESTERTON, *Heretics*, 1905

Enthusiasm, mysticism, plays no great part in religious communities. The virtues jog quietly along a humdrum path. Spirituality is worldly-wise and takes a material form so far as it can, and the possibilities in this direction are far greater than is commonly supposed.

> ANATOLE FRANCE, *The Garden of Epicurus*, 1894

Preachers say, Do as I say, not as I do. But if the physician had the same disease upon him that I have, and he should bid me do one thing, and himself do quite another, could I believe him?

> JOHN SELDEN, *Table Talk*, mid 17th century

A pious man is one who would be an atheist if the king were.

> LA BRUYÈRE, 'Of Fashion', *Characters*, 1688

Religion is built on humility, honour on pride. How to reconcile them must be left to wiser heads than mine.

> MANDEVILLE, *The Fable of the Bees*, 1714

If I lose at play, I blaspheme, and if my fellow loses, he blasphemes, so that God is always sure to be a loser.

DONNE, sermon, 1623

To the frivolous Christianity is certainly not glad tidings, for it wishes first of all to make them serious.

KIERKEGAARD, *Journal*, 1847

Many people believe that they are attracted by God, or by Nature, when they are only repelled by man.

W. R. INGE, *More Lay Thoughts of a Dean*, 1931

In every ascetic morality man worships a part of himself as God and for that he needs to diabolize the other part.

NIETZSCHE, *Human, All Too Human*, 1878–86

As the caterpillar chooses the fairest leaves to lay her eggs on, so the priest lays his curse on the fairest joys.

BLAKE, *The Marriage of Heaven and Hell*, 1790–3

For a priest to turn a man when he lies a-dying, is just like one that has a long time solicited a woman, and cannot obtain his end; at length makes her drunk, and so lies with her.

JOHN SELDEN, *Table Talk*, mid 17th century

It is very dangerous to go into eternity with possibilities which one has oneself prevented from becoming realities. A possibility is a hint from God.

KIERKEGAARD, *Journal*, 1848

The trees reflected in the river – they are unconscious of a spiritual world so near them. So are we.

NATHANIEL HAWTHORNE, *American Notebooks*, 1841–52

There might very well be nothing; nor anyone. No one to notice that there is nothing, and to consider that natural.

But that there is something, and, whatever it may be, the strange thing! I shall never cease being amazed at this.

ANDRÉ GIDE, *Journal*, 1947

God made everything out of nothing. But the nothingness shows through.

VALÉRY, *Mauvaises pensées et autres*, 1942

Fortunately, in her kindness and patience, Nature has never put the fatal question as to the meaning of their lives into the mouths of most people. And where no one asks, no one needs to answer.

JUNG, 'The Development of Personality', 1934

Religion consists of believing that *everything that happens is extraordinarily important*. It can never disappear from the world, precisely for this reason.

CESARE PAVESE, *This Business of Living: Diaries 1935–50*

All religions will pass, but this will remain: simply sitting in a chair and looking in the distance.

V. V. ROZANOV, *Solitaria*, 1912

Mankind

Of all things the measure is Man, of the things that are, that they are, and of the things that are not, that they are not.

PROTAGORAS OF ABDERA (5th century BC)

What is the vanity of the vainest man compared with the vanity which the most modest possesses when, in the midst of nature and the world, he feels himself to be 'man'!

NIETZSCHE, *The Wanderer and His Shadow*, 1880

The wonder is, not that the field of the stars is so vast, but that man has measured it.

ANATOLE FRANCE, *The Garden of Epicurus*, 1894

Man is equally incapable of seeing the nothingness from which he emerges and the infinity in which he is engulfed.

PASCAL, *Pensées*, 1670

Incredible the Lodging
But limited the Guest.

EMILY DICKINSON, *Notebook*, c.1880

It is easier to know man in general than to understand one man in particular.

LA ROCHEFOUCAULD, *Maxims*, 1665

The more one analyses people, the more all reasons for analysis disappear. Sooner or later one comes to that dreadful universal thing called human nature.

OSCAR WILDE, *The Decay of Lying*, 1891

In each of us there is a little of all of us.

LICHTENBERG, *Aphorisms*, 1764–99

Man has a nature, but what is it? Those who have confidently described it, Hobbes, Freud, et cetera, by telling us what we are 'intrinsically', are not our greatest benefactors.

SAUL BELLOW, Moses Herzog in *Herzog*, 1964

All over the world it is customary for people to wish one another a long life. This cannot be ascribed to a knowledge of what life is, but rather to what man is by nature, namely will-to-live.

SCHOPENHAUER, 'Psychological Remarks', *Parerga and Paralipomena*, 1851

Man is a plant which bears thoughts, just as a rose-tree bears roses and an apple-tree bears apples.

ANTOINE FABRE D'OLIVET, *L'Histoire philosophique du genre humain*, 1824

> But I must needs confess, I do not find
> The motions of my mind
> So purified as yet, but at the best
> My body claims in them an interest.

SIR ROBERT AYTON, 'Upon Platonic Love', mid 17th century

Why should a man's mind have been thrown into such close, sad, sensational, inexplicable relations with such a precarious object as his body?

THOMAS HARDY in F. E. Hardy, *The Later Years of Thomas Hardy*, 1930

Of course Celia shits! Who doesn't? And how much worse if she didn't.

D. H. LAWRENCE, *A Propos of Lady Chatterley's Lover*, 1929

What is peculiar in the life of a man consists not in his obedience, but in his opposition, to his instincts. In one direction or another he strives to live a supernatural life.

THOREAU, *Journal*, 1850

We talk of wild animals; but man is the only wild animal. It is man that has broken out. All other animals are tame animals; following the rugged respectability of the tribe or type.

G. K. CHESTERTON, *Orthodoxy*, 1909

I go among the fields and catch a glimpse of a stoat or a fieldmouse peeping out of the withered grass – the creature hath a purpose and its eyes are bright with it. I go amongst the buildings of a city and I see a man hurrying along – to what? the Creature has a purpose and his eyes are bright with it.

KEATS, letter, 1819

Man is a masterpiece of creation, if only because no amount of determinism can prevent him from believing that he acts as a free being.

LICHTENBERG, *Aphorisms*, 1764–99

Of all the marvellous works of the Deity, perhaps there is nothing that angels behold with such supreme astonishment as a proud man.

CHARLES CALEB COLTON, *Lacon*, 1825

If man had created man he would be ashamed of his performance.

MARK TWAIN, *Notebooks*, later 19th century

Everyone has something in his nature which, if he were to express it openly, would of necessity give offence.

GOETHE, *Maxims and Reflections*, early 19th century

He that hath no fools, knaves or beggars in his family was begot by a flash of lightning.

THOMAS FULLER (II), *Gnomologia*, 1732

Following a well-known pronouncement of Kant's which couples the conscience within us with the starry Heavens, a pious man might well be tempted to honour these two things as the masterpieces of creation. The stars are indeed magnificent, but as regards conscience God has done an uneven and careless piece of work.

FREUD, 'Dissection of the Personality', *New Introductory Lectures on Psychoanalysis*, 1933

Without goodness man is a busy, mischievous, wretched thing; no better than a kind of vermin.

SIR FRANCIS BACON, 'Of Goodness', *Essays*, 1597–1625

Man is the only animal that can remain on friendly terms with the victims he intends to eat until he eats them.

SAMUEL BUTLER (II), *Notebooks*, 1912

The world loved man when he smiled. The world became afraid of him when he laughed.

RABINDRANATH TAGORE, *Stray Birds*, 1916

The boa constrictor, when he has had an adequate meal, goes to sleep, and does not wake until he needs another meal. Human beings, for the most part, are not like this.

BERTRAND RUSSELL, *Human Society in Ethics and Politics*, 1954

Whether a man embraces a dupe on the boulevard, or spears his prey in unknown forests, is he not eternal man – that is to say, the most highly perfected beast of prey?

BAUDELAIRE, *Fusées*, 1862

Civilization has rendered man, if not more bloodthirsty, at least a worse (in the sense of a meaner) thirster after blood than before.

DOSTOEVSKY, *Notes from the Underground*, 1864

The bird a nest, the spider a web, man friendship.

BLAKE, *The Marriage of Heaven and Hell*, 1790–3

The soul's immutable core – if there is one – can hardly be amiable. And to love any one for himself perhaps in the end becomes unmeaning.

F. H. BRADLEY, *Aphorisms*, 1930

That man is the noblest of all creatures may also be inferred from the fact that no other creature has yet denied him the title.

LICHTENBERG, *Aphorisms*, 1764–99

Behaviour of such cunning cruelty that only a human being could have thought of or contrived we call 'inhuman', revealing thus some pathetic ideal standard for our species that survives all betrayals.

ROSE MACAULAY, *A Casual Commentary*, 1925

Man is neither angel nor beast, and it is unfortunately the case that anyone trying to act the angel acts the beast.

PASCAL, *Pensées*, 1670

He that can carp in the most eloquent or acute manner at the weaknesses of the human mind is held by his fellows as almost divine.

SPINOZA, *Ethics*, 1677

Things of a nobler and more elevated being may, indeed, reproach ours, but it is against nature for us to contemn and make little account of ourselves; 'tis a disease particular to man, and not discerned in any other creatures, to hate and despise itself.

MONTAIGNE, 'A Custom of the Isle of Cea', *Essays*, 1580–8

What should we think of dogs' monasteries, hermit cats, vegetarian tigers? Of birds who tore off their wings or bulls weeping with remorse? Surely it is in our nature to realize ourselves, yet there remains the deadly flaw by which we feel most guilt when we are most confidently human.

CYRIL CONNOLLY, *The Unquiet Grave*, 1944

We grow weary of being human beings at all – of possessing real, individual flesh and blood. We are *ashamed* of being human – we account it beneath our dignity. Rather, we aim at becoming personalities of a general, a fictitious type.

DOSTOEVSKY, *Notes from the Underground*, 1864

Contempt for human nature is an error of human reason.

VAUVENARGUES, *Reflections and Maxims*, 1746

We must not indulge in unfavourable views of mankind, since by doing it we make bad men believe that they are no worse than others, and we teach the good that they are good in vain.

LANDOR, 'Barrow and Newton', *Imaginary Conversations*, 1824–9

To say that man is made up of strength and weakness, of insight and blindness, of pettiness and grandeur, is not to draw up an indictment against him: it is to define him.

DIDEROT, *Addition aux Pensées philosophiques*, *c*.1762

Where there are humans
you'll find flies,
and Buddhas.

KOBAYASHI ISSA, *c*.1800 (trans. Lucien Stryk and Takashi Ikemoto)

There is no such thing as perpetual tranquillity of mind, while we live here; because life itself is but motion, and can never be without desire, nor without fear, no more than without sense.

HOBBES, *Leviathan*, 1651

Our nature consists in movement; absolute rest is death.

PASCAL, *Pensées*, 1670

We mistake human nature if we wish for a termination of labour, or a scene of repose.

ADAM FERGUSON, *An Essay on the History of Civil Society*, 1767

The world is a vast temple dedicated to Discord.

VOLTAIRE, letter, 1752

A world of dew:
Yet within the dewdrops –
Quarrels.

KOBAYASHI ISSA, *c*.1800 (trans. Geoffrey Bownas and Anthony Thwaite)

It is a folly to expect men to do all that they may reasonably be expected to do.

ARCHBISHOP WHATELY, *Apophthegms*, 1864

The human race consists of the dangerously insane and such as are not.

MARK TWAIN, *Notebooks*, later 19th century

Men will always be mad and those who think they can cure them are the maddest of all.

VOLTAIRE, letter, 1762

On human actions reason tho' you can,
It may be reason, but it is not man.

POPE, *Epistle to Lord Cobham*, 1734

Man's sensitivity to little things and insensitivity to the greatest are the signs of a strange disorder.

PASCAL, *Pensées*, 1670

Most human beings have an almost infinite capacity for taking things for granted.

ALDOUS HUXLEY, *Themes and Variations*, 1950

They who do not understand that a man may be brought to hope that which of all things is the most grievous to him, have not observed with sufficient closeness the perversity of the human mind.

TROLLOPE, *He Knew He Was Right*, 1869

We take issue even with perfection.

PASCAL, *Pensées*, 1670

Man spends his life in reasoning on the past, in complaining of the present, in fearing for the future.

ANTOINE RIVAROL, *Pensées, traits et bons mots*, late 18th century

On the whole, we are meant to look after ourselves; it is certain
Each has to eat for himself, digest for himself, and in general
Care for his own dear life, and see to his own preservation;
Nature's intentions, in most things uncertain, in this are decisive.

CLOUGH, *Amours de Voyage*, 1858

Nothing inclusive of a human Heart could be 'trivial'. The appalling Boon makes all things paltry but itself.

EMILY DICKINSON, letter, 1885

When you are outraged by somebody's impudence, ask yourself at once, 'Can the world exist without impudent people?' It cannot; so do not ask for impossibilities.

MARCUS AURELIUS, *Meditations*, 2nd century

How are we to hope men will pass their lives putting their best foot foremost, and yet will never boast that their better foot is farther advanced and more perfect than in fact it is?

WALTER BAGEHOT, *Literary Studies*, 1879

Each of us in his own person feels that a high-hearted indifference to life would expiate all his short-comings.

WILLIAM JAMES, *Varieties of Religious Experience*, 1902

The human character, however it may be exalted or depressed by a temporary enthusiasm, will return, by degrees, to its proper and natural level, and will resume those passions that seem the most adapted to its present condition.

GIBBON, *The Decline and Fall of the Roman Empire*, 1776–88

How many natures lie in human nature!

PASCAL, *Pensées*, 1670

Life

❀

Life is a great bundle of little things.
OLIVER WENDELL HOLMES sen., *The Professor at the Breakfast Table*, 1859

The components of the world which one loves, and the whole thing, mis–composed, which one hates.
ELIAS CANETTI, *The Human Province*, 1978

The interest in life does not lie in what people do, nor even in their relations to each other, but largely in the power to communicate with a third party, antagonistic, enigmatic, yet perhaps persuadable, which one may call life in general.
VIRGINIA WOOLF, *The Common Reader*, 1925

Life taken in general can be no sacred thing. It has enslaved and brutalized the globe.
SIR CHARLES SHERRINGTON, *Man on his Nature*, 1940

War is the father of all.
HERACLITUS, *Fragments*, 53, *c.*500 BC

No easy fine, no mere apology or formal expiation, will satisfy the world's demands, but every pound of flesh exacted is soaked with all its blood.
WILLIAM JAMES, *The Varieties of Religious Experience*, 1902

The stone fell on the pitcher? Woe to the pitcher. The pitcher fell on the stone? Woe to the pitcher.
RABBINIC SAYING

Things are greater than we, and will not comply with *us*; we, who are less than things, must comply with *them*.
BENJAMIN WHICHCOTE, *Moral and Religious Aphorisms*, 1703

The baby creates the object, but the object was there waiting to be created.

D. W. WINNICOTT, *Playing and Reality*, 1971

All things are strange. One can always sense the strangeness of a thing once it ceases to play any part; when we do not try to find something resembling it and we concentrate on its basic stuff, its intrinsicality.

VALÉRY, *Tel Quel*, 1941–3

Just as people find water whenever they dig, man everywhere finds the incomprehensible, sooner or later.

LICHTENBERG, *Aphorisms*, 1764–99

One need only remind oneself of all that we expect from life to see how very strange it is, and to arrive at the conclusion that man has found his way into it by mistake and does not really belong there.

ITALO SVEVO, *Confessions of Zeno*, 1923

Why shouldn't things be largely absurd, futile, and transitory? They are so, and we are so, and they and we go very well together.

SANTAYANA, *Letters*, 1918

The conviction that the world and thus also man is something that really ought not to be, is calculated to fill us with forbearance towards one another; for what can we expect from beings in such a predicament?

SCHOPENHAUER, 'On the Doctrine of the Suffering of the World', *Parerga and Paralipomena*, 1851

Life is a tragedy wherein we sit as spectators for a while and then act out our part in it.

SWIFT, *Thoughts on Various Subjects*, 1711

There are so many fine and substantial things in the world at any one time, but they are not in touch with each other.

GOETHE, *Maxims and Reflections*, early 19th century

Everything intercepts us from ourselves.

> EMERSON, *Journals*, 1833

Life is what we make it as Whist is what we make it; but not as Chess is what we make it; which ranks higher as a purely intellectual game than either Whist or Life.

> THOMAS HARDY in F. E. Hardy, *The Later Years of Thomas Hardy*, 1930

We learn from experience that not everything which is incredible is untrue.

> CARDINAL DE RETZ, *Memoirs*, 1673–6

We read every day, with astonishment, things which we see every day, without surprise.

> LORD CHESTERFIELD, *Letters*, 1748

Life resembles a novel more often than novels resemble life.

> GEORGE SAND

When all is said and done, no literature can outdo the cynicism of real life; you won't intoxicate with one glass someone who has already drunk up a whole barrel.

> CHEKHOV, letter, 1887

How impossible to describe life! How shameless of literature to poke its nose in everywhere! How can you use a pen to write about – blood!

> ANDREY SINYAVSKY, *A Voice from the Chorus*, 1973

Life is made up of the most differing, unforeseen, contradictory, ill-assorted things; it is brutal, arbitrary, disconnected, full of inexplicable, illogical and contradictory disasters which can only be classified under the heading of 'Other news in brief'.

> MAUPASSANT, *Pierre et Jean*, 1887

> Ceux qui luttent ce sont ceux qui vivent,
> And down here they luttent a very great deal indeed.
> But if life be the desideratum, why grieve, ils vivent.

> STEVIE SMITH, 'Ceux qui luttent . . .', *The Frog Prince*, 1966

What are the facts? Not those in Homer, Shakespeare, or even the
Bible. The facts for most of us are a dark street, crowds, hurry,
commonplaceness, loneliness, and, worse than all, a terrible doubt
which can hardly be named as to the meaning and purpose of the
world.

MARK RUTHERFORD, *Last Pages from a Journal*, 1915

Our civilization is founded on the shambles, and every individual
existence goes out in a lonely spasm of helpless agony.

WILLIAM JAMES, *Varieties of Religious Experience*, 1902

There is so much trouble in coming into the world, and so much
more, as well as meanness, in going out of it, that 'tis hardly worth
while to be here at all.

LORD BOLINGBROKE (1678–1751)

The world is disgracefully managed, one hardly knows to whom to
complain.

RONALD FIRBANK, Mrs Shamefoot in *Vainglory*, 1915

Why should there not be a scale of things, all the way up to God, and
could not then our world be the work of one who did not know his
job properly – an experiment?

LICHTENBERG, *Aphorisms*, 1764–99

What a fine comedy this world would be if one did not play a part in
it!

DIDEROT, *Letters to Sophie Volland*

Life is short, but its ills make it seem long.

PUBLILIUS SYRUS, *Sententiae*, 1st century BC

The shortness of life can neither dissuade us from its pleasures, nor
console us for its pains.

VAUVENARGUES, *Reflections and Maxims*, 1746

The vanity of human life is like a river, constantly passing away, and
yet constantly coming on.

POPE, *Thoughts on Various Subjects*, 1727

Growth is a greater mystery than death. All of us can understand failure, we all contain failure and death within us, but not even the successful man can begin to describe the impalpable elations and apprehensions of growth.

NORMAN MAILER, *Advertisements for Myself*, 1961

Life is one long process of getting tired.

SAMUEL BUTLER (II), *Notebooks*, 1912

The earth keeps some vibration going
There in your heart, and that is you.

EDGAR LEE MASTERS, *Spoon River Anthology*, 1915

Desires & Longings

●

Desire is the very essence of man.

SPINOZA, Ethics, 1677

He who desires, but acts not, breeds pestilence.

BLAKE, The Marriage of Heaven and Hell, 1790–3

There is in a man an upwelling spring of life, energy, love, whatever you like to call it. If a course is not cut for it, it turns the ground round it into a swamp.

MARK RUTHERFORD, More Pages from a Journal, 1910

What nature requires is obtainable, and within easy reach. It's for the superfluous we sweat.

SENECA, Epistles, 1st century

Some desire is necessary to keep life in motion; and he whose real wants are supplied, must admit those of fancy.

DR JOHNSON, Rasselas, 1759

All we really want is otherness, tossing from side to side, and greeting every toss with shouts of welcome, and of contempt for the previous toss.

BERNARD BERENSON, diary, 1954

Much will have more.

EMERSON, Society and Solitude, 1870

The things we are best acquainted with are often the things we lack. This is because we have spent so much time thinking of them.

GERALD BRENAN, Thoughts in a Dry Season, 1978

An aspiration is a joy for ever, a possession as solid as a landed estate.

ROBERT LOUIS STEVENSON, Virginibus Puerisque, 1881

Possessions are generally diminished by possession.

> NIETZSCHE, *The Gay Science*, 1882–7

We grow weary of those things (and perhaps soonest) which we most desire.

> SAMUEL BUTLER (1), *Prose Observations*, 1660–80

If you go expressly to look at the moon, it becomes tinsel.

> EMERSON, 'Nature', *Essays*, Second Series, 1844

Many a man would rather you heard his story than granted his request.

> LORD CHESTERFIELD, *Letters*, 1753

There are certain people who so ardently and passionately desire a thing, that from dread of losing it they leave nothing undone to make them lose it.

> LA BRUYÈRE, 'Of the Affections', *Characters*, 1688

To proportion the eagerness of contest to its importance seems too hard a task for human wisdom. The pride of wit has kept ages busy in the discussion of useless questions, and the pride of power has destroyed armies to gain or keep unprofitable possessions.

> DR JOHNSON, *Thoughts on the Late Transactions respecting Falkland's Islands*, 1771

The value of a thing sometimes lies not in what one attains with it, but in what one pays for it – what it *costs* us.

> NIETZSCHE, *Twilight of the Idols*, 1889

What is easy and obvious is never valued; and even what is *in itself* difficult, if we come to the knowledge of it without difficulty, and without any stretch of thought or judgment, is but little regarded.

> HUME, *A Treatise of Human Nature*, 1739

Man is so made that he can only find relaxation from one kind of labour by taking up another.

> ANATOLE FRANCE, *The Crime of Sylvestre Bonnard*, 1881

The animal needing something knows how much it needs, the man does not.

DEMOCRITUS OF ABDERA, 5th–4th century BC

Limited in his nature, infinite in his desires, man is a fallen god who remembers heaven.

LAMARTINE, *Méditations poétiques*, 1820

Man is an intellectual animal, and therefore an everlasting contradiction to himself. His senses centre in himself, his ideas reach to the ends of the universe; so that he is torn in pieces between the two, without a possibility of its ever being otherwise.

HAZLITT, *Characteristics*, 1823

The average man, who does not know what to do with his life, wants another one which will last forever.

ANATOLE FRANCE, *The Revolt of the Angels*, 1914

With everything that we do, we desire more or less the end; we are impatient to be done with it and glad when it is finished. It is only the end in general, the end of all ends, that we wish, as a rule, to put off as long as possible.

SCHOPENHAUER, 'Psychological Remarks', *Parerga and Paralipomena*, 1851

The soul's longing for infinity, a longing which proclaims its weakness and impotence, is the surest sign of its unworthiness of infinity, which will be for ever denied to it.

HENRY DE MONTHERLANT, 'Explicit Mysterium', 1931

Are we to look at cherry blossoms only in full bloom, the moon only when it is cloudless? To long for the moon while looking on the rain, to lower the blinds and be unaware of the passing of the spring – these are even more deeply moving. Branches about to blossom or gardens strewn with flowers are worthier of our admiration.

YOSHIDA KENKO, *Essays in Idleness*, *c*.1340

The bounded is loathed by its possessor. The same dull round, even of a universe, would soon become a mill with complicated wheels.

BLAKE, 'There is No Natural Religion', 1788

Whatever liberates our spirit without giving us mastery over ourselves is destructive.

GOETHE, *Maxims and Reflections*, early 19th century

Self-satire, disillusion, absence of prejudice may be freedom, but they are not strength.

AMIEL, *Journal*, 1876

I hate to be near the sea, and to hear it raging and roaring like a wild beast in its den. It puts me in mind of the everlasting efforts of the human mind, struggling to be free and ending just where it began.

HAZLITT, *Characteristics*, 1823

Men and women aren't really dogs: they only look like it and behave like it. Somewhere inside there is a great chagrin and a gnawing discontent.

D. H. LAWRENCE, *A Propos of Lady Chatterley's Lover*, 1929

Latent in every man is a venom of amazing bitterness, a black resentment; something that curses and loathes life, a feeling of being trapped, of having trusted and been fooled, of being the helpless prey of impotent rage, blind surrender, the victim of a savage, ruthless power that gives and takes away, enlists a man, drops him, promises and betrays, and – crowning injury – inflicts on him the humiliation of feeling sorry for himself and of regarding this 'power' as an intelligent, sentient being, capable of being touched.

VALÉRY, *Mauvaises pensées et autres*, 1942

Don't despair, not even over the fact that you don't despair.

KAFKA, *Diary*, 1913

The very strategies of despair, and especially the logical strategies involved in the contemplation of suicide, reveal that there is some connection still linking them to life-outside-despair – perhaps only imagined, but imagined still – that despair is unable to sever. Despair would not be so anguished a condition as it is were it as wholly and hopelessly estranged as it believes itself to be.

LESLIE FARBER, *The Ways of the Will*, 1966

Despair itself, if it goes on long enough, can become a kind of sanctuary in which one settles down and feels at ease.

SAINTE-BEUVE, *La vie de Joseph Delorme*, 1829

No person can live, no ego remain intact without hope and will. Even philosophical man who feels motivated to challenge the very ground he stands on, questioning both will and hope as illusory, feels more real for having willed such heroic enquiry; and where man chooses to surrender his sense of having willed the inevitable to gods and leaders, he fervently endows them with what he has renounced for himself.

ERIK ERIKSON, *Insight and Responsibility*, 1966

I can't tell if a straw ever saved a drowning man, but I know that a mere glance is enough to make despair pause. For in truth we who are creatures of impulse are not creatures of despair.

JOSEPH CONRAD, *Chance*, 1913

We are never present with, but always beyond ourselves: fear, desire, hope, still push us on towards the future.

MONTAIGNE, 'That our affections carry themselves beyond us', *Essays*, 1580–8

The love of life is necessary to the vigorous prosecution of any undertaking.

DR JOHNSON, *The Rambler*, 1750–2

At times, our strengths propel us so far forward we can no longer endure our weaknesses and perish from them.

NIETZSCHE, *The Gay Science*, 1882–7

It would not be better if things happened to men just as they wish.

HERACLITUS, *Fragments*, 52, *c.*500 BC

Fears, Hopes, Passions

●

In the human heart new passions are for ever being born; the overthrow of one almost always means the rise of another.

LA ROCHEFOUCAULD, *Maxims*, 1665

It is difficult to overcome one's passions, and impossible to satisfy them.

MARGUERITE DE LA SABLIÈRE, *Pensées chrétiennes*, late 17th century

It is the favourite stratagem of our passions to sham a retreat, and to turn sharp round upon us at the moment we have made up our minds that the day is our own.

GEORGE ELIOT, *Adam Bede*, 1859

Men's feelings are obscure and confused; they are composed of a great number and variety of impressions which defy observation; and words, always too crude and too general, may well indicate them but can never define them.

BENJAMIN CONSTANT, *Adolphe*, 1816

To great evils we submit; we resent little provocations.

HAZLITT, 'On Great and Little Things', 1822

In every one of us the deepest emotions are constantly caused by some absurdly trivial thing, or by nothing at all. Conversely, the great things in our lives – the true occasions for wrath, anguish, rapture, what not – very often leave us quite calm. We never can depend on any right adjustment of emotion to circumstance.

MAX BEERBOHM, *Yet Again*, 1909

All passions exaggerate: it is only because they exaggerate that they are passions.

CHAMFORT, *Maximes et pensées*, 1805

The most sober men, when they walk alone without care and employment of the mind, would be unwilling the vanity and extravagance of their thoughts should be publicly seen: which is a confession that passions unguided are for the most part mere madness.

HOBBES, *Leviathan*, 1651

The sense of power is as strong a principle in the mind as the love of pleasure.

HAZLITT, 'On Poetry in General', 1818

The natural flights of the human mind are not from pleasure to pleasure but from hope to hope.

DR JOHNSON, *The Rambler*, 1750–2

If you do not hope, you will not find what is beyond your hopes.

ST. CLEMENT OF ALEXANDRIA, *Stromateis*, *c*.AD 200

Hope is a waking dream.

ARISTOTLE (4th century BC), cit. Diogenes Laertius, *Lives and Opinions of Eminent Philosophers*

We often call a certainty a hope, to bring it luck.

ELIZABETH BIBESCO, *Haven*, 1951

Blessed is he who expects nothing, for he shall never be disappointed.

POPE, letter, 1727

The sudden disappointment of a hope leaves a scar which the ultimate fulfilment of that hope never entirely removes.

THOMAS HARDY *in* F. E. Hardy, *The Early Life of Thomas Hardy*, 1928

The bitter man must sparkle; when dried out, he is useless. His sparks have to contain hope, which he himself no longer tolerates.

ELIAS CANETTI, *The Human Province*, 1978

A man may destroy everything within himself, love and hate and belief, and even doubt; but as long as he clings to life he cannot destroy fear.

> JOSEPH CONRAD, 'An Outpost of Progress', *Tales of Unrest*,
> 1898

To the man who is afraid everything rustles.

> SOPHOCLES (5th century BC), Fragment 58, *Acrisius*

As cowardly as a coward is, it is not safe to call a coward a coward.

> ANON., *Characters and Observations*, early 18th century

Fear cannot be without hope nor hope without fear.

> SPINOZA, *Ethics*, 1677

Evil is uncertain in the same degree as good, and for the reason that we ought not to hope too securely, we ought not to fear with too much dejection.

> DR JOHNSON, *The Rambler*, 1750–2

The most absurd and the most rash hopes have sometimes been the cause of extraordinary success.

> VAUVENARGUES, *Reflections and Maxims*, 1746

There exist some evils so terrible and some misfortunes so horrible that we dare not think of them, whilst their very aspect makes us shudder; but if they happen to fall on us, we find ourselves stronger than we imagined; we grapple with our ill luck, and behave better than we expected we should.

> LA BRUYÈRE, 'Of Mankind', *Characters*, 1688

Whoever is abandoned by hope has also been abandoned by fear; this is the meaning of the word 'desperate'.

> SCHOPENHAUER, 'Psychological Remarks', *Parerga and
> Paralipomena*, 1851

Anger is one of the sinews of the soul; he that wants it hath a maimed mind.

> THOMAS FULLER (1), *The Holy State and the Profane State*, 1642

A man incorporates anger by concealing it, as Diogenes told Demosthenes, who for fear of being seen in a tavern, withdrew himself the more retiredly into it: 'The more you retire, the more you enter in'.

MONTAIGNE, 'Of anger', *Essays*, 1580–8

Anger is a better sign of the heart than of the head; it is a breaking out of the disease of honesty.

MARQUESS OF HALIFAX, *Moral thoughts and reflections*, late 17th century

A good indignation brings out all one's powers.

EMERSON, *Journals*, 1841

Anger is never sudden. It is born of a long, prior irritation that has ulcerated the spirit and built up an accumulation of force that results in an explosion. It follows that a fine outburst of rage is by no means a sign of a frank, direct nature.

CESARE PAVESE, *This Business of Living: Diaries 1935–50*

He whose face is inflamed with anger shows that the Evil Spirit burns within him.

The Zohar, 13th century

It is easy to fly into a passion – anybody can do that – but to be angry with the right person to the right extent and at the right time and with the right object and in the right way – that is not easy, and it is not everyone who can do it.

ARISTOTLE (4th century BC), *Nicomachean Ethics*

Power is much more easily manifested in destroying than in creating.

WORDSWORTH, Preface to *The Borderers*, 1796

How often, being moved under a false cause, if the person offending makes a good defence and presents us with a just excuse, are we angry against truth and innocence itself?

MONTAIGNE, 'Of anger', *Essays*, 1580–8

Anger always thinks it has power beyond its power.

PUBLILIUS SYRUS, *Sententiae*, 1st century BC

Had Narcissus himself seen his own face when he had been angry, he could never have fallen in love with himself.

THOMAS FULLER (I), *The Holy State and the Profane State*, 1642

An angry look on the face is wholly against nature. If it is assumed frequently, beauty begins to perish, and in the end is quenched beyond rekindling.

MARCUS AURELIUS, *Meditations*, 2nd century

To be angry is to revenge the faults of others upon ourselves.

POPE, *Thoughts on Various Subjects*, 1727

Anger and jealousy can no more bear to lose sight of their objects than love.

GEORGE ELIOT, *The Mill on the Floss*, 1860

Spleen can subsist on any kind of food.

HAZLITT, 'On Wit and Humour', 1818

An ill-humoured man is a prisoner at the mercy of an enemy from whom he can never escape.

SA'DI, *Gulistan*, 1258

> There is a luxury in self-dispraise;
> And inward self-disparagement affords
> To meditative spleen a grateful feast.

WORDSWORTH, *The Excursion*, 1814

If merely 'feeling good' could decide, drunkenness would be the supremely valid human experience.

WILLIAM JAMES, *Varieties of Religious Experience*, 1902

'Tis difficult for the mind, when actuated by any passion, to confine itself to that passion alone, without any change or variation. Human nature is too inconstant to admit of any such regularity.

HUME, *A Treatise of Human Nature*, 1739

Without Contraries is no progression. Attraction and Repulsion, Reason and Energy, Love and Hate, are necessary to Human existence.

BLAKE, *The Marriage of Heaven and Hell*, 1790–3

Sensibility is the more imperious when it is obeyed; abstinence numbs it, abundance excites it.

RÉMY DE GOURMONT, *Epilogues*, 1905

Men's passions are so many roads by which they can be reached.

VAUVENARGUES, *Reflections and Maxims*, 1746

The trip doesn't exist that can set you beyond the reach of cravings, fits of temper, or fears. If it did, the human race would be off there in a body.

SENECA, *Epistles*, 1st century

A philosopher trying to extinguish his passions is like an alchemist putting out his fire.

CHAMFORT, *Maximes et pensées*, 1805

Patience is the Panacea; but where does it grow, or who can swallow it?

WILLIAM SHENSTONE, *Essays on Men and Manners*, 1764

Design & Chance

❀

It may be that the whims of chance are really the importunities of design. But if there is a Design, it aims to look natural and fortuitous; that is how it gets us into its web.

MARY McCARTHY, *On the Contrary*, 1962

Chance understands the royal art of making clear to us that all merit is powerless and unavailing against his favour and grace.

SCHOPENHAUER, 'Counsels and Maxims', *Parerga and Paralipomena*, 1851

The caprices of voluntary agents laugh at calculation. It is not always that there is a strong reason for a great event.

DR JOHNSON, *Thoughts on the Late Transactions Respecting Falkland's Islands*, 1771

At Monte Carlo. This is the temple of Providence where disciples still hourly mark its ways and note the system of its mysteries. Here is the one God whose worshippers prove their faith by their works and in their destruction still trust in Him.

F. H. BRADLEY, *Aphorisms*, 1930

It is not certain that everything is uncertain.

PASCAL, *Pensées*, 1670

As yet the hounds are still playing in the courtyard but their prey will not escape, however fast it may already be charging through the forest.

KAFKA, 'Aphorisms 1917-19', *The Great Wall of China*

A hidden connexion is stronger than an obvious one.

HERACLITUS, *Fragments*, 54, *c.*500 BC

There is a science of *Dynamics* in man's fortunes and nature, as well as of *Mechanics*.

CARLYLE, 'Signs of the Times', 1829

There is always some accident in the best of things, whether thoughts or expression or deeds. The memorable thought, the happy expression, the admirable deed are only partly ours.

THOREAU, *Journal*, 1859

Circumstances are like clouds continually gathering and bursting – While we are laughing the seed of some trouble is put into the wide arable land of events – while we are laughing it sprouts, it grows, and suddenly bears a poison fruit which we must pluck.

KEATS, letter, 1819

So manifold are our interests in life that is not uncommon, on the self-same occasion, for the foundations of a happiness which does not yet exist to be laid down simultaneously with the aggravation of a grief from which we are still suffering.

MARCEL PROUST, *Remembrance of Things Past* (*Swann's Way*, 1913)

Things in our life simply don't go according to set decisions. One glides into a new epoch, and the so-called 'decision' is as a rule only the final summing-up of items long since entered into the ledger by life itself.

FRANZ ROSENZWEIG, letter, 1928

Fate is not an eagle, it creeps like a rat.

ELIZABETH BOWEN, *The House in Paris*, 1938

Once a change of direction has begun, even though it's the wrong one, it still tends to clothe itself as thoroughly in the appurtenances of rightness as if it had been a natural all along.

SCOTT FITZGERALD, *The Crack-Up*, 1945

Need is considered the cause why something came to be; but in truth it is often merely an effect of what has come to be.

NIETZSCHE, *The Gay Science*, 1882–7

Necessity relieves us from the embarrassment of choice.

VAUVENARGUES, *Reflections and Maxims*, 1746

Wherever a man may happen to turn, whatever a man may undertake, he will always end up by returning to that path which nature has marked out for him.

GOETHE, *Autobiography*, 1811

Is the 'goal', the 'purpose' not often enough a beautifying pretext, a self-deception of vanity after the event that does not want to acknowledge that the ship is *following* the current into which it has entered accidentally?

NIETZSCHE, *The Gay Science*, 1882–7

He would like to start from scratch. Where is scratch?

ELIAS CANETTI, *The Human Province*, 1978

Life is a maze in which we take the wrong turning before we have learnt to walk.

CYRIL CONNOLLY, *The Unquiet Grave*, 1944

Since we have explored the maze so long without result, it follows, for poor human reasons, that we cannot have to explore much longer; close by must be the centre, with a champagne luncheon and a piece of ornamental water. How if there were no centre at all, but just one alley after another, and the whole world a labyrinth without end or issue?

ROBERT LOUIS STEVENSON, *Virginibus Puerisque*, 1881

The best way out is always through.

ROBERT FROST, 'A Servant to Servants', 1914

Not every end is a goal. The end of a melody is not its goal; but nonetheless, if the melody had not reached its end it would not have reached its goal either. A parable.

NIETZSCHE, *The Wanderer and His Shadow*, 1880

What are the thoughts of the canvas on which a masterpiece is being painted? 'I am being soiled, brutally treated and concealed from view.' Thus men grumble at their destiny, however fair.

JEAN COCTEAU, *Cock and Harlequin*, 1918

A man may fulfil the object of his existence by asking a question he cannot answer, and attempting a task he cannot achieve.

OLIVER WENDELL HOLMES sen., cit. John Morse, *Life and Letters of O. W. Holmes*

A man should have any number of little aims about which he should be conscious and for which he should have names, but he should have neither name for, nor consciousness concerning, the main aim of his life.

SAMUEL BUTLER (II), *Notebooks*, 1912

Success is relative:
It is what we can make of the mess we have made of things.

T. S. ELIOT, *The Family Reunion*, 1939

A life, admirable at first sight, may have cost so much in imposed liabilities, chores and self-abasement, that, brilliant though it appears, it cannot be considered as other than a failure. Another, which seems to have misfired, is in reality a triumphant success, because it has cost so little.

HENRY DE MONTHERLANT, *Notebooks*, 1930–44

Whatever else we are intended to do, we are not intended to succeed: failure is the fate allotted.

ROBERT LOUIS STEVENSON

The failures and reverses which await men – and one after another sadden the brow of youth – add a dignity to the prospect of human life, which no Arcadian success would do.

THOREAU, *Journal*, 1842

We look back on our life as a thing of broken pieces, because our mistakes and failures are always the first to strike us, and outweigh in our imagination what we have accomplished and attained.

GOETHE, *Maxims and Reflections*, early 19th century

Life always comes to a bad end.
>   MARCEL AYMÉ, *Les Oiseaux de lune*, 1955

If one's prescribed end is to be drowned at sea it is possible to ensure a favourable extent of life by never venturing away from land until the natural end approaches.
>   ERNEST BRAMAH, Ng-Tung in *Kai Lung Unrolls his Mat*, 1928

Nothing ever gets anywhere. The earth keeps turning round and gets nowhere. The moment is the only thing that counts.
>   JEAN COCTEAU, *Professional Secrets*, 1922

If you wish to advance into the infinite, explore the finite in all directions.
>   GOETHE, *Miscellaneous Epigrams*, early 19th century

One must look for one thing only, to find many.
>   CESARE PAVESE, *This Business of Living: Diaries 1935–50*

The least of things with a meaning is worth more in life than the greatest of things without it.
>   JUNG, *Modern Man in Search of a Soul*, 1933

Everything is worthy of notice, for everything can be interpreted.
>   HERMANN HESSE, *The Glass Bead Game*, 1943

Astrology furnishes a splendid proof of the contemptible subjectivity of men. It refers the course of celestial bodies to the miserable ego; it establishes a connection between the comets in heaven and squabbles and rascalities on earth.
>   SCHOPENHAUER, 'Counsels and Maxims', *Parerga and Paralipomena*, 1851

If we lived alone in a featureless desert we should learn to place the individual grains of sand in a moral or aesthetic hierarchy.
>   MICHAEL FRAYN, *Constructions*, 1974

The crest of the flower or the pattern of the lichen may or may not be significant symbols. But there is no stone in the street and no brick in the wall that is not actually a deliberate symbol – a message from some man, as much as if it were a telegram or a post card.

G. K. CHESTERTON, *The Defendant*, 1901

In everything there is an unexplored element because we are prone by habit to use our eyes only in combination with the memory of what others before us have thought about the thing we are looking at. The most insignificant thing contains some little unknown element. We must find it.

MAUPASSANT, Preface to *Pierre et Jean*, 1887

Sophisticated people can hardly understand how vague experience is at bottom, and how truly that vagueness supports whatever clearness is afterwards attained.

SANTAYANA, *The Life of Reason*, 1905–6

A work settles nothing, just as the labour of a whole generation settles nothing. Sons, and the morrow, always start afresh.

CESARE PAVESE, *This Business of Living: Diaries 1935–50*

Individuals

●

Nothing is repeated, and everything is unparalleled.
GONCOURT BROTHERS, *Journal*, 1867

Any attempt at definition of life must start out with the concept of 'individual', otherwise it would not be life.
SIR CHARLES SHERRINGTON, *Man on his Nature*, 1940

Everything that is alive forms an atmosphere around itself.
GOETHE, *Maxims and Reflections*, early 19th century

The nature of the infant is *not* just a new permutation-and-combination of elements contained in the natures of the parents. There is in the nature of the infant that which is utterly unknown in the natures of the parents.
D. H. LAWRENCE, *Psychoanalysis and the Unconscious*, 1921

A person may be indebted for a nose or an eye, for a graceful carriage or a voluble discourse, to a great-aunt or uncle, whose existence he has scarcely heard of.
HAZLITT, 'On Personal Character', 1821

Each one marches in the van. The weakest child is exposed to the fates henceforth as barely as its parents. Parents and relations but entertain the youth; they cannot stand between him and his destiny. This is the one bare side of every man. There is no fence; it is clear before him to the bounds of space.
THOREAU, *Journal*, 1841

> Somewhere at the heart
> of the universe sounds the
> true mystic note: Me.
PETER PORTER, 'Japanese Jokes', *The Last of England*, 1970

However indifferent men are to universal truths, they are keen on those that are individual and particular.

> SCHOPENHAUER, 'Counsels and Maxims', *Parerga and Paralipomena*, 1851

The shoe that fits one person pinches another; there is no recipe for living that suits all cases.

> JUNG, *Modern Man in Search of a Soul*, 1933

The most universal quality is diversity.

> MONTAIGNE, 'Of the resemblance of children to their fathers', *Essays*, 1580–8

There is no proverb which is not true.

> CERVANTES, *Don Quixote*, 1605–15

The best wine is the oldest, the best water the newest.

> BLAKE, *The Marriage of Heaven and Hell*, 1790–3

Some men *must* be too spiritual, some *must* be too sensual. Some *must* be too sympathetic, and some *must* be too proud. We have no desire to say what men *ought* to be. We only wish to say there are all kinds of ways of being, and there is no such thing as human perfection.

> D. H. LAWRENCE, *Fantasia of the Unconscious*, 1922

No birds soars too high, if he soars with his own wings.

> BLAKE, *The Marriage of Heaven and Hell*, 1790–3

The eagle never lost so much time as when he submitted to learn of the crow.

> BLAKE, *The Marriage of Heaven and Hell*, 1790–3

There are people whose defects become them, and others who are ill served by their good qualities.

> LA ROCHEFOUCAULD, *Maxims*, 1665

I do not believe that gifts, whether of mind or character, can be weighed like butter and sugar, not even at Cambridge.

> VIRGINIA WOOLF, *A Room of One's Own*, 1929

Things have various qualities and the soul various tendencies, for nothing presented to the soul is simple, and the soul never applies itself simply to any subject. That is why the same thing makes us laugh and cry.

PASCAL, *Pensées*, 1670

There are as many strata at different levels of life as there are leaves in a book. When on the higher levels we can remember the lower levels, but when on the lower we cannot remember the higher.

THOREAU, *Journal*, 1850

Everything is everywhere. There are tragic elements in superficial things and trivial in the tragic. There is something suffocatingly sinister in what we call pleasure. There is something lyrical about the dress of a whore and something commonplace about the emotions of a lyric poet.

HUGO VON HOFMANNSTHAL, 'Sebastian Melmoth', 1905

People do not think about the events of life as differently as they talk about them.

LICHTENBERG, *Aphorisms*, 1764–99

Most people are other people. Their thoughts are someone else's opinions, their lives a mimicry, their passions a quotation.

OSCAR WILDE, *De Profundis*, 1905

There are persons to whom we never think of applying the ordinary rules of judging. They form a class by themselves, and are curiosities in morals, like nondescripts in natural history. We forgive whatever they do or say, for the singularity of the thing, or because it excites attention. A man who has been hanged is not the worst subject for dissection, and a man who deserves to be hanged may be a very amusing companion or topic of discourse.

HAZLITT, *Characteristics*, 1823

Man is vile, I know, but people are wonderful.

PETER DE VRIES, *Let Me Count the Ways*, 1965

'The individual' is an idea like other ideas.

HAROLD ROSENBERG, *Discovering the Present*, 1973

There is much of mankind that a man can learn only from himself.

WALTER BAGEHOT, *Literary Studies*, 1879

In the course of my life I have seen Frenchmen, Italians, Russians; I even know, thanks to Montesquieu, that one can be a Persian; but *man* I have never met.

JOSEPH DE MAISTRE, *Considérations sur la France*, 1796

The Sense of Identity

●

Searching nature I taste *self* but at one tankard, that of my own being.

GERARD MANLEY HOPKINS, *Journals*, 1880

We have qualities and inclinations so much our own, and so incorporate in us, that we have not the means to feel and recognize them: and of such natural inclinations the body will retain a certain bent, without our knowledge or consent.

MONTAIGNE, 'Of presumption', *Essays*, 1580–8

As a rule a man's face says more of interest than does his tongue; for it is a compendium of all that he will ever say, since it is the monogram of all his thoughts and aspirations. The tongue also expresses only the thoughts of one man, but the face expresses a thought of nature herself.

SCHOPENHAUER, 'On Physiognomy', *Parerga and Paralipomena*, 1851

The voice is a second face.

GERARD BAUER (1888–1967), *Carnets*

The accent of one's birthplace persists in the mind and heart as much as in speech.

LA ROCHEFOUCAULD, *Maxims*, 1665

Becoming accustomed to certain sounds has a profound effect on character; soon one acquires the words and phrases and eventually also the ideas that go with these sounds.

NIETZSCHE, *The Gay Science*, 1882–7

It is through chance that, from among the various individuals of which each of us is composed, one emerges rather than another.

HENRY DE MONTHERLANT, 'Explicit Mysterium', 1931

I cling to my imperfection, as the very essence of my being.
ANATOLE FRANCE, *The Garden of Epicurus*, 1894

In heaven an angel is nobody in particular.
BERNARD SHAW, 'Maxims for Revolutionists', *Man and Superman*, 1903

Every individual is like a company of infantry who leave their trenches and advance in certain places until they have occupied the enemy trench, while elsewhere they are held up or even forced to retreat. Every individual is similar to the line thus formed, with its spearheads and recessions: admirable here, wobbly there, and both at once. That is the touching thing about human beings.
HENRY DE MONTHERLANT, *Notebooks*, 1930–44

At any given moment, our total soul has only a more or less fictitious value, in spite of the rich inventory of its assets, for now some, now others are unrealizable.
MARCEL PROUST, *Remembrance of Things Past* (*Cities of the Plain*, 1921–2)

Let me be nothing if within the compass of myself I do not find the battle of Lepanto, passion against reason, reason against faith, faith against the Devil, and my conscience against all.
SIR THOMAS BROWNE, *Religio Medici*, 1643

A man does not mind being blamed for his faults, and being punished for them, and he patiently suffers much for them; but he becomes impatient if he is required to give them up.
GOETHE, *Maxims and Reflections*, early 19th century

How many pessimists end up by desiring the things they fear, in order to prove that they are right.
ROBERT MALLET (b. 1915), *Apostilles*

In anything it is a mistake to think one can perform an action or behave in a certain way once and no more. What one does, one will do again, indeed has probably already done in the distant past.
CESARE PAVESE, *This Business of Living: Diaries 1935–50*

The rhetoric wherewith I persuade another cannot persuade myself: there is a depraved appetite in us, that will with patience hear the learned instructions of reason, but yet perform no further than agrees to its own irregular humour.

SIR THOMAS BROWNE, *Religio Medici*, 1643

We are dismayed when we find that even disaster cannot cure us of our faults.

VAUVENARGUES, *Reflections and Maxims*, 1746

My fate cannot be mastered; it can only be collaborated with and thereby, to some extent, directed. Nor am I the captain of my soul; I am only its noisiest passenger.

ALDOUS HUXLEY, *Adonis and the Alphabet*, 1956

If disorder is the rule with you, you will be penalized for installing order.

VALÉRY, *Tel Quel*, 1941–3

The educated man tries to repress the inferior one in himself, without realizing that by this he forces the latter to become revolutionary.

JUNG, *Psychology and Religion*, 1940

Motives are symptoms of weakness, and supplements for the deficient energy of the living principle, the law within us.

COLERIDGE, *Aids to Reflection*, 1825

We negate and must negate because something is us wants to live and affirm – something that we perhaps do not know or see as yet.

NIETZSCHE, *The Gay Science*, 1882–7

Self-sacrifice is too often the 'great sacrifice' of trade, the giving cheap what is worth nothing. To know what one wants, and to scruple at no means that will get it, may be a harder self-surrender.

F. H. BRADLEY, *Aphorisms*, 1930

Formula of my happiness: a Yes, a No, a straight line, a goal . . .

NIETZSCHE, *Twilight of the Idols*, 1889

An imaginative man is apt to see, in his life, the story of his life; and is thereby led to conduct himself in life in such a manner as to make a good story of it rather than a good life.

SIR HENRY TAYLOR, *The Statesman*, 1836

To know your ruling passion, examine your castles in the air.

ARCHBISHOP WHATELY, *Apophthegms*, 1864

We dream much of paradise, or rather of a number of successive paradises, but each of them is, long before we die, a paradise lost, in which we should feel ourselves lost too.

MARCEL PROUST, *Remembrance of Things Past (Cities of the Plain, 1921–2)*

One's real life is so often the life that one does not lead.

OSCAR WILDE, L'Envoi to 'Rose-leaf and Apple-leaf', 1882

When I think of all the books I have read, and of the wise words I have heard spoken, and of the anxiety I have given to parents and grandparents, and of the hopes that I have had, all life weighed in the scales of my own life seems to me preparation for something that never happens.

W. B. YEATS, *Autobiography*, 1938

I carry in my world that flourishes the worlds that have failed.

RABINDRANATH TAGORE, *Stray Birds*, 1916

We live beyond any tale we happen to enact.

V. S. PRITCHETT, *The Myth Makers*, 1979

Arriving at each new city, the traveller finds again a past of his that he did not know he had: the foreignness of what you no longer are or no longer possess lies in wait for you in foreign, unpossessed places.

ITALO CALVINO, *Invisible Cities*, 1972

Are you not the future of all the memories stored within you? The future of a past?

VALÉRY, *Mauvaises pensées et autres*, 1942

People often say that this or that person has not yet found himself. But the self is not something one finds, it is something one creates.

THOMAS SZASZ, *The Second Sin*, 1974

One does what one is; one becomes what one does.

ROBERT MUSIL, *Kleine Prosa*, *c*.1930

There may be intelligence or sparks of the divinity in millions – but they are not Souls till they acquire identities, till each one is personally itself.

KEATS, letter, 1819

You should aim to be independent of any one vote, of any one fashion, of any one century.

GRACIÁN, *The Art of Worldly Wisdom*, 1647

A man may be so much of everything that he is nothing of anything.

DR JOHNSON in Boswell's *Life of Johnson*, 1783

One of the unpardonable sins, in the eyes of most people, is for a man to go about unlabelled. The world regards such a person as the police do an unmuzzled dog, not under proper control.

T. H. HUXLEY, *Evolution and Ethics*, 1893

The Platonic type or idea of each of us, towards which we tend, sits behind the high brick walls of the county lunatic asylum. Paranoiacs, schizophrenics, melancholics, manic depressives, people who believe they are God or the Emperor Napoleon, people who sit motionless like statues, people who move about all the time, people who suffer from a total recall of memory, people who never stop talking – among them we see our purified images, our completed models.

GERALD BRENAN, *Thoughts in a Dry Season*, 1978

You are the problem. No scholar to be found far and wide.

KAFKA, 'Aphorisms 1917–19', *The Great Wall of China*

Whatever you may be sure of, be sure of this: that you are dreadfully like other people.

JAMES RUSSELL LOWELL, *My Study Windows*, 1871

Self-Love

❀

He that considers how little he dwells upon the condition of others will learn how little the attention of others is attracted by himself.

DR JOHNSON, *The Rambler*, 1750–2

How comes it that our memories are good enough to retain even the minutest details of what has befallen us, but not to recollect how many times we have recounted them to the same person?

LA ROCHEFOUCAULD, *Maxims*, 1665

We are more anxious to speak than to be heard.

THOREAU, *Journal*, 1841

Everybody has his own theatre, in which he is manager, actor, prompter, playwright, scene-shifter, boxkeeper, doorkeeper, all in one, and audience into the bargain.

JULIUS HARE, *Guesses at Truth*, 1827

To others we are not ourselves but a performer in their lives cast for a part we do not even know that we are playing.

ELIZABETH BIBESCO, *Haven*, 1951

We lack the sense of our own visibility as we lack that of distances, imagining as quite close to us the interested attention of people who on the contrary never give us a thought, and not suspecting that we are at that same moment the sole preoccupation of others.

MARCEL PROUST, *Remembrance of Things Past* (*Cities of the Plain*, 1921–2)

A man cannot look in the mirror at his own image with the eyes of a stranger; his moral egoism constantly whispers in his ear a precautionary 'it is not another ego but my ego that I see'.

SCHOPENHAUER, 'Psychological Remarks', *Parerga and Paralipomena*, 1851

No wonder fops so much enjoy looking at themselves in the mirror; they see themselves whole. If the philosopher had a mirror in which, like the fop, he could see himself whole, he would never get away from it.

LICHTENBERG, *Aphorisms*, 1764–99

Self-love is subtler than the subtlest man in the world.

LA ROCHEFOUCAULD, *Maxims*, 1665

Vanity dies hard; in some obstinate cases it outlives the man.

ROBERT LOUIS STEVENSON, *Prince Otto*, 1885

Most people complain of fortune, few of nature; and the kinder they think the latter has been to them, the more they murmur at what they call the injustice of the former.

LORD CHESTERFIELD, 'Upon Affectation', *The World*, 1755

To love oneself is the beginning of a life-long romance.

OSCAR WILDE, 'Phrases and Philosophies for the Use of the Young', 1894

Can we imagine it possible, that while human nature remains the same, men will ever become entirely indifferent to their power, riches, beauty or personal merit, and that their pride and vanity will not be affected by these advantages?

HUME, *A Treatise of Human Nature*, 1739

The Arch-flatterer, with whom all the petty flatterers have intelligence, is a man's self.

SIR FRANCIS BACON, 'On Love', *Essays*, 1597–1625

Men sometimes feel injured by praise because it assigns a limit to their merit.

VAUVENARGUES, *Reflections and Maxims*, 1746

If we happen to be praised on account of qualities which we formerly despised, our estimation of those qualities immediately rises.

LEOPARDI, *Pensieri*, 1834–7

We are so vain that we even care for the opinion of those we don't care for.

MARIA VON EBNER-ESCHENBACH, *Aphorisms*, 1880

We all think we are exceptional, and are surprised to find ourselves criticized just like anyone else.

COMTESSE DIANE, *Maximes de la vie*, 1908

Praise shames me, for I secretly beg for it.

RABINDRANATH TAGORE, *Stray Birds*, 1916

Just as it is always said of slander that something always sticks when people boldly slander, so it might be said of self-praise (if it is not entirely shameful and ridiculous) that if we praise ourselves fearlessly, something will always stick.

SIR FRANCIS BACON, *De Augmentis scientiarum*, 1623

A dignity which has to be contended for is not worth a quarrel; for it is of the essence of real dignity to be self-sustained, and no man's dignity can be asserted without being impaired.

SIR HENRY TAYLOR, *The Statesman*, 1836

Whoever desires the character of a proud man ought to conceal his vanity.

SWIFT, *Thoughts on Various Subjects*, 1711

Men are much more willing to have their weaknesses and their imperfections known, than their crimes.

LORD CHESTERFIELD, *Letters*, 1748

Vanity is like some men, who are very useful if they are kept under, and else not to be endured.

MARQUESS OF HALIFAX, *Moral thoughts and reflections*, late 17th century

Vanity, like murder, will out.

HANNAH COWLEY, *The Belle's Stratagem*, 1782

One is vain by nature, modest by necessity.

PIERRE REVERDY (1889–1960), *En vrac*

None so empty, as those who are full of themselves.

> BENJAMIN WHICHCOTE, *Moral and Religious Aphorisms*, 1703

Conceit is the finest armour a man can wear.

> JEROME K. JEROME, *The Idle Thoughts of an Idle Fellow*, 1889

Every man has a right to be conceited until he is successful.

> BENJAMIN DISRAELI

I've never any pity for conceited people, because I think they carry their comfort about with them.

> GEORGE ELIOT, *The Mill on the Floss*, 1860

Every man is under that complicated disease, and that riddling distemper, not to be content with the most, and yet to be proud of the least thing he hath; that when he looks upon men, he despises them, because he is some kind of officer, and when he looks upon God, he murmurs at Him, because He made him not a king.

> DONNE, sermon, 1627

He that overvalues himself will undervalue others, and he that undervalues others will oppress them.

> DR JOHNSON, *Sermons*, later 18th century

We measure the excellency of other men, by some excellency we conceive to be in ourselves.

> JOHN SELDEN, *Table Talk*, mid 17th century

Personal resentment, though no laudable motive to satire, can add great force to general principle. Self-love is a busy prompter.

> DR JOHNSON, 'Dryden', *Lives of the Poets*, 1779–81

We are so presumptuous that we think we can separate our personal interest from that of humanity, and slander mankind without compromising ourselves.

> VAUVENARGUES, *Reflections and Maxims*, 1746

Pride worthy of the name does not rise up against superior strength.

It yields as quickly as possible and retires into itself, proud of what it is and disdainful of what it is not.

RÉMY DE GOURMONT, *A Night in Luxembourg*, 1906

There is false modesty, but there is no false pride.

JULES RENARD, *Journal*, 1909

Nobody hates a proud man more than a proud man.

ANON., *Characters and Observations*, early 18th century

Fly pride, says the peacock.

SHAKESPEARE, *The Comedy of Errors*, 1592-3

The book written against fame and learning has the author's name on the title-page.

EMERSON, *Journals*, 1857

Vanity is other people's pride.

SACHA GUITRY, *Jusqu'à nouvel ordre*, 1913

Be modest! It is the kind of pride least likely to offend.

JULES RENARD, *Journal*, 1895

Vanity is the more odious and shocking to everybody, because everybody, without exception, has vanity; and two vanities can never love one another.

LORD CHESTERFIELD, *Letters*, 1766

Egoism in a man strikes us unpleasantly because it betrays our poverty. 'I cannot dole out my abundance to my neighbour, for if I do I shall be left with very little myself.'

LEO SHESTOV, *All Things are Possible*, 1905

Try to arrange your life in such a way that you can afford to be disinterested. It is the most expensive of all luxuries, and the one best worth having.

W. R. INGE, *More Lay Thoughts of a Dean*, 1931

Intolerance itself is a form of egoism, and to condemn egoism intolerantly is to share it.

SANTAYANA, *Winds of Doctrine*, 1913

The 'neighbour' praises selflessness because it brings him advantages. If the neighbour himself were 'selfless' in his thinking, he would repudiate this diminution of strength, this mutilation for *his* benefit.

NIETZSCHE, *The Gay Science*, 1882–7

Is it against reason or justice to love ourselves? And why is self-love always a vice?

VAUVENARGUES, *Reflections and Maxims*, 1746

Self-love rightly defined is far from being a fault. A man who loveth himself right will do everything else right.

MARQUESS OF HALIFAX, *Miscellaneous thoughts and reflections*, late 17th century

You can never get rid of what is part of you, even if you throw it away.

GOETHE, *Maxims and Reflections*, early 19th century

That unsharable feeling which each one of us has of the pinch of his individual destiny as he privately feels it rolling out on fortune's wheel may be disparaged for its egotism, may be sneered at as unscientific, but it is the one thing that fills up the measure of our concrete actuality, and any would-be existent that should lack such a feeling, or its analogue, would be a piece of reality only half made up.

WILLIAM JAMES, *The Varieties of Religious Experience*, 1902

However we may be reproached for our vanity we sometimes need to be assured of our merits and to have our most obvious advantages pointed out to us.

VAUVENARGUES, *Reflections and Maxims*, 1746

Self-love resembles the instrument by which we perpetuate the species. It is necessary, it is dear to us, it gives us pleasure, and it has to be concealed.

VOLTAIRE, 'Self-love', *Philosophical Dictionary*, 1764

'The ego is hateful,' you say. Not mine. I should have liked it in another; should I be hard to please because it is mine?

ANDRÉ GIDE, *Journal*, 1896

Perhaps one should not think so much of oneself, though it is an interesting subject.

NORMAN DOUGLAS, *An Almanac*, 1945

I am the only person in the world I should like to know thoroughly.

OSCAR WILDE, *Lady Windermere's Fan*, 1891

He who has nothing external that can divert him, must find pleasure in his own thoughts, and must conceive himself what he is not; for who is pleased with what he is?

DR JOHNSON, *Rasselas*, 1759

When people do not respect us we are sharply offended; yet deep down in his heart no man much respects himself.

MARK TWAIN, *Notebooks*, later 19th century

There are many things we despise in order that we may not have to despise ourselves.

VAUVENARGUES, *Reflections and Maxims*, 1746

The men who really believe in themselves are all in lunatic asylums.

G. K. CHESTERTON, *Orthodoxy*, 1909

We hate the thing we fear, the thing we know may be true and may have a certain affinity with ourselves, for each man hates himself.

CESARE PAVESE, *This Business of Living: Diaries 1935–50*

Self-love seems so often unrequited.

ANTHONY POWELL, *The Acceptance World*, 1955

How shall we expect charity towards others, when we are uncharitable to ourselves?

SIR THOMAS BROWNE, *Religio Medici*, 1643

Whoever is dissatisfied with himself is continually ready for revenge, and we others will have to be his victims, if only by having to endure his ugly sight. For the sight of what is ugly makes one bad and gloomy.

NIETZSCHE, *The Gay Science*, 1882–7

The most dangerous of our prejudices reign in ourselves against ourselves. To dissolve them is a creative act.

HUGO VON HOFMANNSTHAL, *The Book of Friends*, 1922

Once dismiss the view you take, and you are out of danger. Who, then, is hindering such dismissal?

MARCUS AURELIUS, *Meditations*, 2nd century

Some conjurors say that number three is the magic number, and some say number seven. It's neither, my friend, neither. It's number one.

DICKENS, Fagin in *Oliver Twist*, 1837–8

Self-Knowledge

Up to a certain point every man is what he thinks he is.

F. H. BRADLEY, *Aphorisms*, 1930

It is an error to suppose that no man understands his own character. Most persons know even their failings very well, only they persist in giving them names different from those usually assigned by the rest of the world.

SIR ARTHUR HELPS, *Thoughts in the Cloister and the Crowd*, 1835

People love as self-recognition what they hate as an accusation.

ELIAS CANETTI, *The Human Province*, 1978

The proof that men know their own weak points better than is commonly supposed is that they never make a mistake when you hear them discussing their own behaviour. The very self-love that blinds them as a rule now opens their eyes and gives them such clear vision that they omit or disguise the slightest thing that might be disapproved of.

LA ROCHEFOUCAULD, *Maxims*, 1665

Any one is to be pitied who has just sense enough to perceive his deficiencies.

HAZLITT, *Characteristics*, 1823

No one quality engrosses us purely and universally. Were it not the sign of a fool to talk to one's self, there would hardly be a day or hour wherein I might not be heard to grumble and mutter to myself and against myself, 'Confound the fool!' and yet I do not think that to be my definition.

MONTAIGNE, 'That we laugh and cry for the same thing', *Essays*, 1580–8

True modesty and true pride are much the same thing: both consist in setting a just value on ourselves – neither more nor less.

HAZLITT, *Characteristics*, 1823

Between the ages of twenty and forty we are engaged in the process of discovering who we are, which involves learning the difference between accidental limitations which it is our duty to outgrow and the necessary limitations of our nature beyond which we cannot trespass with impunity.

W. H. AUDEN, *The Dyer's Hand*, 1963

It is so many years before one can believe enough in what one feels even to know what the feeling is.

W. B. YEATS, *Autobiography*, 1938

It is not impossibilities which fill us with the deepest despair, but possibilities which we have failed to realize.

ROBERT MALLET (b. 1915), *Apostilles*

In order to live at peace with ourselves, we almost always disguise our impotence or weakness as calculated actions and systems, and so we satisfy that part of us which is observing the other.

BENJAMIN CONSTANT, *Adolphe*, 1816

We make out of the quarrel with others, rhetoric, but of the quarrel with ourselves, poetry.

W. B. YEATS, 'Anima Hominis', 1917

We can obviously make a wrong use of self-knowledge, just as we can of any other knowledge.

JUNG, interview, 1943

If only we could treat ourselves as we treat other men, looking at their withdrawn faces and crediting them with some mysterious, irresistible power. Instead, we know all our own faults, our misgivings, and are reduced to hoping for some unconscious force to surge up from our inmost being and act with a subtlety all its own.

CESARE PAVESE, *This Business of Living: Diaries 1935–50*

We are, I know not how, double in ourselves, which is the cause that what we believe we do not believe, and cannot disengage ourselves from what we condemn.

MONTAIGNE, 'Of glory', *Essays*, 1580–8

I cannot tell what part of me deceives the other.

GEORG BÜCHNER, *Danton's Death*, 1835

It is a great relief when for a few moments in the day we can retire to our chamber and be completely true to ourselves. It leavens the rest of our hours. In that moment I will be nakedly as vicious as I am – this false life of mine shall have a being at length.

THOREAU, *Journal*, 1841

'I have done that,' says my memory. 'I cannot have done that' – says my pride, and remains adamant. At last – memory yields.

NIETZSCHE, *Beyond Good and Evil*, 1886

When one has made a mistake, one says: 'Another time I shall know what to do,' and what one should say is: 'I already know what I shall really do another time.'

CESARE PAVESE, *This Business of Living: Diaries 1935–50*

The innocent are so few that two of them seldom meet – when they do meet, their victims lie strewn all around.

ELIZABETH BOWEN, *The Death of the Heart*, 1938

What is familiar is what we are used to; and what we are used to is most difficult to 'Know' – that is, to see as a problem; that is, to see as strange, as distant, as 'outside us'.

NIETZSCHE, *The Gay Science*, 1882–7

We discover in ourselves what others hide from us, and we recognize in others what we hide from ourselves.

VAUVENARGUES, *Reflections and Maxims*, 1746

We alone know that those whom we really resemble are not at all those whom we seem to resemble.

JEAN ROSTAND, *Journal d'un Caractère*, 1931

The world judge of men by their ability in their profession, and we judge of ourselves by the same test; for it is that on which our success in life depends. Yet how often do our talents and pursuits lie in different directions! The best painters are not always the cleverest men; and an author who makes an unfavourable or doubtful impression on the public may in himself be a person of rare and agreeable qualifications.

HAZLITT, *Characteristics*, 1823

Almost every man wastes part of his life in attempts to display qualities which he does not possess, and to gain applause which he cannot keep.

DR JOHNSON, *The Rambler*, 1750–2

Many know how to please, but know not when they have ceased to give pleasure.

SIR ARTHUR HELPS, *Thoughts in the Cloister and the Crowd*, 1835

Our years, our debts, and our enemies are always more numerous than we imagine.

CHARLES NODIER (1780–1844)

He that is much flattered soon learns to flatter himself; we are commonly taught our duty by fear or shame, and how can they act upon the man who hears nothing but his own praises?

DR JOHNSON, 'Swift', *Lives of the Poets*, 1779–81

We bestow on others praise in which we do not believe, on condition that in return they bestow upon us praise in which we do.

JEAN ROSTAND, *De la vanité*, 1925

They say princes learn no art truly, but the art of horsemanship. The reason is, the brave beast is no flatterer. He will throw a prince as soon as his groom.

BEN JONSON, *Timber; or Discoveries*, 1640

A stumble may prevent a fall.

THOMAS FULLER (II), *Gnomologia*, 1732

The vices we scoff at in others laugh at us within ourselves.

SIR THOMAS BROWNE, *Christian Morals*, mid 17th century

People seem not to see that their opinion of the world is also a confession of character.

EMERSON, 'Worship', *The Conduct of Life*, 1860

Somebody's boring me . . . I think it's me.

DYLAN THOMAS

While we study with attention the vanity of human life, and turn all our thoughts towards the empty and transitory nature of riches and honours, we are, perhaps, all the while flattering our natural indolence.

HUME, *Philosophical Essays Concerning Human Understanding*, 1748

It is one thing to praise discipline, and another to submit to it.

CERVANTES, *The Dialogue of the Dogs*, 1613

When you meet someone better than yourself, turn your thoughts to becoming his equal. When you meet someone not as good as you are, look within and examine your own self.

CONFUCIUS, *Analects*, 5th century BC

Wherever an inferiority complex exists, there is a good reason for it. There is always something inferior there, although not just where we persuade ourselves that it is.

JUNG, interview, 1943

Very few people in this world would care to listen to the real defence of their own characters. The real defence, the defence which belongs to the Day of Judgment, would make such damaging admissions, would clear away so many artificial virtues, would tell such tragedies of weakness and failure, that a man would sooner be misunderstood and censured by the world than exposed to that awful and merciless eulogy.

G. K. CHESTERTON, *Robert Browning*, 1902

Tell me what you think you are and I will tell you what you are not.

AMIEL, *Journal intime*, 1866

Self-Doubt

❧

There is no creature whose inward being is so strong that it is not greatly determined by what lies outside it.

GEORGE ELIOT, *Middlemarch*, 1871–2

I now perceive one immense omission in my *Psychology* – the deepest principle of Human Nature is the *craving to be appreciated*.

WILLIAM JAMES, *Letters*, 1896

Our lives are greedy pilgrimages in search of hungry recipients.

ELIZABETH BIBESCO, *Haven*, 1951

Nothing could better prove the mythical character of self-consciousness than our extreme sensitiveness to alien opinions; for if a man really knew himself he would utterly despise the ignorant notions others might form on a subject in which he had such matchless opportunities for observation.

SANTAYANA, *The Life of Reason*, 1905–6

The craving to be understood may in the end be merest egoism.

F. H. BRADLEY, *Aphorisms*, 1930

Life for both sexes is arduous, difficult, a perpetual struggle. It calls for gigantic courage and strength. More than anything, perhaps, creatures of illusion as we are, it calls for confidence in oneself. Without self-confidence we are babes in the cradle. And how can we generate this imponderable quality, which is yet so invaluable, most quickly? By thinking that other people are inferior to oneself.

VIRGINIA WOOLF, *A Room of One's Own*, 1929

I often marvel that while each man loves himself more than anyone else, he sets less value on his own estimate than on the opinions of others.

MARCUS AURELIUS, *Meditations*, 2nd century

The image of myself which I try to create in my own mind in order that I may love myself is very different from the image which I try to create in the minds of others in order that they may love me.

w. h. AUDEN, *The Dyer's Hand*, 1963

Wrongs are often forgiven, but contempt never is. Our pride remembers it for ever.

LORD CHESTERFIELD, *Letters*, 1748

The necessity of repelling unjust contempt forces the most modest man into a feeling of pride and self-consciousness.

COLERIDGE, *Omniana*, 1812

If your body were to be put at the disposal of a stranger, you would certainly be indignant. Then aren't you ashamed of putting your mind at the disposal of chance acquaintance, by allowing yourself to be upset if he happens to abuse you?

EPICTETUS, *Enchiridion*, 1st century

A man who likes being praised does not despise his fellow men. One who dreads criticism makes a bogey of their opinion of him. Both praise and criticism lead us to believe that someone can give us *much more than he possesses*.

VALÉRY, *Mauvaises pensées et autres*, 1942

It is easier to cope with a bad conscience than with a bad reputation.

NIETZSCHE, *The Gay Science*, 1882–7

We recognize that flattery is poison, but its perfume intoxicates us.

MARQUIS DE LA GRANGE, *Pensées*, 1872

Sometimes we think we dislike flattery, but it is only the way it is done that we dislike.

LA ROCHEFOUCAULD, *Maxims*, 1665

The flatterer does not think highly enough of himself or of others.

LA BRUYÈRE, 'Of Opinions', *Characters*, 1688

They who are seldom gorged to the full with praises may be safely

fed with gross compliments; for the appetite must be satisfied before
it is disgusted.

DR JOHNSON, *The Rambler*, 1750–2

Plagiaries are delighted with praises, which they are conscious they
do not deserve; but this is a kind of castle building, where the
imagination amuses itself with its own fictions, and strives to render
them firm and stable by a sympathy with the sentiments of others.

HUME, *A Treatise of Human Nature*, 1739

The anxiety to be admired is a loveless passion, ever strongest with
regard to those by whom we are least known and cared for, loud on
the hustings, gay in the ballroom, mute and sullen at the family
fireside.

COLERIDGE, *Aids to Reflection*, 1825

When we ask advice we are usually looking for an accomplice.

MARQUIS DE LA GRANGE, *Pensées*, 1872

Awful disillusion of arriving at centre of supposed authority and
finding need of flattery so as to be reinforced in that authority.

SCOTT FITZGERALD, *The Crack-Up*, 1945

Magnificent characters suffer very differently from what their
admirers imagine. They suffer most keenly from their ignoble and
petty agitations of some evil moments –briefly, from their doubts
about their own magnificence – not from the sacrifices and martyr-
doms that their task demands from them.

NIETZSCHE, *The Gay Science*, 1882–7

Generally those who boast most of contentment have least of it.
Their very boasting shows that they want something, and basely
beg it, namely, commendation.

THOMAS FULLER (I), *The Holy State and the Profane State*, 1642

When we feel that we lack whatever is needed to secure someone
else's esteem, we are very close to hating him.

VAUVENARGUES, *Reflections and Maxims*, 1746

How slight and insignificant is the thing which casts down or
restores a mind greedy for praise.

HORACE, *Epistles*, 20–*c*.8 BC

A jealous man is very quick in his application: he knows how to find
a double edge in an invective, and to draw a satire on himself out of a
panegyrick on another.

ADDISON, *The Spectator*, 1711–12

We resent all criticism which denies us anything that lies in our line
of advance.

EMERSON

Ridicule often checks what is absurd, and fully as often smothers that
which is noble.

SIR WALTER SCOTT, *Quentin Durward*, 1823

A great deal of talent is lost to the world for the want of a little
courage.

SYDNEY SMITH, *Elementary Sketches of Moral Philosophy*, 1804–6

Many would be cowards if they had courage enough.

THOMAS FULLER (II), *Gnomologia*, 1732

No one likes to be pitied for his faults.

VAUVENARGUES, *Reflections and Maxims*, 1746

To show pity is felt as a sign of contempt because one has clearly
ceased to be an object of *fear* as soon as one is pitied.

NIETZSCHE, *The Wanderer and His Shadow*, 1880

It can well come to pass that any one, while sadly regarding his
weakness, should imagine that he is despised by all, and that while all
other men are thinking of nothing less than of despising him.

SPINOZA, *Ethics*, 1677

'Please, oh please drop the subject! Don't talk to me about what I'm
discussing with myself all the time in my mind!'

VALÉRY, *Mauvaises pensées et autres*, 1942

To condemn oneself can also be a means of restoring the feeling of
power after a defeat.

NIETZSCHE, *Daybreak*, 1881

If you want people to envy you your sorrow or your shame, look as
if you were proud of it. If you have enough of the actor in you, rest
assured, you will become the hero of the day.

LEO SHESTOV, *All Things are Possible*, 1905

Jealousy is the fear or apprehension of superiority; Envy our uneasiness under it.

WILLIAM SHENSTONE, *Essays on Men and Manners*, 1764

What is best about a great victory is that it liberates the victor from
the fear of defeat. 'Why not be defeated some time, too?' he says to
himself; 'Now I am rich enough for that.'

NIETZSCHE, *The Gay Science*, 1882–7

When men are easy in themselves, they let others remain so.

LORD SHAFTESBURY, *Characteristics*, 1711

One Among Many

❀

We all come down to dinner, but each has a room to himself.
WALTER BAGEHOT, *Literary Studies*, 1879

Those who think they have no need of others become unreasonable.
VAUVENARGUES, *Reflections and Maxims*, 1746

He that relieth upon himself will be oppressed by others with offers of their service.
MARQUESS OF HALIFAX, *Miscellaneous thoughts and reflections*, late 17th century

Man loves company even if it is only that of a small burning candle.
LICHTENBERG, *Aphorisms*, 1764–99

Man cannot long survive without air, water, and sleep. Next in importance comes food. And close on its heels, solitude.
THOMAS SZASZ, *The Second Sin*, 1974

When boys and girls go out to play there is always someone left behind, and the boy who is left behind is no use to the girl who is left behind.
PAUL POTTS, *Dante Called You Beatrice*, 1960

People who cannot bear to be alone are generally the worst company.
ALBERT GUINON, *c*.1900

It is well known that evils are alleviated by the fact that we bear them in common. People seem to regard boredom as one of these and therefore get together in order to be bored in common.
SCHOPENHAUER, 'Counsels and Maxims', *Parerga and Paralipomena*, 1851

One can acquire anything in solitude except character.

STENDHAL, *Love*, 1822

Everyone alters and is altered by everyone else. We are all the time taking in portions of one another or else reacting against them, and by these involuntary acquisitions and repulsions modifying our natures.

GERALD BRENAN, *Thoughts in a Dry Season*, 1978

When people are free to do as they please, they usually imitate each other.

ERIC HOFFER, *The Passionate State of Mind*, 1955

To do just the opposite is also a form of imitation.

LICHTENBERG, *Aphorisms*, 1764–99

There is no perfectly epicurean corner; there is no perfectly irresponsible place. Everywhere men have made the way for us with sweat and submission. We may fling ourselves into a hammock in a fit of divine carelessness. But we are glad that the net-maker did not make the hammock in a fit of divine carelessness.

G. K. CHESTERTON, *Heretics*, 1905

Let satirists laugh to their hearts' content at human affairs, let theologians revile them, and let the melancholy praise as much as they can the rude and barbarous isolated life: let them despise men and admire the brutes – despite all this, men will find that they can prepare with mutual aid far more easily what they need, and avoid far more easily the perils which beset them on all sides, by united forces: to say nothing of how much better it is, and more worthy of our knowledge, to regard the deeds of men rather than those of brutes.

SPINOZA, *Ethics*, 1677

To be happy, we must not be too concerned with others.

ALBERT CAMUS, Jean-Baptiste Clamance in *The Fall*, 1956

Don't shout for help at night. You may wake your neighbours.

STANISLAW LEC, *Unkempt Thoughts*, 1962

The world is quickly bored by the recital of misfortunes, and willingly avoids the sight of distress.

SOMERSET MAUGHAM, *The Moon and Sixpence*, 1919

The man who cannot live with charity, sharing other men's pain, is punished by feeling his own with intolerable anguish.

CESARE PAVESE, *This Business of Living: Diaries 1935–50*

There is a certain distance at which each person we know is naturally placed from us. It varies with each, and we must not attempt to alter it. We may clasp him who is close, and we are not to pull closer him who is more remote.

MARK RUTHERFORD, *More Pages from a Journal*, 1910

No man lives without jostling and being jostled; in all ways he has to elbow himself through the world, giving and receiving offence.

CARLYLE, 'Sir Walter Scott', 1838

Character calls forth character.

GOETHE, *Maxims and Reflections*, early 19th century

We don't ask others to be faultless; we only ask that their faults should not incommode our own.

'GYP', late 19th century

It astounds us to come upon other egoists, as though we alone had the right to be selfish, and to be filled with eagerness to live.

JULES RENARD, *Journal*, 1887

Impeded aggressiveness seems to involve a grave injury. It really seems as though it is necessary for us to destroy some other thing or person in order not to destroy ourselves.

FREUD, 'Anxiety and Instinctual Life', *New Introductory Lectures on Psychoanalysis*, 1933

How can you say my life is not a success? Have I not for more than sixty years got enough to eat and escaped being eaten?

LOGAN PEARSALL SMITH, *Last Words*, 1933

What men call social virtues, good fellowship, is commonly but the virtue of pigs in a litter, which lie close together to keep each other warm. It brings men together in crowds and mobs in bar-rooms and elsewhere, but it does not deserve the name of virtue.

THOREAU, *Journal*, 1852

We are by all odds the most persistently and obsessively social of all species, more dependent on each other than the famous social insects, and really, when you look at us, infinitely more imaginative and deft at social living.

LEWIS THOMAS, *The Medusa and the Snail*, 1979

Whoever live at a different end of the town from me, I look upon as persons out of the world, and only myself and the scene about me to be in it.

SWIFT, *Thoughts on Various Subjects*, 1711

Many pains are incident to a man of delicacy, which the unfeeling world cannot be persuaded to pity; and which, when they are separated from their peculiar and personal circumstances, will never be considered as important enough to claim attention or deserve redress.

DR JOHNSON, *The Rambler*, 1750–2

The moment we care for anything deeply, the world – that is, all the other miscellaneous interests – becomes our enemy.

G. K. CHESTERTON, *Heretics*, 1905

Let us stay at home: there we are decent. Let us not go out: our defects wait for us at the door, like flies.

JULES RENARD, *Journal*, 1898

I never come back home with quite the same moral character I went out with; something or other becomes unsettled where I had achieved internal peace, some one or other of the things I had put to flight reappears on the scene.

SENECA, *Epistles*, 1st century

No man can have society upon his own terms. If he seeks it, he must serve it too.

EMERSON, *Journals*, 1833

The moment you enter society, you draw the key from your heart and put it in your pocket. Those who fail to do so are fools.

GOETHE, conversation with Lavater, 1774

It must be admitted that there are some parts of the soul which we must entirely *paralyse* before we can live happily in this world.

CHAMFORT, *Maximes et pensées*, 1805

As soon as we attract enough attention in the world to play a part in it, we are set rolling like a ball which will never again be at rest.

PRINCE DE LIGNE, *Mes écarts*, 1796

Happy that few of us are aware of the world until we are already in league with it.

ELIZABETH BOWEN, *The Death of the Heart*, 1938

We become charlatans without realizing it, and actors without wanting to.

AMIEL, *Journal intime*, 1866

Almost from the cradle to the grave one has an audience to whom one is playing up. The story of these audiences succeeding one another, their character and quality should be treated as an important part of a biography or an autobiography.

BERNARD BERENSON, notebook, *c.*1939

The world is a country which nobody ever yet knew by description; one must travel through it one's self to be acquainted with it.

LORD CHESTERFIELD, *Letters*, 1747

If a man wishes to know the origin of human society, to know what society, philosophically speaking, really is, let him not go into the British Museum; let him go into society.

G. K. CHESTERTON, *Heretics*, 1905

Society and the World are like a library where at first glance all seems in order, for the books are arranged according to their shapes and sizes, but where, on closer scrutiny, there is seen to be utter confusion, because there has been no grouping under subject matter, class, or author.

CHAMFORT, *Maximes et pensées*, 1805

Pretend not thou to scorn the pomp of the world before thou knowest it.

THOMAS FULLER (II), *Introductio ad Prudentiam*, 1731

If you wish to become a philosopher you must not be disheartened by the first distressing discoveries you make in your study of human beings. To learn these thoroughly you must triumph over the dissatisfactions they afford you, as an anatomist triumphs over Nature and his bodily disgust in order to become proficient in his calling.

CHAMFORT, *Maximes et pensées*, 1805

Real misanthropes are not found in solitude, but in the world; since it is experience of life, and not philosophy, which produces real hatred of mankind.

LEOPARDI, *Pensieri*, 1834–7

It is the fools and the knaves that make the wheels of the World turn. They *are* the World; those few who have sense or honesty sneak up and down single, but never go in herds.

MARQUESS OF HALIFAX, *Moral thoughts and reflections*, late 17th century

Every man has a mob self and an individual self, in varying proportions.

D. H. LAWRENCE, 'Pornography and Obscenity', 1929

There is an accumulative cruelty in a number of men, though none in particular are ill-natured.

MARQUESS OF HALIFAX, *Political thoughts and reflections*, late 17th century

Everyone in a crowd has the power to throw dirt: nine out of ten have the inclination.

HAZLITT, 'On Reading Old Books', 1821

What the crowd requires is mediocrity of the highest order.

> AUGUSTE PRÉAULT (1809–79)

The stacking together of the paintings of the great masters in museums is a catastrophe, and a collection of a hundred good intellects produces collectively one idiot.

> JUNG, book review, 1934

The public! the public! How many fools does it take to make up a public?

> CHAMFORT, *Caractères et anecdotes*, 1771

A man of correct insight among those who are duped and deluded resembles one whose watch is right while all the clocks in the town give the wrong time. He alone knows the correct time, but of what use is this to him? The whole world is guided by the clocks that show the wrong time.

> SCHOPENHAUER, 'Counsels and Maxims', *Parerga and Paralipomena*, 1851

How can one be glad of the world, unless one is flying to it for refuge?

> KAFKA, 'Aphorisms 1917–19', *The Great Wall of China*

To be too much troubled is a worse way of over-valuing the World than the being too much pleased.

> MARQUESS OF HALIFAX, *Moral thoughts and reflections*, late 17th century

The world will, in the end, follow only those who have despised as well as served it.

> SAMUEL BUTLER (II), *Notebooks*, 1912

There are moments when Society seems really to value itself at its proper worth. I have frequently come to the conclusion that it looks up to those who care nothing at all about it.

> CHAMFORT, *Maximes et pensées*, 1805

One is not superior merely because one sees the world in an odious light.

> CHATEAUBRIAND

No one is so completely disenchanted with the world, or knows it so thoroughly, or is so utterly disgusted with it, that when it begins to smile upon him he does not become partially reconciled to it.

LEOPARDI, *Pensieri*, 1834–7

The world will commonly end by making men that which it thinks them. If a man could be satisfied that the world was convinced that he was indifferent to the objects of ambition, then he might more easily be actually indifferent to them; but as the world must always be understood to assume that a man is aiming at such objects, the non-attainment of them seems to place him in a position of defeat.

SIR HENRY TAYLOR, *The Statesman*, 1836

Others are to us like the 'characters' of fiction, eternal and incorrigible; the surprises they give us turn out in the end to have been predictable – unexpected variations on the theme of being themselves, of the *principio individuationis*. But it is just this principle that we cannot see in ourselves.

MARY McCARTHY, *On the Contrary*, 1962

The men we see in each other do not give us the image and likeness of man. The men we see are whipped through the world; they are harried, wrinkled, anxious; they all seem the hacks of some invisible riders.

EMERSON, 'Domestic Life', *Society and Solitude*, 1870

It is good to know what a man is, and also what the world takes him for. But you do not understand him until you have learnt how he understands himself.

F. H. BRADLEY, *Aphorisms*, 1930

We never remark any passion or principle in others, of which, in some degree or other, we may not find a parallel in ourselves.

HUME, *A Treatise of Human Nature*, 1739

Attributing our own temptations to others, we give them credit for victories they have never won.

ELIZABETH BIBESCO, *Haven*, 1951

The world will find out that part of your character which concerns it:

that which especially concerns yourself, it will leave for you to discover.

SIR ARTHUR HELPS, *Thoughts in the Cloister and the Crowd*, 1835

There exists scarcely any man so accomplished, or so necessary to those around him, that he does not have some failing which will diminish their regret at his loss.

LA BRUYÈRE, 'Of Personal Merit', *Characters*, 1688

It was perhaps ordained by Providence, to hinder us from tyrannizing over one another, that no individual should be of such importance, as to cause, by his retirement or death, any chasm in the world.

DR JOHNSON, *The Rambler*, 1750–2

Soon you will have forgotten the world, and the world will have forgotten you.

MARCUS AURELIUS, *Meditations*, 2nd century

Nobody is forgotten when it is convenient to remember him.

BENJAMIN DISRAELI

Be prosperous and gay, require our services – never, and we will be your friends. This is not what Society says, but it is the principle on which it acts.

LADY BLESSINGTON, 'Night Thought Book', 1834

Society is immoral and immortal; it can afford to commit any kind of folly, and indulge in any kind of vice; it cannot be killed, and the fragments that survive can always laugh at the dead.

HENRY ADAMS, *The Education of Henry Adams*, 1907

You may break your heart, but men will still go on as before.

MARCUS AURELIUS, *Meditations*, 2nd century

Fame & Reputation

●

We are so presumptuous that we should like to be known all over the world, even by people who will only come when we are no more. Such is our vanity that the good opinion of half a dozen of the people around us gives us pleasure and satisfaction.

PASCAL, *Pensées*, 1670

Fame is sometimes like unto a kind of mushroom, which Pliny recounts to be the greatest miracle in nature, because growing and having no root.

THOMAS FULLER (I), *The Holy State and the Profane State*, 1642

Wealth is like sea-water; the more we drink, the thirstier we become; and the same is true of fame.

SCHOPENHAUER, 'What a Man has', *Parerga and Paralipomena*, 1851

The more you are talked about, the more you will wish to be talked about. The condemned murderer who is allowed to see the account of his trial in the Press is indignant if he finds a newspaper which has reported it inadequately. And the more he finds about himself in other newspapers, the more indignant he will be with the one whose reports are meagre. Politicians and literary men are in the same case.

BERTRAND RUSSELL, *Human Society in Ethics and Politics*, 1954

Fame is so sweet that we love anything with which we connect it, even death.

PASCAL, *Pensées*, 1670

Avoid shame, but do not seek glory; nothing so expensive as glory.

SYDNEY SMITH in Lady Holland, *Memoir*, 1855

Contempt of fame begets contempt of virtue.

BEN JONSON, *Sejanus*, 1605

Most celebrated men live in a condition of prostitution.
                                   SAINTE-BEUVE, *Notebooks*, 1876

Many a man would have been a veritable Phoenix if he had been the
first of the sort. Those who come first are the heirs of Fame; the
others get only a younger brother's allowance.
                          GRACIÁN, *The Art of Worldly Wisdom*, 1647

Popularity is a crime from the moment it is sought; it is only a virtue
where men have it whether they will or no.
                   MARQUESS OF HALIFAX, *Moral thoughts and reflections*, late 17th
                   century

As disdain displeases and offends more than hatred, so esteem is
more welcome than benevolence; and men generally desire much
more to be esteemed than to be loved.
                                         LEOPARDI, *Pensieri*, 1837

The more one pleases generally, the less one pleases profoundly.
                                         STENDHAL, *Love*, 1822

We seek our happiness outside ourselves, and in the opinion of men
whom we know to be flatterers, insincere, unjust, full of envy,
caprice and prejudice. How absurd!
                         LA BRUYÈRE, 'Of Mankind', *Characters*, 1688

When Princes break their miserable etiquette it is always in favour of
some girl or jester, and never for a man of worth. When women
make themselves conspicuous, it is never for an upright man, always
for a *creature*. In a word, when we throw off the yoke of public
opinion, it is seldom for the purpose of rising above it, but nearly
always to fall below.
                             CHAMFORT, *Maximes et pensées*, 1805

The world is not unkind, and reprobates are worse than their reputations.
                     LOGAN PEARSALL SMITH, *Afterthoughts*, 1931

It often happens that our good points are only loved and praised, because their lustre is tempered by our defects. It is, indeed, no rare thing to be loved rather for our failings than for our good qualities.

JOUBERT, *Pensées*, 1842

It is difficult to esteem a man as he desires to be esteemed.

VAUVENARGUES, *Reflections and Maxims*, 1746

Men are rewarded and punished not for what they do, but rather for how their acts are defined. This is why men are more interested in better justifying themselves than in better behaving themselves.

THOMAS SZASZ, *The Second Sin*, 1974

Respect is often paid in proportion as it is claimed.

DR JOHNSON, *The Idler*, 1758

A sense of one's own dignity is as admirable when kept to oneself as it is ridiculous when displayed to others.

LA ROCHEFOUCAULD, *Maxims*, 1665

Knowledge may give weight, but accomplishments add lustre, and many more people see than weigh.

LORD CHESTERFIELD, *Letters*, 1750

Men hold moral virtues of little account, and worship physical and intellectual gifts. A man who can say of himself, quite coolly and, so he thinks, without offending against modesty, that he is kind, constant, loyal, sincere, fair-minded, grateful, dares not to say that he is lively, that he has fine teeth or a soft skin: that would be going too far.

LA BRUYÈRE, 'Of Mankind', *Characters*, 1688

Fools invent fashions, and wise men are fain to follow them.

SAMUEL BUTLER (I), *Prose Observations*, 1660–80

Fashion, *n.* A despot whom the wise ridicule and obey.

AMBROSE BIERCE, *The Devil's Dictionary*, 1906

Dress is a very foolish thing, and yet it is a very foolish thing for a man not to be well dressed.

LORD CHESTERFIELD, *Letters*, 1745

A man in fashion does not last long, for fashions pass, but if he happens to be a man of ability, he is not quite destroyed, and something of him still subsists; he is still admirable, he is merely less admired.

LA BRUYÈRE, 'Of Fashion', *Characters*, 1688

There are persons who, when they cease to shock us, cease to interest us.

F. H. BRADLEY, *Aphorisms*, 1930

Those who support startling paradoxes in society must expect severe treatment. By the articles of war, the conquerors never spare those who maintain indefensible positions.

SIR ARTHUR HELPS, *Thoughts in the Cloister and the Crowd*, 1835

There are but three ways for a man to revenge himself of a censorious world: to despise it, to return the like, or to endeavour to live so as to avoid it. The first of these is usually pretended; the last is almost impossible; the universal practice is for the second.

SWIFT, *Thoughts on Various Subjects*, 1711

Men shut their doors against a setting sun.

SHAKESPEARE, *Timon of Athens*, 1607–8

The very best have had their calumniators, the very worst their panegyrists.

CHARLES CALEB COLTON, *Lacon*, 1825

Those are most desirous of honour and glory who cry out loudest at its abuse and the vanity of the world.

SPINOZA, *Ethics*, 1677

Why long for glory, which one despises as soon as one has it? But that is precisely what the ambitious man wants: having it in order to be able to despise it.

JEAN ROSTAND, *De la vanité*, 1925

The Arts of Success

The shortest and best way to make your fortune is to let people see clearly that it is in their interests to promote yours.

LA BRUYÈRE, 'Of the Gifts of Fortune', *Characters*, 1688

Knowledge, sense, honesty, learning, good behaviour are the chief things towards making a man's fortune, next to interest and opportunity.

ANON., *Characters and Observations*, early 18th century

The clever man often worries; the loyal person is often overworked.

'MR TUT-TUT', *A Night's Talk*, Chinese, 17th century

Merit envies success, and success takes itself for merit.

JEAN ROSTAND, *De la vanité*, 1925

Success in ordinary life depends far more on negative than on positive qualities.

CHURTON COLLINS, aphorisms in the *English Review*, 1914

Fortune sometimes uses our faults for our advancement; some people are so tiresome that their merits would go unrewarded were it not that we want to get them out of the way.

LA ROCHEFOUCAULD, *Maxims*, 1665

There is reason to think the most celebrated philosophers would have been bunglers at business; but the reason is because they despised it.

MARQUESS OF HALIFAX, *Moral thoughts and reflections*, late 17th century

Prizes bring bad luck. Academic prizes, prizes for virtue, decorations, all these inventions of the devil encourage hypocrisy, and freeze the spontaneous upsurge of a free heart.

BAUDELAIRE, *Curiosités esthétiques*, 1868

The reason why fools and knaves thrive better in the world than wiser and honester men is because they are nearer to the general temper of mankind, which is nothing but a mixture of cheat and folly, which those that understand and mean better cannot comply with, but entertain themselves with another kind of fool's paradise of what should be, not what is; while those that know no better take naturally to it, and get the start of them.

SAMUEL BUTLER (I), *Prose Observations*, 1660–80

The nearest way to honour is to have none at all.

SAMUEL BUTLER (I), *Prose Observations*, 1660–80

A man with a career can have no time to waste upon his wife and friends; he has to devote it wholly to his enemies.

JOHN OLIVER HOBBES (1867–1906)

The only means to gain one's ends with people are force and cunning. Love also, they say; but that is to wait for sunshine, and life needs every moment.

GOETHE, conversation with Riemer, 1810

Never contend with a man who has nothing to lose.

GRACIÁN, *The Art of Worldly Wisdom*, 1647

The path of social advancement is, and must be, strewn with broken friendships.

H. G. WELLS, *Kipps*, 1905

A man has made great progress in cunning when he does not seem too clever to others.

LA BRUYÈRE, 'Of the Court', *Characters*, 1688

Never tell your resolution beforehand.

JOHN SELDEN, *Table Talk*, mid 17th century

The best way to keep one's word is not to give it.

NAPOLEON, *Maxims*, early 19th century

Ambition often puts men upon doing the meanest offices; so climb-
ing is performed in the same posture with creeping.

SWIFT, *Thoughts on Various Subjects*, 1711

Few things are more shocking to those who practise the arts of
success than the frank description of those arts.

LOGAN PEARSALL SMITH, *Reperusals and Re-collections*, 1936

No one is safe from flattery, therefore the art of flattery is infinitely
various; the crowd of blackmailers is legion, therefore the flow of
rumours is difficult to stop.

'MR TUT-TUT', *A Night's Talk*, Chinese, 17th century

'Tis an old maxim in the schools,
That flattery's the food of fools;
Yet now and then your men of wit
Will condescend to take a bit.

SWIFT, *Cadenus and Vanessa*, 1713

We speak in the presence of people who are vain, just like ourselves,
and their vanity suffers in proportion as ours is satisfied.

MONTESQUIEU

If you want to succeed in the world it is necessary, when entering a
salon, that your vanity should bow to that of others.

MADAME DE GENLIS (1746–1830)

It seems that in our social life, a minor echo of what occurs in love,
the best way to get oneself sought after is to withhold oneself.

MARCEL PROUST, *Remembrance of Things Past* (*The Captive*,
1923)

The greatest of all secrets is knowing how to reduce the force of
envy.

CARDINAL DE RETZ, *Memoirs*, 1673–6

There is no need to show your ability before everyone.

GRACIÁN, *The Art of Worldly Wisdom*, 1647

Mutual praise may stem from a genuine harmony of views, but in a field infested by charlatans it more commonly occurs as an unprincipled collusion which enables the partners to circumvent the customary taboo on boasting.

STANISLAV ANDRESKI, *Social Sciences as Sorcery*, 1972

If you wish to win a man's heart, allow him to confute you.

BENJAMIN DISRAELI, *Vivian Grey*, 1826

Excusations, cessions, modesty itself well governed, are but arts of ostentation.

SIR FRANCIS BACON, 'Of Vain-Glory', *Essays*, 1597–1625

Yield to a man's tastes and he will yield to your interests.

EDWARD BULWER-LYTTON, *Paul Clifford*, 1835

Birds are taken with pipes that imitate their own voices, and men with those sayings that are most agreeable to their own opinions.

SAMUEL BUTLER (1), *Prose Observations*, 1660–80

A compliment is a forensic anaesthetic. Many people will complacently undergo a fatal interrogation if they be well flattered all the while; and more men are likely to be caught by a compliment to their ability than by a tribute to their virtue.

MR JUSTICE DARLING, *Scintillae Juris*, 1889

It is a grace in flattery to let fall your compliments as that you shall seem to consider them to be a matter of indifference to him to whom they are addressed; for thus one flattery will include another – and that other perhaps the most agreeable – being that of attributing to the party a peculiar absence of self-love.

SIR HENRY TAYLOR, *The Statesman*, 1836

What really flatters a man is that you think him worth flattering.

BERNARD SHAW, *John Bull's Other Island*, 1907

Never claim as a right what you can ask as a favour.

CHURTON COLLINS, aphorisms in the *English Review*, 1914

It is the nature of men to be bound by the benefits they confer as much as by those they receive.

MACHIAVELLI, *The Prince*, 1513

Remember that in giving any reason at all for refusing, you lay some foundation for a future request.

SIR ARTHUR HELPS, *Essays Written in Intervals of Business*, 1841

We often make people pay dearly for what we think we give them.

COMTESSE DIANE, *Maximes de la vie*, 1908

There is a hook in every benefit, that sticks in his jaws that takes that benefit, and draws him whither the benefactor will.

DONNE, sermon, *c*.1625

Many a man loves the memory of his benefactor, that would be loth to have him alive again.

ANON., *Characters and Observations*, early 18th century

One must not depend on one thing or trust to only one resource, however pre-eminent. Everything should be kept double, especially the causes of success, of favour, or of esteem.

GRACIÁN, *The Art of Worldly Wisdom*, 1647

No one who deserves confidence ever solicits it.

CHURTON COLLINS, aphorisms in the *English Review*, 1914

Quack and dupe are upper side, and under, of the selfsame substance; controvertible personages.

CARLYLE, *Past and Present*, 1843

A market is a place set apart for men to deceive and get the better of one another.

ANACHARSIS (*c*.600 BC), cit. Diogenes Laertius, *Lives and Opinions of Eminent Philosophers*

What we think an unreasonable price when we are to buy, we think just and equitable when we are to sell.

ANON., *Characters and Observations*, early 18th century

People of the same trade seldom meet together but the conversation ends in a conspiracy against the public, or in some diversion to raise prices.

ADAM SMITH, *The Wealth of Nations*, 1776

One now and then meets with people on whose face, in whose manner, in whose words, one may read a bill giving notice that they are *to be let or sold*. They also profess to be furnished; but everybody knows what the furniture of a ready-furnished house usually is.

JULIUS HARE, *Guesses at Truth*, 1827

Crafty men deal in generalizations.

ANON.

A wise man will keep his suspicions muzzled, but he will keep them awake.

MARQUESS OF HALIFAX, *Miscellaneous thoughts and reflections*, late 17th century

How many 'coming men' one has known! Where on earth do they all go to?

SIR ARTHUR PINERO

Action & Achievement

❀

There is no such thing as a great talent without great will-power.

BALZAC, *La Muse du Département*, 1843

There are no mute inglorious Miltons, save in the hallucinations of poets. The one sound test of a Milton is that he functions as a Milton.

H. L. MENCKEN, *Prejudices: Third Series*, 1922

Between vague wavering Capability and fixed indubitable Performance, what a difference!

CARLYLE, *Sartor Resartus*, 1833

An unfulfilled vocation drains the colour from a man's entire existence.

BALZAC, *La Maison Nucingen*, 1838

Men despise great projects when they do not feel themselves capable of great successes.

VAUVENARGUES, *Reflections and Maxims*, 1746

Those that have done nothing in life, are not qualified to judge of those that have done little.

DR JOHNSON, *Plan of an English Dictionary*, 1747

Action is consolatory. It is the enemy of thought and the friend of flattering illusions.

JOSEPH CONRAD, *Nostromo*, 1904

The first undertakers in all great attempts commonly miscarry, and leave the advantages of their losses to those that come after them.

SAMUEL BUTLER (I), *Prose Observations*, 1660–80

It is better to be adventurous than cautious, because fortune is a woman.

MACHIAVELLI, *The Prince*, 1517

Good swimmers are oftenest drowned.

THOMAS FULLER (II), *Gnomologia*, 1732

Nothing will ever be attempted, if all possible objections must be first overcome.

DR JOHNSON, *Rasselas*, 1759

No one is more liable to make mistakes than the man who acts only on reflection.

VAUVENARGUES, *Reflections and Maxims*, 1746

There is always a multitude of reasons both in favour of doing a thing and against doing it. The art of debate lies in presenting them; the art of life lies in neglecting ninety-nine hundredths of them.

MARK RUTHERFORD, *More Pages from a Journal*, 1910

In accomplishing anything definite a man renounces everything else.

SANTAYANA, *The Life of Reason*, 1905–6

The pretext for indecisiveness is commonly mature deliberation; but in reality indecisive men occupy themselves less in deliberation than others; for to him who fears to decide, deliberation (which has a foretaste of that fear) soon becomes intolerably irksome, and the mind escapes from the anxiety of it into alien themes.

SIR HENRY TAYLOR, *The Statesman*, 1836

Decide, *v.i.* To succumb to the preponderance of one set of influences over another set.

AMBROSE BIERCE, *The Devil's Dictionary*, 1906

Irresolute men are sometimes very persistent in their undertakings, because if they gave up their design they would have to make a second resolution.

LEOPARDI, 'Sayings of Filippo Ottonieri', *Essays and Dialogues*, 1824–32

At the last moment there is always a reason not existing before –
namely, the impossibility of further vacillation.

GEORGE ELIOT, *Felix Holt*, 1866

For a thing to remain undone nothing more is needed than to think it
done.

GRACIÁN, *The Art of Worldly Wisdom*, 1647

No task is a long one but the task on which one dare not start. It
becomes a nightmare.

BAUDELAIRE, *My Heart Laid Bare*, 1864–6

There is an old saying 'well begun is half done' – 'tis a bad one. I
would use instead – Not begun at all until half done.

KEATS, letter, 1817

Arrears of small things to be attended to, if allowed to accumulate,
worry and depress like unpaid debts. The main work should always
stand aside for these, not these for the main work, as large debts
should stand aside for small ones, or truth for common charity and
good feeling. If we attend continually and promptly to the little that
we can do, we shall ere long be surprised to find how little remains
that we cannot do.

SAMUEL BUTLER (II), *Notebooks*, 1912

As a general rule, the shorter the interval that separates us from our
planned objective the longer it seems to us, because we apply to it a
more minute scale of measurement, or simply because it occurs to us
to measure it.

MARCEL PROUST, *Remembrance of Things Past* (*The Guermantes
Way*, 1920–1)

Never undertake anything unless you have the heart to ask Heaven's
blessing on your undertaking!

LICHTENBERG, *Aphorisms*, 1764–99

The test of a vocation is the love of the drudgery it involves.

LOGAN PEARSALL SMITH, *Afterthoughts*, 1931

All professional men are handicapped by not being allowed to ignore things which are useless.

GOETHE, *Maxims and Reflections*, early 19th century

There is no kind of idleness by which we are so easily seduced as that which dignifies itself by the appearance of business.

DR JOHNSON, *The Idler*, 1758

We make a mistake if we believe that only the violent passions like ambition and love can subdue the others. Laziness, for all her languor, is nevertheless often mistress: she permeates every aim and action in life and imperceptibly eats away and destroys passions and virtues alike.

LA ROCHEFOUCAULD, *Maxims*, 1665

A lazy hand is no argument of a contented heart.

THOMAS FULLER (I), *The Holy State and the Profane State*, 1642

The lazy are always wanting to do something.

VAUVENARGUES, *Reflections and Maxims*, 1746

Failure is not the only punishment for laziness: there is also the success of others.

JULES RENARD, *Journal*, 1898

If a soldier or a labourer complains of the hardship of his lot, set him to do nothing.

PASCAL, *Pensées*, 1670

His weariness is that of the gladiator after the combat; his work was the whitewashing of a corner in a state official's office.

KAFKA, 'Aphorisms 1917–19', *The Great Wall of China*

House-keeping ain't no joke.

LOUISA MAY ALCOTT, *Little Women*, 1868

There are tracts in my life that are bare and silent. They are the open spaces where my busy days had their light and air.

RABINDRANATH TAGORE, *Stray Birds*, 1916

But men must know, that in this theatre of man's life it is reserved only for God and angels to be lookers on.

SIR FRANCIS BACON, *The Advancement of Learning*, 1605

The way to get things done is not to mind who gets the credit of doing them.

BENJAMIN JOWETT

Money & Rank

●

If we did not see it with our own eyes, could we ever imagine the
extraordinary disproportion created between men by a larger or
smaller degree of wealth?

LA BRUYÈRE, 'Of the Gifts of Fortune', *Characters*, 1688

The purse strings tie us to our kind.

WALTER BAGEHOT, *Literary Studies*, 1879

He that has nothing but merit to support him, is in a fair way to
starve.

ANON., *Characters and Observations*, early 18th century

Every single instance of a friend's insincerity increases our dependence on the efficacy of money.

WILLIAM SHENSTONE, *Essays on Men and Manners*, 1764

Money makes a man laugh.

JOHN SELDEN, *Table Talk*, mid 17th century

Gold is the soul of all civil life, that can resolve all things into itself,
and turn itself into all things.

SAMUEL BUTLER (I), *Prose Observations*, 1660–80

When I think of all the sorrow and the barrenness that has been
wrought in my life by want of a few more pounds per annum than I
was able to earn, I stand aghast at money's significance.

GEORGE GISSING, *The Private Papers of Henry Ryecroft*, 1903

Those who have some means think that the most important thing in
the world is love. The poor know that it is money.

GERALD BRENAN, *Thoughts in a Dry Season*, 1978

I sit and worry
about money who very
soon will have to die.

PETER PORTER, 'Japanese Jokes', *The Last of England*, 1970

One must be poor to know the luxury of giving.

GEORGE ELIOT, *Middlemarch*, 1872

It is easy enough to say that poverty is no crime. No; if it were men wouldn't be ashamed of it. It is a blunder, though, and is punished as such. A poor man is despised the whole world over.

JEROME K. JEROME, *Idle Thoughts of an Idle Fellow*, 1889

'Tis as hard f'r a rich man to enther th' kingdom iv Hiven as it is f'r a poor man to get out iv Purgatory.

FINLEY PETER DUNNE, *Mr. Dooley's Opinions*, 1900

There is one advantage of being poor – a doctor will cure you faster.

KIN HUBBARD, *Abe Martin's Sayings*, 1915

It's no great step for a poor man to the grave.
He's lived his life out only half-alive.

But when the man of plenty nears the end of his,
Death yawns beneath him like a precipice.

PALLADAS (4th–5th century), *The Greek Anthology* (trans. Tony Harrison)

Respectable means rich, and decent means poor. I should die if I heard my family called decent.

THOMAS LOVE PEACOCK, Lady Clarinda in *Crotchet Castle*, 1831

We may see the small value God has for riches by the people he gives them to.

POPE, *Thoughts on Various Subjects*, 1727

Wealth by which some people think to get a reputation, does but expose the more their weaknesses and follies.

ANON., *Characters and Observations*, early 18th century

With the great part of rich people, the chief employment of riches consists in the parade of riches.

ADAM SMITH, *The Wealth of Nations*, 1776

No man divulges his revenue, or at least which way it comes in; but everyone publishes his acquisitions.

MONTAIGNE, 'Of the education of children', *Essays*, 1580

Kleptomaniac, *n*. A rich thief.

AMBROSE BIERCE, *The Devil's Dictionary*, 1906

To be clever enough to get all that money, one must be stupid enough to want it.

G. K. CHESTERTON, *The Innocence of Father Brown*, 1911

There is nothing so habit-forming as money.

DON MARQUIS (1878–1937)

Plenty of people despise money, but few know how to give it away.

LA ROCHEFOUCAULD, *Maxims*, 1665

When you hear a man talk of nothing but his father or grandfather, or some great-uncle, what they said and did, what places of honour or profit they filled, you may then take it for granted that he has no merit of his own to recommend him.

ANON., *Characters and Observations*, early 18th century

Genealogy, *n*. An account of one's descent from a man who did not particularly care to trace his own.

AMBROSE BIERCE, *The Devil's Dictionary*, 1906

Great families in England bear date from William the Conqueror; the rest from Adam and Eve.

ANON., *Characters and Observations*, early 18th century

If a man in the street proclaimed, with rude feudal rhetoric, that he was the Earl of Doncaster, he would be arrested as a lunatic; but if it were discovered that he really was the Earl of Doncaster, he would simply be cut as a cad. No poetical prose must be expected from earls as a class.

G. K. CHESTERTON, *The Defendant*, 1902

Kings are naturally lovers of low company.

EDMUND BURKE, *Speech on the Economical Reform*, 1780

The difference between what is commonly called ordinary company and good company, is only hearing the same things said in a little room, or in a large saloon, at small tables or at great tables, before two candles or twenty sconces.

POPE, *Thoughts on Various Subjects*, 1727

Pope's scorn of the Great is too often repeated to be real; no man thinks much of that which he despises.

DR JOHNSON, 'Pope', *Lives of the Poets*, 1779–81

Snobbishness is an insidious endemic, but it is rarely a mortal malady.

WALTER BAGEHOT, *Literary Studies*, 1879

People in the fashionable world are driven to commit as many ugly actions through snobbery as wretches are through misery.

ROBERT DE FLERS and FRANCIS DE CROISSET, *Les Précieuses de Genève*, 1929

To a man of the world the universe is a suburb.

ELIZABETH BIBESCO, *Haven*, 1951

The best-treated, most favoured and intelligent part of any society is often the most ungrateful. Ingratitude, however, is its social function.

SAUL BELLOW, Moses Herzog in *Herzog*, 1964

A person of bourgeois origin goes through life with some expectation of getting what he wants, within reasonable limits. Hence the fact that in times of stress 'educated' people tend to come to the front.

GEORGE ORWELL, *The Road to Wigan Pier*, 1937

Take care how thou offendest men raised from low condition.

THOMAS FULLER (II), *Introductio ad Prudentiam*, 1731

If you have been put in your place long enough, you begin to act like the place.

RANDALL JARRELL, *A Sad Heart at the Supermarket*, 1965

Social injustice is such a familiar phenomenon, it has such a sturdy constitution, that it is readily regarded as something natural even by its victims.

MARCEL AYMÉ, *Silhouette du Scandale*, 1938

This love of place, and precedency, it rocks us in our cradles, it lies down with us in our graves.

DONNE, sermon, 1619

One man is no more than another if he does no more than another.

CERVANTES, *Don Quixote*, 1605–15

The rebel angels fly in ranks.

HENRI PETIT (1900–78), *Les Justes Solitudes*

As favour and riches forsake a man, we discover in him the foolishness they concealed, and which no-one perceived before.

LA BRUYÈRE, 'Of the Gifts of Fortune', *Characters*, 1688

The Social Fabric

●

Drinking together in the evening we are human.
When dawn comes, animals
We rise up against each other.

ANTIMEDON (*c.* 1st century BC), *The Greek Anthology* (trans. Peter Jay)

Success and miscarriage have the same effects in all conditions. The prosperous are feared, hated and flattered; and the unfortunate avoided, pitied and despised.

DR JOHNSON, *The Idler*, 1758

When a man is down, 'down with him!'.

CERVANTES, *Don Quixote*, 1605–15

It is not at all uncommon for someone to arrive at a scene of brutality or injustice and, with a sympathetic murmur or heroic flourish, attack the victim. It happens all the time.

RENATA ADLER, *Speedboat*, 1977

To make one's fortune is so fine a phrase, and of such charming import, that it is universally used; it is to be met with in all languages, is pleasing to strangers and to barbarians, is to be found at court and in the city, has made its way into cloisters and scaled the walls of monasteries and convents; there is no place so sacred where it has not penetrated, no desert or solitude where it is unknown.

LA BRUYÈRE, 'Of the Gifts of Fortune', *Characters*, 1688

A curate hopes to be a rector, a rector a dean, and a dean to be a bishop: a bishop hopes to be a greater bishop. Well, this is merry living, if a life of hope be a life of pleasure. But an archbishop, alas! has nothing to hope for; he must exercise his patience, he's like to be content, he's at the tip-top of preferment.

ANON., *Characters and Observations*, early 18th century

Ambition, *n*. An overmastering desire to be vilified by enemies
while living and made ridiculous by friends when dead.

AMBROSE BIERCE, *The Devil's Dictionary*, 1906

A slave has but one master; an ambitious man has as many masters as
there are people who may be useful in bettering his position.

LA BRUYÈRE, 'Of the Court', *Characters*, 1688

Men in business are in as much danger from those at work under
them as from those that work against them.

MARQUESS OF HALIFAX, *Political thoughts and reflections*, late 17th
century

The effect of power and publicity on all men is the aggravation of
self, a sort of tumor that ends by killing the victim's sympathies.

HENRY ADAMS, *The Education of Henry Adams*, 1907

It is folly of too many to mistake the echo of a London coffee-house
for the voice of the kingdom.

SWIFT, *The Conduct of the Allies*, 1711

The danger of success is that it makes us forget the world's dreadful
injustice.

JULES RENARD, *Journal*, 1908

Like power in any shape, a full stomach always holds a dose of
insolence, and this dose expresses itself first of all in the well-fed
lecturing the starving.

CHEKHOV, letter, 1891

Of all the preposterous assumptions of humanity over humanity,
nothing exceeds most of the criticisms made on the habits of the
poor by the well-housed, well-warmed, and well-fed.

HERMAN MELVILLE, 'Poor Man's Pudding and Rich Man's
Crumbs', 1854

It is only the poor who are forbidden to beg.

ANATOLE FRANCE, *Crainquebille*, 1901

Labor, *n*. One of the processes by which A acquires property for B.
AMBROSE BIERCE, *The Devil's Dictionary*, 1906

Nowhere more naively than in banknotes does capitalism display itself in solemn earnest. The innocent cupids frolicking about numbers, the goddesses holding tablets of the law, the stalwart heroes sheathing their swords before monetary units are a world of their own: ornamenting the façade of hell.
WALTER BENJAMIN, *One-Way Street*, 1925–6

Regarded as a means, the businessman is tolerable; regarded as an end he is not so satisfactory.
JOHN MAYNARD KEYNES, *Essays in Persuasion*, 1933

To have a horror of the bourgeois is bourgeois.
JULES RENARD, *Journal*, 1889

Three-fourths of the demands existing in the world are romantic; founded on visions, idealisms, hopes and affections; and the regulation of the purse is, in its essence, regulation of the imagination and the heart.
RUSKIN, *Unto This Last*, 1860

Promise – large promise – is the soul of an advertisement.
DR JOHNSON, *The Idler*, 1758

Many priceless things can be bought.
MARIA VON EBNER-ESCHENBACH, *Aphorisms*, 1880

There is but one sorrow which is lasting, and that is one produced by the loss of property; time, which alleviates all others, sharpens this; we feel it every moment during the course of our lives when we miss the fortune we have lost.
LA BRUYÈRE, 'Of the Gifts of Fortune', *Characters*, 1688

Commerce, however we may please ourselves with the contrary opinion, is one of the daughters of fortune, inconstant and deceitful as her mother.
DR JOHNSON, *The Universal Visiter*, 1756

The gambling known as business looks with austere disfavour upon the business known as gambling.

AMBROSE BIERCE, *The Devil's Dictionary*, 1906

A 'sound' banker, alas, is not one who sees danger and avoids it, but one who, when he is ruined, is ruined in a conventional and orthodox way along with his fellows, so that no one can really blame him.

JOHN MAYNARD KEYNES, *Essays in Persuasion*, 1933

It is more dangerous to be a great prophet or poet than to promote twenty companies for swindling simple folk out of their savings.

BERNARD SHAW, Preface to *Misalliance*, 1914

A man is robbed on the Stock Exchange, just as he is killed in a war, by people whom he never sees.

ALFRED CAPUS, *La Bourse ou la vie*, 1901

You never expected justice from a company, did you? They have neither a soul to lose, nor a body to kick.

SYDNEY SMITH in Lady Holland, *Memoir*, 1855

The usual trade and commerce is cheating all round by consent.

THOMAS FULLER (II), *Gnomologia*, 1732

Found a Society of Honest Men, and all the thieves will join it.

ALAIN, *Propos d'un Normand*, 1906–14

Successful and fortunate crime is called virtue.

SENECA, *Hercules Furens*, 1st century

When knaves complain of one another as if they were honest men, they ought to be laughed at as if they were fools.

MARQUESS OF HALIFAX, *Moral thoughts and reflections*, late 17th century

Thieves respect property. They merely wish the property to become their property that they may more perfectly respect it.

G. K. CHESTERTON, *The Man who was Thursday*, 1908

Property is not theft, but a good deal of theft becomes property.

R. H. TAWNEY, *The Acquisitive Society*, 1921

People say law but they mean wealth.

EMERSON, *Journals*, 1841

Justice is the sanction of established injustice.

ANATOLE FRANCE, *Crainquebille*, 1901

Among barbarous peoples there exists a species of customs whose purpose appears to be custom in general: minute and fundamentally superfluous stipulations which, however, keep continually in the consciousness the constant proximity of custom, the perpetual compulsion to practise customs: so as to strengthen the mighty proposition with which civilization begins: any custom is better than no custom.

NIETZSCHE, *Daybreak*, 1881

The people should fight for their law as for their city wall.

HERACLITUS, *Fragments*, 82, *c*.500 BC

Lawful and settled authority is seldom resisted when it is well employed.

DR JOHNSON, *The Rambler*, 1750–2

Justice to others is charity for ourselves.

MONTESQUIEU, *Persian Letters*, 1721

The law does not content itself with classifying and punishing crime. It invents crime.

NORMAN DOUGLAS, *An Almanac*, 1945

'*Rex non potest peccari*' – Ahem!

MR JUSTICE DARLING, *Scintillae Juris*, 1889

Lawyers are the only persons in whom ignorance of the law is not punished.

JEREMY BENTHAM

A client is fain to hire a lawyer to keep from the injury of other lawyers – as Christians that travel in Turkey are forced to hire Janissaries, to protect them from the insolencies of other Turks.

SAMUEL BUTLER (I), *Prose Observations*, 1660–80

Justice must not only be done, it must be seen to be believed.

BEACHCOMBER

Judges, like the criminal classes, have their lighter moments.

OSCAR WILDE, 'Sententiae', *A Critic in Pall Mall*, 1919

Because punishment does not annihilate crime, it is folly to say it does not lessen it. It did not stop the murder of Mrs. Donatty; but how many Mrs. Donattys has it kept alive!

SYDNEY SMITH, *Edinburgh Review*, 1824

It is fairly obvious that those who are in favour of the death penalty have more affinity with murderers than those who are not.

RÉMY DE GOURMONT, *Pensées inédites*, 1920

There are some acts of justice which corrupt those who perform them.

JOUBERT, *Pensées*, 1842

No one who has not sat in prison knows what the State is like.

LEO TOLSTOY

Few are mended by imprisonment; and he whose crimes have made confinement necessary, seldom makes any other use of his enlargement, than to do with greater cunning what he did before with less.

DR JOHNSON, *The False Alarm*, 1770

Imprisonment is as irrevocable as death.

BERNARD SHAW, 'Maxims for Revolutionists', *Man and Superman*, 1903

The worst evil of being in prison is that one can never bar one's door.

STENDHAL, *The Red and the Black*, 1830

Wherever there are enclosing walls, there are abuses behind them.
                    NORMAN DOUGLAS, *An Almanac*, 1945

The dispensing of injustice is always in the right hands.
                    STANISLAW LEC, *Unkempt Thoughts*, 1962

The tyrant grinds down his slaves and they don't turn against him; they crush those beneath them.
                    EMILY BRONTË, Heathcliff in *Wuthering Heights*, 1847

To be feared is to fear: no one has been able to strike terror into others and at the same time enjoy peace of mind himself.
                    SENECA, *Epistles*, 1st century

Oddly, submission to powerful, frightening, even terrible persons, like tyrants and generals, is not experienced as nearly so painful as is submission to unknown and uninteresting persons, which is what all luminaries of industry are.
                    NIETZSCHE, *The Gay Science*, 1882–7

The boss's room bristles with weapons. The apparent comfort that disarms those entering is in reality a hidden arsenal.
                    WALTER BENJAMIN, *One-Way Street*, 1925–6

Machinery is aggressive. The weaver becomes a web, the machinist a machine. If you do not use the tools, they use you.
                    EMERSON, 'Works and Days', *Society and Solitude*, 1870

Invention is the mother of necessity.
                    THORSTEIN VEBLEN

The mass of men must satisfy the needs of the social organism in which they live far more than the social organism must satisfy them.
                    NORMAN MAILER, *Advertisements for Myself*, 1961

There is a rage to organize which is the sworn enemy of order.
                    GEORGES DUHAMEL, *Vie des martyrs*, 1917

'Give me your tired, your poor, your huddled masses yearning to be free, provided they have satisfactorily filled out forms 3584–A through 3597–Q.'

DWIGHT MACDONALD, *Against the American Grain*, 1963
(revised inscription for the Statue of Liberty)

I see the woman with a scarf twisted round her hair and a cigarette in her mouth. She has put the tea tray down upon the file on which my future depends.

JOHN BETJEMAN, *First and Last Loves*, 1952

No grand idea was ever born in a conference, but a lot of foolish ideas have died there.

SCOTT FITZGERALD, *The Crack-Up*, 1945

Riches, knowledge and honour are but several sorts of power.

HOBBES, *Leviathan*, 1651

We love to overlook the boundaries which we do not wish to pass; and as the Roman satirist remarks, he that has no design to take the life of another is yet glad to have it in his hands.

DR JOHNSON, *The Rambler*, 1750–2

Everyone has observed how much more dogs are animated when they hunt in a pack, than when they pursue their game apart. We might, perhaps, be at a loss to explain this phenomenon, if we had not experience of a similar in ourselves.

HUME, *A Treatise of Human Nature*, 1739

Happy the man who is hated on his own account.

JEAN ROSTAND, *Journal d'un caractère*, 1931

It wasn't the black market which gave the Jews a bad name; it was the Jews who gave the black market a bad name.

attrib. SIR LEWIS NAMIER

A banker who flees in an aeroplane, gangsters who make away with the child of a national hero, a girl who turns into a boy, a house painter who becomes Caesar: we can put a name to all these novelistic episodes which have been composed by an indefatigable journalist who doesn't care much about verisimilitude.

ROBERT BRASILLACH, *Pierre Corneille*, 1938

Sometimes in life situations develop that only the half-crazy can get out of.

LA ROCHEFOUCAULD, *Maxims*, 1665

Politics

❀

Nothing appears more surprising to those who consider human affairs with a philosophical eye, than the easiness with which the many are governed by the few.

HUME, 'First Principles of Government', *Essays*, 1742

The offhand decision of some commonplace mind high in office at a critical moment influences the course of events for a hundred years.

THOMAS HARDY in F. E. Hardy, *The Early Life of Thomas Hardy*, 1928

There are no wise few. Every aristocracy that has ever existed has behaved, in all essential points, exactly like a small mob.

G. K. CHESTERTON, *Heretics*, 1905

In civil business; what first? boldness; what second and third? boldness; and yet boldness is a child of ignorance and baseness.

SIR FRANCIS BACON, 'Of Boldness', *Essays*, 1597–1625

If it is true that vice can never be done away with, the science of government consists of making it contribute to the public good.

VAUVENARGUES, *Reflections and Maxims*, 1746

Circumstances (which with some gentlemen pass for nothing) give in reality to every political principle its distinguishing colour and discriminating effect. The circumstances are what render every civil and political scheme beneficial or noxious to mankind.

EDMUND BURKE, *Reflections on the Revolution in France*, 1790

In politics nothing is contemptible.

BENJAMIN DISRAELI, *Vivian Grey*, 1826–7

There are no small steps in great affairs.

CARDINAL DE RETZ, *Memoirs*, 1673–6

Everything in our political life tends to hide from us that there is anything wiser than our ordinary selves.

MATTHEW ARNOLD, *Culture and Anarchy*, 1869

The Government of the World is a great thing, but it is a very coarse one, too, compared with the fineness of speculative knowledge.

MARQUESS OF HALIFAX, *Moral thoughts and reflections*, late 17th century

An attitude of permanent indignation signifies great mental poverty. Politics compels its votaries to take that line and you can see their minds growing more and more impoverished every day, from one burst of righteous anger to the next.

VALÉRY, *Tel Quel*, 1941–3

Vain hope to make men happy by politics!

CARLYLE, *Journal*, 1831

What matters most about political ideas is the underlying emotions, the music, to which ideas are a mere libretto, often of very inferior quality.

SIR LEWIS NAMIER, *Personalities and Powers*, 1955

Practical men, who believe themselves to be quite exempt from any intellectual influences, are usually the slaves of some defunct economist. Madmen in authority, who hear voices in the air, are distilling their frenzy from some academic scribbler of a few years back.

JOHN MAYNARD KEYNES, *General Theory of Employment, Interest and Money*, 1936

Government by Idea tends to take in everything, to make the whole of society obedient to the idea. Spaces not so governed are unconquered, beyond the border, unconverted, unconvinced, a future -danger.

LORD ACTON, MSS notes, Cambridge, late 19th century

Every central government worships uniformity: uniformity relieves it from inquiry into an infinity of details, which must be attended to if rules have to be adapted to different men, instead of indiscriminately subjecting all men to the same rule.

DE TOCQUEVILLE, *Democracy in America*, 1835

The worst enemy of life, freedom and the common decencies is total anarchy; their second worst enemy is total efficiency.

ALDOUS HUXLEY, *Adonis and the Alphabet*, 1956

There has never been a perfect government, because men have passions; and if they did not have passions, there would be no need for government.

VOLTAIRE, *Politique et législation: Idées républicaines*, 18th century

Private passions grow tired and wear themselves out; political passions, never.

LAMARTINE

One of the chief problems a modern society has to face is how to provide an outlet for the intellectual's restless energies and yet deny him power. How to make and keep him a paper tiger.

ERIC HOFFER, in Calvin Tomkins, *Eric Hoffer: An American Odyssey*, 1969

An intellectual hatred is the worst.

W. B. YEATS, 'A Prayer for My Daughter', 1919

In all political regulations, good cannot be complete, it can only be predominant.

DR JOHNSON, *Journey to the Western Islands*, 1775

Abstract liberty, like other mere abstractions, is not to be found.

EDMUND BURKE, *Speech on Conciliation with the American Colonies*, 1775

Liberty is the right to do whatever the law permits.

MONTESQUIEU, *De l'esprit des lois*, 1748

The *sense* of liberty is a message read between the lines of constraint. Real liberty is as transparent, as odourless and tasteless, as water.

MICHAEL FRAYN, *Constructions*, 1974

The battle of Marathon is more important, even as an event in English history, than the battle of Hastings.

JOHN STUART MILL, 'Grote's History of Greece', 1846

O Freedom, what liberties are taken in thy name!

DANIEL GEORGE, *The Perpetual Pessimist*, 1963

Man persuades himself that he is emancipated every time that he decorates a new servitude with the name of liberty.

ACHILLE TOURNIER, 19th century

The chains which men bear they have imposed upon themselves; strike them off, and they will weep for their lost security.

JOHN PASSMORE, *The Perfectibility of Man*, 1970

Servitude debases men to the point where they end up liking it.

VAUVENARGUES, *Reflections and Maxims*, 1746

You can fool too many of the people too much of the time.

JAMES THURBER, *Fables for Our Time*, 1940

What makes equality such a difficult business is that we only want it with our superiors.

HENRY BECQUE, *Querelles littéraires*, 1890

Whatever may be the general endeavour of a community to render its members equal and alike, the personal pride of individuals will always seek to rise above the line, and to form somewhere an inequality to their own advantage.

DE TOCQUEVILLE, *Democracy in America*, 1835

We who are liberal and progressive know that the poor are our equals in every sense except that of being equal to us.

LIONEL TRILLING, *The Liberal Imagination*, 1950

Equality may perhaps be a right, but no power on earth can ever turn it into a fact.

BALZAC, *La Duchesse de Langeais*, 1834

That such dreadful and bloody happenings have surrounded this doctrine of equality has given this 'modern idea' *par excellence* a kind of glory and lurid glow, so that the Revolution as a *spectacle* has seduced even the noblest spirits.

NIETZSCHE, *Twilight of the Idols*, 1888

Only one more indispensable massacre of Capitalists or Communists or Fascists or Christians or Heretics, and there we are – there we are in the Golden Future.

ALDOUS HUXLEY, *Time Must Have a Stop*, 1944

Brotherhood, solidarity, unity, love: they all mean these but not those, you but not them.

MICHAEL FRAYN, *Constructions*, 1974

That all men should be brothers is the dream of people who have no brothers.

CHARLES CHINCHOLLES, *Pensées de tout le monde*, 1880

Extreme hopes are born of extreme misery.

BERTRAND RUSSELL, *Unpopular Essays*, 1950

The idea of a perfect and immortal commonwealth will always be found as chimerical as that of a perfect and immortal man.

HUME, *History of Great Britain*, 1754–62

Powerful imaginations are conservative.

HUGO VON HOFMANNSTHAL, *The Book of Friends*, 1922

Conservatism is primarily based on a proper recognition of human limitations, and cannot be argued in a spirit of self-glorifying logic.

SIR LEWIS NAMIER, *Vanished Supremacies*, 1958

We read occasionally in conservative literature alternations of sentences, the first an appeal to the coarsest prejudice – the next a subtle hint to a craving and insatiable scepticism.

WALTER BAGEHOT, *Literary Studies*, 1879

Season for reform – *Not* when we are at war, for then all is hurry and confusion, and our minds too heated and agitated to set about so serious an affair. *Not* when we are at peace, for then it would be madness to disturb the tranquillity of the nation.

> CHARLES PIGOTT, *A Political Dictionary: explaining the True Meaning of Words*, 1795

He that goeth about to persuade a multitude, that they are not so well governed as they ought to be, shall never want attentive and favourable hearers.

> RICHARD HOOKER, *Ecclesiastical Polity*, 1594

To worship the people is to be worshipped.

> SIR FRANCIS BACON, *De Augmentis Scientiarum*, 1623

It is a general error to imagine the loudest complainers for the public to be the most anxious for its welfare.

> EDMUND BURKE, *Observations on a publication entitled 'The Present State of the Nation'*, 1769

It is one of the consolations of middle-aged reformers that the good they inculcate must live after them if it is to live at all.

> SAKI, *Beasts and Super-Beasts*, 1914

Reforms are less to be dreaded than revolutions, for they cause less reaction.

> MR JUSTICE DARLING, *Scintillae Juris*, 1889

One of the surest ways of killing a tree is to lay bare its roots. It is the same with institutions. We must not be too ready to disinter the origins of those we wish to preserve. All beginnings are small.

> JOUBERT, *Pensées*, 1842

Revolutionary movements attract those who are not good enough for established institutions as well as those who are too good for them.

> BERNARD SHAW, *Androcles and the Lion*, 1913

All revolutions invariably encourage bad characters and potential criminals. Traitors throw off the mask; they cannot contain themselves amidst the general confusion that seems to promise easy victims.

DELACROIX, *Journal*, 1860

When they were burning John Huss, a gentle little old lady came carrying her faggot to add it to the pile.

ALBERT CAMUS, *Carnets*, 1942–51

When the populace is excited, one cannot conceive how calm can be restored; and when it is peaceful, one cannot see how calm can be disturbed.

LA BRUYÈRE, 'Of the Sovereign and the State', *Characters*, 1688

Among those who dislike oppression are many who like to oppress.

NAPOLEON, *Maxims*, early 19th century

By a revolution in the state, the fawning sycophant of yesterday is converted into the austere critic of the present hour.

EDMUND BURKE, *Reflections on the Revolution in France*, 1790

Revolution is not the up-rising against the existing order, but the setting-up of a new order contradictory to the traditional one.

JOSÉ ORTEGA Y GASSET, *The Revolt of the Masses*, 1929

When smashing monuments, save the pedestals – they always come in handy.

STANISLAW LEC, *Unkempt Thoughts*, 1962

The 'people' who exercise the power are not always the same people over whom it is exercised.

JOHN STUART MILL, *On Liberty*, 1859

The nature of man is intricate; the objects of society are of the greatest possible complexity; and therefore no simple disposition or direction of power can be suitable either to man's nature, or to the quality of his affairs.

EDMUND BURKE, *Reflections on the Revolution in France*, 1790

Every despotism has a specially keen and hostile instinct for whatever keeps up human dignity and independence.

AMIEL, *Journal*, 1852

It takes in reality only one to make a quarrel. It is useless for the sheep to pass resolutions in favour of vegetarianism while the wolf remains of a different opinion.

W. R. INGE, *Outspoken Essays*, First Series, 1919

In matters of government, justice means force as well as virtue.

NAPOLEON, *Maxims*, early 19th century

A certain *quantum* of power must always exist in the community, in some hands, and under some appelation.

EDMUND BURKE, *Reflections on the Revolution in France*, 1790

There must in every society be some power or other from which there is no appeal, which admits no restrictions, which pervades the whole mass of the community.

DR JOHNSON, *Taxation No Tyranny*, 1775

Power ought to serve as a check to power.

MONTESQUIEU, *De l'esprit des lois*, 1748

Power will intoxicate the best hearts, as wine the strongest heads.

CHARLES CALEB COLTON, *Lacon*, 1825

The wise become as the unwise in the enchanted chambers of Power, whose lamps make every face the same colour.

LANDOR, 'Demosthenes and Eubulides', *Imaginary Conversations*, 1824–9

Power worship blurs political judgment because it leads, almost unavoidably, to the belief that present trends will continue. Whoever is winning at the moment will always seem to be invincible.

GEORGE ORWELL, 'James Burnham and the Managerial Revolution', 1946

All the armed prophets conquered, all the unarmed ones perished.

MACHIAVELLI, *The Prince*, 1513

Eleven men well armed will certainly subdue one single man in his shirt.

SWIFT, *Drapier's Letters*, 1724

The public weal requires that men should betray, and lie, and massacre.

MONTAIGNE, 'Of profit and honesty', *Essays*, 1580–8

At bottom, every state regards another as a gang of robbers who will fall upon it as soon as there is an opportunity.

SCHOPENHAUER, 'On Jurisprudence and Politics', *Parerga and Paralipomena*, 1851

Does anyone suppose that the love of country in an Englishman implies any friendly feeling or disposition to serve another bearing the same name?

HAZLITT, 'On the Pleasure of Hating', 1826

A nation is only at peace when it's at war.

HUGH KINGSMILL

The real working class, though they hate war and are immune to jingoism, are never really pacifist, because their life teaches them something different.

GEORGE ORWELL, 'No, Not One', 1941

Different races and nationalities cherish different ideals of society that stink in each other's nostrils with an offensiveness beyond the power of any but the most monstrous private deed.

REBECCA WEST, *Black Lamb and Grey Falcon*, 1941

A healthy nation is as unconscious of its nationality as a healthy man of his bones. But if you break a nation's nationality it will think of nothing else but getting it set again.

BERNARD SHAW, Preface to *John Bull's Other Island*, 1904

> Few even wish they could read
> the lost annals
> of a cudgelled people.
>
> W. H. AUDEN, 'Marginalia', *City Without Walls*, 1969

There are only chosen peoples: all who still exist.

> ELIAS CANETTI, *The Human Province*, 1978

How is the world ruled and how do wars start? Diplomats tell lies to journalists and then believe what they read.

> KARL KRAUS, *Aphorisms and More Aphorisms*, 1909

War hath no fury like a non-combatant.

> C. E. MONTAGUE, *Disenchantment*, 1922

The art of war is to dispose one's troops so that they are everywhere at the same time.

> NAPOLEON to King Joseph, 1806

War does not feed on fixed rations.

> ARCHIDAMUS, cit. Plutarch's *Moralia*

Wars begin when you will, but they do not end when you please.

> MACHIAVELLI, *History of Florence*, 1521–5

The quickest way of ending a war is to lose it.

> GEORGE ORWELL, 'Second Thoughts on James Burnham', 1946

No victor believes in chance.

> NIETZSCHE, *The Gay Science*, 1882–7

To find a new country and invade it has always been the same.

> DR JOHNSON, Introduction to *The World Displayed*, 1759

Freebooter, *n.* A conqueror in a small way of business, whose annexations lack the sanctifying merit of magnitude.

> AMBROSE BIERCE, *The Devil's Dictionary*, 1906

The use of force alone is temporary. It may subdue for a moment, but it does not remove the necessity of subduing again: and a nation is not governed which is perpetually to be conquered.

> EDMUND BURKE, *Speech on Conciliation with the American Colonies*, 1775

A subjick race is on'y funny whin it's ra-aly subjick.
FINLEY PETER DUNNE, *Mr. Dooley Says*, 1910

Finality is not the language of politics.
BENJAMIN DISRAELI, speech, House of Commons, 1859

The high sentiments always win in the end, the leaders who offer blood, toil, tears and sweat always get more out of their followers than those who offer safety and a good time. When it comes to the pinch, human beings are heroic.
GEORGE ORWELL, 'The Art of Donald McGill', 1941

Political necessities sometimes turn out to be political mistakes.
BERNARD SHAW, *St. Joan*, 1923

Rulers

●

As mankind is made, the keeping it in order is an ill-natured office.
MARQUESS OF HALIFAX, *Political thoughts and reflections*, late 17th century

Many have ruled well who could not perhaps define a Commonwealth.
SIR THOMAS BROWNE, *Christian Morals*, mid 17th century

A king is a thing men have made for their own sakes, for quietness' sake. Just as in a family one man is appointed to buy the meat.
JOHN SELDEN, *Table Talk*, mid 17th century

What grimaces, what capers, leaps and chuckles prime ministers, presidents, and kings must indulge in, in the privacy of their bedrooms, so as to avenge their systems on the daylong strain imposed on them!
VALÉRY, *Tel Quel*, 1941–3

The poor unfortunates who inhabit the monastery of La Trappe are wretched people who have not had quite enough courage to kill themselves. I except the leaders, who enjoy the pleasure of being leaders.
STENDHAL, *Love*, 1822

All rising to great place is by a winding stair.
SIR FRANCIS BACON, 'Of Great Place', *Essays*, 1597–1625

None climbs so high as he who knows not whither he is going.
OLIVER CROMWELL

How many weak shoulders have craved heavy burdens!
JOUBERT, *Pensées*, 1842

It is wonderful how soon men acquire talents for offices of trust and importance. The higher the situation, the higher the opinion it gives us of ourselves; and as is our confidence, so is our capacity. We assume an equality with circumstance.

HAZLITT, *Characteristics*, 1823

Being a general calls for different talents from being a soldier.

LIVY, *History of Rome*

An idol is not the worse for being of coarse materials; a king should be a common-place man. Otherwise he is superior in his own nature, and not dependent on our bounty or caprice.

HAZLITT, 'On the Spirit of Monarchy', 1823

Those who insist on the dignity of their office, show they have not deserved it.

GRACIÁN, *The Art of Worldly Wisdom*, 1647

A man born to obey will obey even on a throne.

VAUVENARGUES, *Reflections and Maxims*, 1746

Monarchs are always surrounded with refined spirits, so penetrating that they frequently discover in their masters great qualities, invisible to vulgar eyes, and which, did they not publish them to mankind, would be unobserved for ever.

DR JOHNSON, *Marmor Norfolciense*, 1739

When men get by pleasing and lose by serving, the choice is so easy that nobody can miss it.

MARQUESS OF HALIFAX, *Political thoughts and reflections*, late 17th century

Great men, like great cities, have many crooked arts, and dark alleys in their hearts, whereby he that knows them may save himself much time and trouble.

CHARLES CALEB COLTON, *Lacon*, 1825

To enjoy a prince's favour does not rule out the possibility of merit, but neither does it argue for its existence.

LA BRUYÈRE, 'Of Opinions', *Characters*, 1688

When a prince giveth any man a very extravagant reward it looketh as if it was rather for an ill thing than a good one.

> MARQUESS OF HALIFAX, *Political thoughts and reflections*, late 17th century

Even the best-intentioned of great men need a few scoundrels around them; there are some things you cannot ask an honest man to do.

> LA BRUYÈRE, *Characters*, 1688

The most dangerous follower is he whose defection would destroy the whole party: that is to say, the best follower.

> NIETZSCHE, *The Wanderer and His Shadow*, 1880

He was a wise fellow that, being bid to ask what he would of the king, desired he might know none of his secrets.

> SHAKESPEARE, *Pericles*, 1608–9

A great man ought never to pry too minutely into things, least of all in unpleasant matters. For though it is important to know all, it is not necessary to know all about all.

> GRACIÁN, *The Art of Worldly Wisdom*, 1647

Courtesy is the politic witchery of great personages.

> GRACIÁN, *The Art of Worldly Wisdom*, 1647

The civilities of the great are never thrown away.

> DR JOHNSON, *Memoirs of the King of Prussia*, 1756

Though men in great positions are easily flattered, we are still more easily flattered when in their company.

> VAUVENARGUES, *Reflections and Maxims*, 1746

Ministers say what one wants them to say, so that one may do what they want one to do.

> VICTOR HUGO, *Notebook*, 1820

It is not in human nature that a statesman should not desire to satisfy the man whom he sees and who sees him, in preference to the

unembodied name or idea of a man who is separated from him by
lands or seas; or that he should not prefer the interests of the man
who is there, to those of the multitude which is an abstraction.

SIR HENRY TAYLOR, *The Statesman*, 1836

It is impossible that a man who is false to his friends and neighbours
should be true to the public.

BISHOP BERKELEY, *Maxims Concerning Patriotism*, 1750

Politicians neither love nor hate. Interest, not sentiment, directs
them.

LORD CHESTERFIELD, *Letters*, 1748

The man who is selling newspapers outside the Houses of Parliament can safely leave his papers to go for a drink and his cap beside
them: anyone who takes a paper is sure to drop a copper into the cap.
But the men who are inside the Houses of Parliament – they cannot
trust one another like that, still less can the Government they compose trust other governments. No caps upon the pavement here.

E. M. FORSTER, *Two Cheers for Democracy*, 1951

The oldest, wisest politician grows not more human so, but is
merely a gray wharf rat at last.

THOREAU, *Journal*, 1853

He who has the greatest power put into his hands will only become
the more impatient of any restraint in the use of it.

HAZLITT, 'On the Spirit of Monarchy', 1823

In all supremacy of power, there is inherent a prerogative to pardon.

BENJAMIN WHICHCOTE, *Moral and Religious Aphorisms*, 1703

A great man does enough for us when he refrains from doing us
harm.

BEAUMARCHAIS, *The Barber of Seville*, 1775

To have the welfare and the lives of millions placed at our disposal, is
a sort of warrant, a challenge to squander them without mercy.

HAZLITT, 'On the Spirit of Monarchy', 1823

Princes have this remaining of humanity, that they think themselves obliged not to make war without a reason.

> DR JOHNSON, *Memoirs of the King of Prussia*, 1756

> Small tyrants, threatened by big,
> sincerely believe
> they love Liberty.

> W. H. AUDEN, 'Marginalia', *City Without Walls*, 1969

Courts are, unquestionably, the seats of politeness and good-breeding; were they not so, they would be the seats of slaughter and desolation.

> LORD CHESTERFIELD, *Letters*, 1749

The court does not satisfy a man, but it prevents him from being satisfied with anything else.

> LA BRUYÈRE, 'Of the Court', *Characters*, 1688

A party spirit betrays the greatest man to act as meanly as the vulgar herd.

> LA BRUYÈRE, 'Of Mankind', *Characters*, 1688

Party is the madness of many for the gain of a few.

> SWIFT, *Thoughts on Various Subjects*, 1711

Official dignity tends to increase in inverse ratio to the importance of the country in which the office is held.

> ALDOUS HUXLEY, *Beyond the Mexique Bay*, 1934

Princes glory *in Arcanis*, that they have secrets which no man shall know, and, God knows, they have hearts which know not themselves; thoughts and purposes indigested fall upon them and surprise them.

> DONNE, sermon, 1628

> Weak kings are subject to flashes of temper
> Ruled by their emotions. So are strong ones.

> GAVIN EWART, 'The Law Allows Cruel Experiments on Friendly Animals', *The Pleasures of the Flesh*, 1966

People who have power respond simply. They have no minds but their own.

IVY COMPTON-BURNETT, *The Mighty and their Fall*, 1961

Men in high places, from having less personal interest in the characters of others – being safe from them – are commonly less acute observers, and with their progressive elevation in life become, as more and more indifferent to what other men are, so more and more ignorant of them.

SIR HENRY TAYLOR, *The Statesman*, 1836

Princes had need, in tender matters and ticklish times, to beware what they say: especially in these short speeches, which fly abroad like darts, and are thought to be shot out of their secret intentions.

SIR FRANCIS BACON, 'Of Sedition and Troubles', *Essays*, 1597–1625

It is even more damaging for a minister to say foolish things than to do them.

CARDINAL DE RETZ, *Memoirs*, 1673–6

Authority is never without hate.

EURIPIDES, *Ion*, *c*.411 BC

Fortune soon tires of carrying anyone long on her shoulders.

GRACIÁN, *The Art of Worldly Wisdom*, 1647

We see men fall from high estate on account of the very faults through which they attained it.

LA BRUYÈRE, 'Of the Court', *Characters*, 1688

Rats and conquerors must expect no mercy in misfortune.

CHARLES CALEB COLTON, *Lacon*, 1825

However many people a tyrant slaughters he cannot kill his successor.

SENECA, adapted from a remark in Dio's *Roman History*, 1st century

To a surprising extent the war-lords in shining armour, the apostles of the martial virtues, tend not to die fighting when the time comes. History is full of ignominious getaways by the great and famous.

GEORGE ORWELL, 'Who Are the War Criminals?', 1942

Fortune rarely accompanies anyone to the door.

GRACIÁN, *The Art of Worldly Wisdom*, 1647

The favourites of fortune or fame topple from their pedestals before our eyes without diverting us from ambition.

VAUVENARGUES, *Reflections and Maxims*, 1746

Who whom? As Lenin said.
  Who rules whom?
  Who hands out the soup to whom?
  Who is a better person than whom?
  Who is more democratic than whom?
  Who says 'Who whom' to whom?

MICHAEL FRAYN, *Constructions*, 1974

Friends & Foes

He that has no one to love or confide in, has little to hope. He wants the radical principle of happiness.

DR JOHNSON, *Rasselas*, 1759

Life is to be fortified by many friendships. To love, and to be loved, is the greatest happiness of existence.

SYDNEY SMITH in Lady Holland, *Memoir*, 1855

To be attached to the subdivisions, to love the little platoon we belong to in society, is the first principle (the germ as it were) of public affections.

EDMUND BURKE, *Reflections on the Revolution in France*, 1790

There is little friendship in the world, and least of all between equals.

SIR FRANCIS BACON, 'Of Friendship and Followers', *Essays*, 1597–1625

He who has never struggled with his fellow-creatures is a stranger to half the sentiments of mankind.

ADAM FERGUSON, *An Essay on the History of Civil Society*, 1767

Friend is sometimes a word devoid of meaning; *enemy*, never.

VICTOR HUGO, *Tas de pierres*, mid 19th century

Enemies publish themselves. They declare war. The friend never declares his love.

THOREAU, *Journal*, 1856

A true friend is the most precious of all possessions and the one we take least thought about acquiring.

LA ROCHEFOUCAULD, *Maxims*, 1665

If the first law of friendship is that it has to be cultivated, the second law is to be indulgent when the first law has been neglected.

VOLTAIRE, letter, 1740

We have fewer friends than we imagine, but more than we know.

HUGO VON HOFMANNSTHAL, *The Book of Friends*, 1922

We have three kinds of friends: those who love us, those who are indifferent to us, and those who hate us.

CHAMFORT, *Characters and anecdotes*, 1771

It is more shameful to distrust one's friends than to be deceived by them.

LA ROCHEFOUCAULD, *Maxims*, 1665

It is not so much our friends' help that helps us as the confident knowledge that they will help us.

EPICURUS, 3rd century BC

Of what help is anyone who can only be approached with the right words?

ELIZABETH BIBESCO, *Haven*, 1951

In prosperity our friends know us; in adversity we know our friends.

CHURTON COLLINS, aphorisms in the *English Review*, 1914

When a man laughs at his troubles he loses a good many friends. They never forgive the loss of their prerogative.

H. L. MENCKEN, *A Book of Burlesques*, 1928

Since we are mortal, friendships are best kept to a moderate level, rather than sharing the very depths of our souls.

EURIPIDES, *Hippolytus*, 428 BC

True friendship is never serene.

MADAME DE SÉVIGNÉ, letter, 1671

Don't go to visit your friend in the hour of his disgrace.
>RABBI SIMEON BEN ELEAZAR (2nd century AD), *Ethics of the Fathers*

Job endured everything – until his friends came to comfort him, then he grew impatient.
>KIERKEGAARD, *Journal*, 1849

We are not greatly pleased by our friends respecting our good qualities if they also venture to perceive our faults.
>VAUVENARGUES, *Reflections and Maxims*, 1746

How much easier to make pets of our friends' weaknesses than to put up with their strengths.
>ELIZABETH BIBESCO, *Haven*, 1951

Never speak ill of yourself, your friends will always say enough on that subject.
>TALLEYRAND

'There is a report that Piso is dead; it is a great loss; he was an honest man, who deserved to live longer; he was intelligent and agreeable, resolute and courageous, to be depended upon, generous and faithful.' Add: 'provided he is really dead'.
>LA BRUYÈRE, 'Of Opinions', *Characters*, 1688

It takes your enemy and your friend, working together, to hurt you to the heart; the one to slander you and the other to get the news to you.
>MARK TWAIN, *Following the Equator*, 1897

There is no feeling of liberty like that of escape from half-friends.
>EDWARD BULWER-LYTTON, *Weeds and Wild Flowers*, 1826

He whose friendship is worth having, must hate and be hated.
>WILLIAM MAGINN, *The Maxims of Sir Morgan O'Doherty, Bart.*, 1849

It is easier to forgive an Enemy than to forgive a Friend.
>BLAKE, *Jerusalem*, 1804

People imagine that friendship is a peaceful divinity, whose gentle chains succeed to those of love when we have settled down to a time of life which gives us, or is supposed to give us, the taste for calm attachments. Nothing is more false. Friendship, dull-coloured and pale as she is, has her storms, and unhappily reconciliations are more difficult.

DELACROIX, letter, 1860

Cosmus Duke of Florence had a desperate saying, against perfidious or neglecting friends, as if those wrongs were unpardonable: You shall read (saith he) that we are commanded to forgive our enemies; but you never read that we are commanded to forgive our friends.

SIR FRANCIS BACON, 'Of Revenge', *Essays*, 1597–1625

To make our peace with a friend, with whom we had broken, is a weakness for which we shall have to atone when at the first opportunity he again does the very same thing that has brought about the breach; indeed he does it again with more audacity and assurance because he is secretly aware of his being indispensable.

SCHOPENHAUER, 'Counsels and Maxims', *Parerga and Paralipomena*, 1851

He that advised thee not to let the sun set on thine anger did not command thee to trust a deceiving enemy the next morning.

THOMAS FULLER (II), *Introductio ad Prudentiam*, 1731

He who has a thousand friends has not a friend to spare.
And he who has one enemy will meet him everywhere.

ALI IBN-ABI-TALIB, *Sentences*, 7th century

The art of living is more like wrestling than dancing.

MARCUS AURELIUS, *Meditations*, 2nd century

There are no two people on this earth who could not be turned into deadly enemies by a devilishly contrived indiscretion.

HUGO VON HOFMANNSTHAL, *The Book of Friends*, 1922

There is no one who does not represent a danger to someone.

MADAME DE SÉVIGNÉ, letter, 1675

Everybody is not capable of being a friend, but anybody has it in his power to be an enemy.

> ANON., *Characters and Observations*, early 18th century

No viper so little, but hath its venom.

> THOMAS FULLER (II), *Gnomologia*, 1732

A great enemy is a great object that inviteth precaution, which maketh him less dangerous than a mean one.

> MARQUESS OF HALIFAX, *Miscellaneous thoughts and reflections*, late 17th century

The man that is once hated, both his good and evil deeds oppress him.

> BEN JONSON, *Timber; or Discoveries*, 1640

An enemy's virtues are not the thing we least dislike about him.

> JEAN ROSTAND, *Julien ou une Conscience*, 1928

It is a general mistake to think the men we like are good for everything, and those we do not, good for nothing.

> MARQUESS OF HALIFAX, *Miscellaneous thoughts and reflections*, late 17th century

Pay attention to your enemies, for they are the first to discover your mistakes.

> ANTISTHENES (5th–4th century BC), cit. Diogenes Laertius, *Lives and Opinions of Eminent Philosophers*

He that wrestles with us strengthens our nerves, and sharpens our skill. Our antagonist is our helper.

> EDMUND BURKE, *Reflections on the Revolution in France*, 1790

What makes our opponents useful is that they allow us to believe that without them we would be able to realize our ideals.

> JEAN ROSTAND, *Journal d'un Caractère*, 1931

There is a jealousy in hating too: we want to have our enemy to ourselves.

> NIETZSCHE, *Nachgelassene Fragmente*, 1882–9

From the true antagonist boundless courage flows into you.

> KAFKA, 'Aphorisms 1917–19', *The Great Wall of China*

Though a quarrel in the streets is a thing to be hated, the energies displayed in it are fine; the commonest man shows a grace in his quarrel.

> KEATS, letter, 1819

In all private quarrels the duller nature is triumphant by reason of dullness.

> GEORGE ELIOT, *Felix Holt*, 1866

All our foes are mortal.

> VALÉRY, *Tel Quel*, 1941–3

There is no finer revenge than that which *others* inflict on your enemy. Moreover, it has the advantage of leaving you the role of a generous man.

> CESARE PAVESE, *This Business of Living: Diaries 1935–50*

Sometimes one greatly dislikes a person for no particular reason – and then that person goes and does something hateful.

> *The Pillow Book of Sei Shonagon*, 10th century

It is wonderful to see men secretly meditating how to harm each other, yet forced to help each other against their inclinations and intentions.

> VAUVENARGUES, *Reflections and Maxims*, 1746

A wise man gets more use from his enemies than a fool from his friends. Caution thrives well when rivalry and ill-will are next-door neighbours.

> GRACIÁN, *The Art of Worldly Wisdom*, 1647

Man is a social animal who dislikes his fellow men.

> DELACROIX, *Journal*, 1852

The man exactly situated between our enemy and ourselves, seems nearer to our enemy. This is the result of that optical law which makes a fountain jet appear less distant from the far side of the basin than from the side on which we stand.

CHAMFORT, *Maximes et pensées*, 1805

All men naturally hate each other. We have used concupiscence as best we can to make it serve the common good, but this is mere sham and a false image of charity, for essentially it is just hate.

PASCAL, *Pensées*, 1670

Life is not worth living for the man who has not even one good friend.

DEMOCRITUS OF ABDERA, 5th–4th century BC

Think of the myriad enmities, suspicions, animosities, and conflicts that are now vanished with the dust and ashes of the men who knew them; and fret no more.

MARCUS AURELIUS, *Meditations*, 2nd century

To be able to live among men and women we must allow everyone to exist with his given individuality. If we condemn another man absolutely, there is nothing for him but to treat us as a mortal enemy; for we are willing to grant him the right to exist only on condition that he becomes different from what he invariably is.

SCHOPENHAUER, 'Counsels and Maxims', *Parerga and Paralipomena*, 1851

Every man is obliged to be just and honest, but every man is not obliged to be a friend.

ANON., *Characters and Observations*, early 18th century

If there were only two men in the world, how would they get on? They would help one another, harm one another, flatter one another, slander one another, fight one another, make it up; they could neither live together nor do without one another.

VOLTAIRE, *Philosophical Dictionary*, 1764

Sympathies & Antipathies

❀

Some people are moulded by their admirations, others by their hostilities.

ELIZABETH BOWEN, *The Death of the Heart*, 1938

There are those in whom the sight of a man at once stirs feelings of hostility in that their innermost being exclaims 'not-I'. And there are others in whom that sight at once arouses feelings of friendly interest and sympathy; their true nature exclaims 'I once more!'

SCHOPENHAUER, 'On Ethics', *Parerga and Paralipomena*, 1851

It is obviously impossible to love all men in any strict and true sense. What is meant by loving all men, is to feel well disposed towards all men, to be ready to assist them, and to act towards those who come in our way as if we loved them.

J. H. NEWMAN, *Parochial and Plain Sermons*, 1837–42

A patronizing disposition always has its meaner side.

GEORGE ELIOT, *Adam Bede*, 1859

There are people whom I wish well, and only wish that I could wish better.

GOETHE, *Maxims and Reflections*, early 19th century

It is flattering some men to endure them.

MARQUESS OF HALIFAX, *Moral thoughts and reflections*, late 17th century

In the presence of some people we inevitably depart from ourselves: we are inaccurate, say things we do not feel, and talk nonsense. When we get home we are conscious that we have made fools of ourselves. Never go near these people.

MARK RUTHERFORD, *More Pages from a Journal*, 1910

There is a sort of man who goes through the world in a succession of quarrels, always able to make out that he is in the right, although he never ceases to put other men in the wrong. The least that can be said of such a person is that he has an unhappy aptitude for eliciting whatever evil there may be in the natures with which he comes in contact; and a man who is sure to cause injuries to him wherever he goes, is almost as great an evil and inconvenience as if he were himself the wrongdoer.

SIR HENRY TAYLOR, *The Statesman*, 1836

The reasons which any man offers to you for his own conduct, betray his opinion of your character.

SIR ARTHUR HELPS, *Thoughts in the Cloister and the Crowd*, 1835

A man's interest is not a sufficient ground to suspect him, if his nature doth not concur in it.

MARQUESS OF HALIFAX, *Miscellaneous thoughts and reflections*, late 17th century

There is a way of asking us for our reasons that leads us not only to forget our best reasons but also to conceive a stubborn aversion to all reasons. This way of asking makes people very stupid and is a trick used by tyrannical people.

NIETZSCHE, *The Gay Science*, 1882–7

Some men's No is more highly prized than the Yes of others; for a gilded No is more satisfactory than a dry Yes.

GRACIÁN, *The Art of Worldly Wisdom*, 1647

Some actions are called malicious because they are done by ugly people.

LICHTENBERG, *Aphorisms*, 1764–99

Personalize your sympathies; depersonalize your antipathies.

W. R. INGE, *More Lay Thoughts of a Dean*, 1931

We can scarcely hate anyone that we know. If you come into a room where a man is, you find, in general, that he has a nose upon his face. 'There's sympathy!' This alone is a diversion to your unqualified contempt.

HAZLITT, 'Why Distant Objects Please', 1822

Ignorance alone makes monsters or bugbears; our actual acquain
tances are all very common-place people.

HAZLITT, 'Why Distant Objects Please', 18:

In daily life we are more often liked for our defects than for ou
qualities.

LA ROCHEFOUCAULD, Maxims, 16(

In every character, even the most unamiable, there is some redeem
ing quality, which, making itself evident, will please far more tha
any simulated virtues.

LEOPARDI, Pensieri, 1834-

We all have a dark feeling of resistance towards people we have neve
met, and a profound and manly dislike of the authors we have neve
read.

G. K. CHESTERTON, Robert Browning, 19(

Such seems to be the disposition of man, that whatever makes
distinction produces rivalry.

DR JOHNSON, Journey to the Western Islands, 17:

As soon as there were two, there was pride.

DONNE, sermon, 16:

'Tis not the great disproportion betwixt ourself and another, whic
produces envy; but on the contrary, our proximity.

HUME, A Treatise of Human Nature, 17:

Potter bears a grudge against potter, and craftsman against craft:
man, and beggar is envious of beggar, and bard of bard.

HESIOD, Works and Days, 8th century I

Where there is no comparison, no envy; and therefore kings are no
envied, but by kings.

SIR FRANCIS BACON, 'Of Envy', Essays, 1597–16:

A rebuff or a cold look from those who are above us in rank ma
make us hate them, but a greeting or a smile soon reconciles us.

LA BRUYÈRE, 'Of the Great', Characters, 16(

The player envies only the player, the poet envies only the poet.
                    HAZLITT, 'Envy', *Sketches and Essays*, 1839

Men contend with the living, not with the dead; to these ascribing
more than due, that they may obscure the glory of the other.
                              HOBBES, *Leviathan*, 1651

The dullard's envy of brilliant men is always assuaged by the suspicion that they will come to a bad end.
                    MAX BEERBOHM, *Zuleika Dobson*, 1911

Envy is a gadding passion, and walketh the streets, and doth not
keep home.
                    SIR FRANCIS BACON, 'Of Envy', *Essays*, 1597–1625

It's surprising how the world – particularly human nature – is often
most precisely observed by those who do not like what they see.
Perhaps their feelings are more ambiguous than they suppose.
                    MICHAEL FRAYN, *Constructions*, 1974

Men of cold passions have quick eyes.
                    NATHANIEL HAWTHORNE, *American Notebooks*, 1837–40

Unlike true admiration, which, because it is free of conscious will
always has the option of silence, envy's imitation of admiration
clamours for public acknowledgment; the more stinging the envy,
the more ardently must the envious one dramatize himself as an
admirer whose passion overshadows and shames the more reticent
responses of others.
                    LESLIE FARBER, *The Ways of the Will*, 1966

We spend our time envying people whom we wouldn't wish to be.
                    JEAN ROSTAND, *Journal d'un caractère*, 1931

A man is undone when envy will not vouchsafe to look upon him.
                    MARQUESS OF HALIFAX, *Moral thoughts and reflections*, late 17th
                    century

He that laughs at mischief done, only wanted an opportunity to have done it himself.

ANON., *Characters and Observations*, early 18th century

In our relations with people who are bashful about their feelings, we must be capable of dissimulation; they feel a sudden hatred against anyone who catches them in a tender, enthusiastic, or elevated feeling, as if he had seen their secrets. If you want to make them feel good at such moments, you have to make them laugh or voice some cold but witty sarcasm; then their feeling freezes and they regain power over themselves.

NIETZSCHE, *The Gay Science*, 1882–7

A cruel story runs on wheels, and every hand oils the wheels as they run.

OUIDA, *Moths*, 1880

It is essential to the sanity of mankind that each one should think the other crazy – a condition with which the cynicism of human nature so cordially complies, one could wish it were a concurrence upon a subject more noble.

EMILY DICKINSON, notebook, *c.*1880

We all have strength enough to endure the troubles of others.

LA ROCHEFOUCAULD, *Maxims*, 1665

I don't think we injye other people's sufferin, Hinnissy. It isn't acshally injyement. But we feel betther f'r it.

FINLEY PETER DUNNE, *Observations by Mr. Dooley*, 1902

Someone is glad that I, Theodoros, am dead.
Another will be glad when that someone is dead.
We are all in arrears to death.

SIMONIDES (6th–5th century BC), *The Greek Anthology* (trans. Peter Jay)

Pride and hatred invigorate the soul; and love and humility enfeeble it.

HUME, *A Treatise of Human Nature*, 1739

The offender never pardons.

> GEORGE HERBERT, *Jacula Prudentum*, 1651

Beware of the man who does not return your blow: he neither forgives you nor allows you to forgive yourself.

> BERNARD SHAW, 'Maxims for Revolutionists', *Man and Superman*, 1903

To refrain from imitation is the best revenge.

> MARCUS AURELIUS, *Meditations*, 2nd century

You gave him an opportunity of showing greatness of character and he did not seize it. He will never forgive you for that.

> NIETZSCHE, *Assorted Opinions and Maxims*, 1886

The magnanimous person – or at least the type of magnanimity that has always been considered most impressive – appears to me as an extremely vengeful person who beholds satisfaction so close at hand and who drains it so fully and thoroughly to the last drop, in *anticipation*, that a tremendous and quick nausea follows this quick orgy, and he now rises 'above himself'.

> NIETZSCHE, *The Gay Science*, 1882–7

To forgive is human, to forget divine.

> JAMES GRAND, *c*.1980

All the while thou studiest revenge, thou art tearing thy own wound open.

> THOMAS FULLER (II), *Introductio ad Prudentiam*, 1731

There are many occasions in life where it is possible to effect by forgiveness every object which you propose to effect by resentment.

> SYDNEY SMITH, sermon: 'The Forgiveness of Injuries'

How often could things be remedied by a word. How often is it left unspoken.

> NORMAN DOUGLAS, *An Almanac*, 1945

Men, Women, Marriage

●

It takes all sorts to make a sex.

SAKI, The Square Egg, 1924

There is more difference within the sexes than between them.

IVY COMPTON-BURNETT, Mother and Son, 1955

Man is a creature who lives not upon bread alone, but principally by catchwords; and the little rift between the sexes is astonishingly widened by simply teaching one set of catchwords to the girls and another to the boys.

ROBERT LOUIS STEVENSON, Virginibus Puerisque, 1881

Women have served all these centuries as looking-glasses possessing the magic and delicious power of reflecting the figure of man at twice its natural size.

VIRGINIA WOOLF, A Room of One's Own, 1929

An intelligent woman is a woman with whom one can be as stupid as one wants.

VALÉRY, Mauvaises pensées et autres, 1941

Women's Rights are men's duties.

KARL KRAUS, Aphorisms and More Aphorisms, 1909

A woman's guess is much more accurate than a man's certainty.

RUDYARD KIPLING, Plain Tales from the Hills, 1888

I like a man who talks me to death, provided he is amusing; it saves so much trouble.

MARY SHELLEY, letter, 1840

Women deprived of the company of men pine, men deprived of the company of women become stupid.

CHEKHOV, *Notebooks*, 1892–1904

Marriage may often be a stormy lake, but celibacy is almost always a muddy horse-pond.

THOMAS LOVE PEACOCK, *Melincourt*, 1817

Of all actions of a man's life, his marriage does least concern other people; yet of all actions of our life, 'tis the most meddled with by other people.

JOHN SELDEN, *Table Talk*, mid 17th century

In matters of religion and matrimony I never give any advice, because I will not have anybody's torments in this world or the next laid to my charge.

LORD CHESTERFIELD, *Letters*, 1765

The hardest task of a girl's life is to prove to a man that his intentions are serious.

HELEN ROWLAND, *Reflections of a Bachelor Girl*, 1903

A lady's imagination is very rapid; it jumps from admiration to love, from love to matrimony, in a moment.

JANE AUSTEN, Darcy in *Pride and Prejudice*, 1813

It is proverbial that from a hungry tiger and an affectionate woman there is no escape.

ERNEST BRAMAH, *Kai Lung Unrolls his Mat*, 1928

To take a wife merely as an agreeable and rational companion, will commonly be found to be a grand mistake.

LORD CHESTERFIELD, *Letters*, 1765

Most people marry upon mingled motives, between convenience and inclination.

DR JOHNSON, *Life of Sir Thomas Browne*, 1756

No woman marries for money: they are all clever enough, before marrying a millionaire, to fall in love with him first.

CESARE PAVESE, *This Business of Living: Diaries 1935–50*

All tragedies are finish'd by a death,
All comedies are ended by a marriage.

LORD BYRON, *Don Juan*, 1819–24

Taking numbers into account, I should think more mental suffering has been undergone in the streets leading from St George's, Hanover Square, than in the condemned cells of Newgate.

SAMUEL BUTLER (II), *The Way of All Flesh*, 1903

But for his funeral train which the bridegroom sees in the distance,
Would he so joyfully, think you, fall in with the marriage-procession?

CLOUGH, *Amours de Voyage*, 1858

Love pleases more than marriage, for the reason that romances are more enjoyable than history.

CHAMFORT, *Maximes et pensées*, 1805

A poet may praise many whom he would be afraid to marry.

DR JOHNSON, 'Waller', *Lives of the Poets*, 1783

Love is blind, but marriage restores its sight.

LICHTENBERG, *Aphorisms*, 1764–99

People insist on confusing marriage and love on the one hand, and love and happiness on the other. But they have nothing in common. That is why, the absence of love being more frequent than love, there are happy marriages.

ALBERT CAMUS, *Carnets*, 1942–51

The particular charm of marriage is the duologue, the permanent conversation between two people who talk over everything and everyone till death breaks the record. It is this back-chat which, in the long run, makes a reciprocal equality more intoxicating than any form of servitude or domination.

CYRIL CONNOLLY, *The Unquiet Grave*, 1944

Good marriages do exist, but not delectable ones.

> LA ROCHEFOUCAULD, *Maxims*, 1665

What they do in Heaven we are ignorant of; what they do *not* we are told expressly; that they neither marry, nor are given in marriage.

> SWIFT, *Thoughts on Various Subjects*, 1711

Of all serious things, marriage is the most ludicrous.

> BEAUMARCHAIS, *The Marriage of Figaro*, 1778

It destroys one's nerves to be amiable every day to the same human being.

> BENJAMIN DISRAELI, *The Young Duke*, 1831

Marriage makes us cherish our faults.

> JEAN ROSTAND, *Le Mariage*, 1927

A different taste in jokes is a great strain on the affections.

> GEORGE ELIOT, *Daniel Deronda*, 1876

There are some men in the world who behave with the greatest complaisance, civility and good nature to all ladies whatsoever; except one.

> ANON., *Characters and Observations*, early 18th century

A married couple are well suited when both partners usually feel the need for a quarrel at the same time.

> JEAN ROSTAND, *Le Mariage*, 1927

A husband should not insult his wife publicly, at parties. He should insult her in the privacy of the home.

> JAMES THURBER, *Thurber Country*, 1953

A woman springs a sudden reproach upon you which provokes a hot retort – and then she will presently ask you to apologize.

> MARK TWAIN, *Notebooks*, later 19th century

O the pleasure of counting the melancholy clock by a snoring husband!

GEORGE FARQUHAR, *The Beaux' Strategem*, 1707

Each one of an affectionate couple may be willing, as we say, to die for the other, yet unwilling to utter the agreeable word at the right moment.

MEREDITH, *On the Idea of Comedy*, 1877

The fundamental trouble with marriage is that it shakes a man's confidence in himself, and so greatly diminishes his general competence and effectiveness. His habit of mind becomes that of a commander who has lost a decisive and calamitous battle. He never quite trusts himself thereafter.

H. L. MENCKEN, *Prejudices: Second Series*, 1920

How men hate waiting while their wives shop for clothes and trinkets; how women hate waiting, often for much of their lives, while their husbands shop for fame and glory.

THOMAS SZASZ, *The Second Sin*, 1974

In the sex-war thoughtlessness is the weapon of the male, vindictiveness of the female.

CYRIL CONNOLLY, *The Unquiet Grave*, 1944

Never feel remorse for what you have thought about your wife; she has thought much worse things about you.

JEAN ROSTAND, *Le Mariage*, 1927

Divorce is so entirely natural, that, in many houses, he sleeps each night between the husband and the wife.

CHAMFORT, *Maximes et pensées*, 1805

The one charm of marriage is that it makes a life of deception absolutely necessary for both parties.

OSCAR WILDE, *The Picture of Dorian Gray*, 1891

The chains of marriage are so heavy that it takes two to bear them, and sometimes three.

ALEXANDRE DUMAS *fils*, cit. Treich, *L'Esprit d'Alexandre Dumas*

They that marry where they do not love, will love where they do not marry.

THOMAS FULLER (I), *The Holy State and the Profane State*, 1642

In married life three is company and two is none.

OSCAR WILDE, *The Importance of Being Earnest*, 1895

Very often the only thing that comes between a charming man and a charming woman is the fact that they are married to each other.

ROBERT DE FLERS and GASTON CAILLAVET, *La Belle Aventure*, 1914

There are women whose infidelities are the only link they still have with their husbands.

SACHA GUITRY, *Elles et toi*, 1948

When a man steals your wife, there is no better revenge than to let him keep her.

SACHA GUITRY, *Elles et toi*, 1948

Twenty years of romance makes a woman look like a ruin; but twenty years of marriage make her something like a public building.

OSCAR WILDE, *A Woman of No Importance*, 1893

There is a tide in the affairs of women
Which, taken at the flood, leads – God knows where.

LORD BYRON, *Don Juan*, 1819–24

When the fine eyes of a woman are veiled with tears it is the man who no longer sees clearly.

ACHILLE TOURNIER, 19th century

Women are never stronger than when they arm themselves with their weaknesses.

MADAME DU DEFFAND, letter to Voltaire

A man never knows how to say goodbye; a woman never knows when to say it.

HELEN ROWLAND, *Reflections of a Bachelor Girl*, 1903

Some women are not beautiful – they only look as though they are.
                    KARL KRAUS, *Aphorisms and More Aphorisms*, 1909

Nothing is more moving than beauty which is unaware of itself, except for ugliness which is.
                    ROBERT MALLET (b. 1915), *Apostilles*

The tongue of a woman is capable of producing sound, which admits of no comparison either for frightfulness or harmony.
                    ANON., *Characters and Observations*, early 18th century

The more serious the face, the more beautiful the smile.
                    CHATEAUBRIAND, *Mémoires d'Outre-Tombe*, 1849–50

Love, Jealousy, Libido

●

In love, everything is true, everything is false; and it is the one subject on which one cannot express an absurdity.

CHAMFORT, *Maximes et pensées*, 1805

Love is the bright foreigner, the foreign self.

EMERSON, 'Compensation', *Essays*, First Series, 1841

Love is the affection of a mind that has nothing better to engage it.

THEOPHRASTUS, 3rd century BC

Any time that is not spent on love is wasted.

TASSO

If intelligence were taken out of my life, it would only be more or less reduced. If I had no one to love, it would be ruined.

HENRY DE MONTHERLANT, 'Explicit Mysterium', 1931

Absence sharpens love, presence strengthens it.

THOMAS FULLER (II), *Gnomologia*, 1732

Love is a capricious creature which desires everything and can be contented with almost nothing.

MADELEINE DE SCUDÉRY, 'De l'amour', *Choix de pensées*, 17th century

Love begins with love; and the warmest friendship cannot change even to the coldest love.

LA BRUYÈRE, 'Of the Affections', *Characters*, 1688

When you really want love you will find it waiting for you.

OSCAR WILDE, *De Profundis*, 1905

When we are not in love too much, we are not in love enough.
COMTE DE BUSSY-RABUTIN, *Maximes d'amour*, 17th century

I have every reason to love you. What I lack is the unreason.
ROBERT MALLET (b. 1915), *Apostilles*

There is nothing like desire for preventing the thing one says from bearing any resemblance to what one has in one's mind.
MARCEL PROUST, *Remembrance of Things Past* (*The Guermantes Way*, 1920–1)

Love makes mutes of those who habitually speak most fluently.
MADELEINE DE SCUDÉRY, 'De l'amour', *Choix de pensées*, 17th century

To hide a passion is inconceivable: not because the human subject is too weak, but because passion is in its essence made to be seen: *I want you to know that I am hiding something from you*, that is the active paradox I must resolve: I want you to know that I don't want to show my feelings: that is the message I address to the other.
ROLAND BARTHES, *A Lover's Discourse*, 1977

It would seem that love never seeks real perfection, and even fears it. It delights only in the perfection it has itself imagined; it is like those kings who recognize no greatness except in their own works.
CHAMFORT, *Maximes et pensées*, 1805

Love seeks to escape from itself, to mingle itself with its victim, as a victor nation with the vanquished – and yet at the same time to retain the privileges of a conqueror.
BAUDELAIRE, *Fusées*, 1862

It is the terrible deception of love that it begins by engaging us in play not with a woman of the external world but with a doll fashioned in our brain – the only woman moreover that we have always at our disposal, the only one we shall ever possess.
MARCEL PROUST, *Remembrance of Things Past* (*The Guermantes Way*, 1920–1)

Two people who are in love are attached above all else to their names.

WALTER BENJAMIN, *One-Way Street*, 1925–6

That girl in the omnibus had one of those faces of marvellous beauty which are seen casually in the streets but never among one's friends. Where do these women come from? Who marries them? Who knows them?

THOMAS HARDY in F. E. Hardy, *The Early Life of Thomas Hardy*, 1928

Beauty is like a glass that will burn, though it has no heat in itself.

ANON., *Characters and Observations*, early 18th century

Perhaps men who cannot love passionately are those who feel the effect of beauty most keenly; at any rate this is the strongest impression women can make on them.

STENDHAL, *Love*, 1822

When a plain-looking woman is loved it can only be very passionately; for either her influence over her lover is irresistible, or she has secret charms more powerful than those of beauty.

LA BRUYÈRE, 'Of the Affections', *Characters*, 1688

There are beautiful flowers that are scentless, and beautiful women that are unlovable.

HOUELLÉ, 19th century

It would be impossible to 'love' anyone or anything one knew *completely*. Love is directed towards what lies hidden in its object.

VALÉRY, *Tel Quel*, 1941–3

It is a certain sign of love to want to know, *to relive*, the childhood of the other.

CESARE PAVESE, *This Business of Living: Diaries 1935–50*

When one feels oneself smitten by love for a woman, one should say to oneself, 'Who are the people around her, What kind of life has she led?' All one's future happiness lies in the answer.

ALFRED DE VIGNY, *Journal d'un poète*, mid 19th century

Love makes up for the lack of long memories by a sort of magic. All other affections need a past: love creates a past which envelops us, as if by enchantment.

BENJAMIN CONSTANT, *Adolphe*, 1816

Should an obstacle prevent union, at once the fantasy of a contented, shared old age is at hand.

WALTER BENJAMIN, *One-Way Street*, 1925–6

People often say that, by pointing out to a man the faults of his mistress, you succeed only in strengthening his attachment to her, because he does not believe you; yet how much more if he does!

MARCEL PROUST, *Remembrance of Things Past* (*Swann in Love*, 1913)

A man doesn't dream about a woman because he thinks her 'mysterious'; he decides that she is 'mysterious' to justify his dreaming about her.

HENRY DE MONTHERLANT, 'The Goddess Cypris', 1944

To the lover the loved one appears always as solitary.

WALTER BENJAMIN, *One-Way Street*, 1925–6

What we take, in the presence of the beloved object, is merely a negative, which we develop later, when we are back at home, and have once again found at our disposal that inner darkroom the entrance to which is barred to us so long as we are with other people.

MARCEL PROUST, *Remembrance of Things Past* (*Within a Budding Grove*, 1919)

Friendship is a disinterested commerce between equals; love, an abject intercourse between tyrants and slaves.

OLIVER GOLDSMITH, *The Good-Natured Man*, 1768

The beloved object is successively the malady and the remedy that suspends and aggravates it.

MARCEL PROUST, *Remembrance of Things Past* (*Cities of the Plain*, 1921–2)

To love is to suffer, to be loved is to cause suffering.

COMTESSE DIANE, *Maximes de la vie*, 1908

The pleasure of love is loving, and we get more happiness from the passion we feel than from the passion we inspire.

LA ROCHEFOUCAULD, *Maxims*, 1665

As for being loved, not only does it serve no purpose, it almost always brings disaster. It must be admitted that this is one of the risks you run in loving someone.

HENRY DE MONTHERLANT, 'Explicit Mysterium', 1931

If love is judged by its visible effects it looks more like hatred than friendship.

LA ROCHEFOUCAULD, *Maxims*, 1665

Love, that is ignorant, and hatred, have almost the same ends: many foolish lovers wish the same to their friends, which their enemies would. As to wish a friend banished, that they might accompany him in exile; or some great want, that they might relieve him; or a disease, that they might sit by him.

BEN JONSON, *Timber: or Discoveries*, 1640

Love is a kind of warfare.

OVID, *Ars Amatoria*, c.1 BC

The anger of lovers renews their love.

TERENCE, *The Woman of Andros*, 166 BC

He who loves without jealousy does not truly love.

The Zohar, 13th century

It is the property of love to make us at once more distrustful and more credulous, to make us suspect the loved one, more readily than we should suspect anyone else, and be convinced more easily by her denials.

MARCEL PROUST, *Remembrance of Things Past* (*Cities of the Plain*, 1921–2)

An absence, the declining of an invitation to dinner, an unintentional, unconscious harshness are of more service than all the cosmetics and fine clothes in the world.

> MARCEL PROUST, *Remembrance of Things Past* (*The Guermantes Way*, 1920–1)

Inquisitiveness as seldom cures jealousy, as drinking in a fever quenches the thirst.

> WILLIAM WYCHERLEY, *Love in a Wood*, 1672

A jealous man always finds more than he is looking for.

> MADELEINE DE SCUDÉRY, 'De la jalousie', *Choix de pensées*, 17th century

It is astonishing what a want of imagination jealousy, which spends its time making petty suppositions that are false, shows when it comes to discovering what is true.

> MARCEL PROUST, *Remembrance of Things Past* (*The Fugitive*, 1925)

A man may deceive a woman by a pretence of love, provided he is not really in love with someone else.

> LA BRUYÈRE, 'Of Women', *Characters*, 1688

Under certain circumstances a woman will tolerate a man's conversation about his love for another woman, but the whole emphasis must lie on love, not on the object of that love.

> HUGO VON HOFMANNSTHAL, *The Book of Friends*, 1922

I have seen a man discover that his rival was beloved, and the latter fail to perceive it because of his passion.

> STENDHAL, *Love*, 1822

It has always been one of the more mysterious aspects of jealousy that, not only is it independent of envy, but that, often, the less respect – or potential envy – the jealous one feels for his rival, the more he is tortured by his jealousy.

> LESLIE FARBER, *The Ways of the Will*, 1966

As a rule the person found out in a betrayal of love holds, all the same, the superior position of the two. It is the betrayed one who is humiliated.

ADA LEVERSON, *Love's Shadow*, 1908

Surely, once the name of jealousy has been applied to an unjust, perverse and unfounded suspicion, that other jealousy which is a just and natural feeling, founded on reason and experience, deserves another name.

LA BRUYÈRE, 'Of the Affections', *Characters*, 1688

Selfishness is one of the qualities apt to inspire love.

NATHANIEL HAWTHORNE, *American Notebooks*, 1837–40

A woman without the vanity which delights in her power of attracting would be by that very fact without power to attract.

COVENTRY PATMORE, *Religio Poetae*, 1893

She who would long retain her power must use her lover ill.

OVID, *Amores*, c.16 BC

Coquettes know how to please, not how to love, which is why men love them so much.

PIERRE MARIVAUX, *Lettres sur les habitants de Paris*, 1717–18

Your true jilt uses men like chess-men, she never dwells so long on any single man as to overlook another who may prove more advantageous; nor gives one another's place, until she has seen that it is for her interest; but if one is more useful to her than others, brings him in over the heads of all others.

POPE, *Thoughts on Various Subjects*, 1727

It is easier to keep half a dozen lovers guessing than to keep one lover after he has stopped guessing.

HELEN ROWLAND, *Reflections of a Bachelor Girl*, 1903

Lovers' vows do not reach the ears of the gods.

CALLIMACHUS, *Epigrams*, 3rd century BC

This being in love is great – you get a lot of compliments and begin to think you are a great guy.

SCOTT FITZGERALD, *The Crack-Up*, 1945

The power of love consists mainly in the privilege that Potentate possesses of coining, circulating, and making current those false-hoods between man and woman, that would not pass for one moment, either between woman and woman, or man and man.

CHARLES CALEB COLTON, *Lacon*, 1825

We must not ridicule a passion which he who never felt never was happy, and he who laughs at never deserves to feel.

DR JOHNSON

A passionate nature always loves women, but one who loves women is not necessarily a passionate nature.

CHANG CH'AO, *Sweet Dream Shadows*, mid 17th century

Sex is the one thing you cannot really swindle; and it is the centre of the worst swindling of all, emotional swindling.

D. H. LAWRENCE, *A Propos of Lady Chatterley's Lover*, 1929

Dreaming is the poor retreat of the lazy, hopeless and imperfect lover.

CONGREVE, *Love for Love*, 1695

A voice from a jar of vaseline: 'This too is love'.

GAVIN EWART, 'Lifelines', *The Deceptive Grin of the Gravel Porters*, 1968

Venereal disease extends its influence much further than might appear at first glance. Since Cupid's quiver also contains poisoned arrows, the relations between the sexes have assumed a strange, hostile and even diabolical element.

SCHOPENHAUER, 'What a Man represents', *Parerga and Paralipomena*, 1851

The blood of youth burns not with such excess
As gravity's revolt to wantonness.

SHAKESPEARE, *Love's Labour's Lost*, 1594–5

A whore is like a crocodile that fastens upon her prey with her tail.

SAMUEL BUTLER (1), *Prose Observations*, 1660–80

Traditionally, sex has been a very private, secretive activity. Herein perhaps lies its powerful force for uniting people in a strong bond. As we make sex less secretive, we may rob it of its power to hold men and women together.

THOMAS SZASZ, *The Second Sin*, 1974

The angel of disgust guards the seeds of life. Just as moral prohibitions have as their end their own safety, some boundary to the exploration of the bodies of others, some economy in knowledge, is asked for, that potency be conserved.

JOHN UPDIKE, 'An Interesting Emendation', *Picked-Up Pieces*, 1975

No woman so naked as one you can see to be naked underneath her clothes.

MICHAEL FRAYN, *Constructions*, 1974

'Tis an affect worth consideration, that they, who are masters in the trade, prescribe as a remedy for amorous passions the full and free view of the body a man desires; so that, to cool his ardour, there needs no more but at full liberty to see and contemplate what he loves.

MONTAIGNE, 'Apology for Raimond de Sebonde', *Essays*, 1580–8

Beauty is still supposed to arouse desire. This is not the case. Beauty has nothing to do with the physical jerks under the coverlet. Ugliness is one of the most reliable stimulants.

HENRY DE MONTHERLANT, 'The Goddess Cypris', 1944

A mother who says 'My son will only marry a blonde' does not suspect that her remark corresponds to the worst sexual imbroglios. Travesties, mingling of the sexes, torturing of animals, chains and insults.

JEAN COCTEAU, *Opium*, 1930

There is no unhappier creature on earth than a fetishist who yearns for a woman's shoe and has to embrace the whole woman.

> KARL KRAUS, *Aphorisms and More Aphorisms*, 1909

Of all sexual aberrations, chastity is the strangest.

> ANATOLE FRANCE

That very tickling and sting which are in certain pleasures, and that seem to raise us above simple health and insensibility: that active, moving, and, I know not how, itching and biting pleasure, even that pleasure itself aims at nothing but insensibility as its mark.

> MONTAIGNE, 'Apology for Raimond de Sebonde', *Essays*, 1580–8

Our extremest pleasure has some air of groaning and complaining in it; would you not say that it is dying of pain?

> MONTAIGNE, 'That we taste nothing pure', *Essays*, 1580–8

On the brink of being satiated, desire still appears infinite.

> JEAN ROSTAND, *Journal d'un Caractère*, 1931

In order to possess, one must first have desired.

> MARCEL PROUST, *Remembrance of Things Past* (*The Captive*, 1923)

Love, like fortune, turns upon a wheel, and is very much given to rising and falling.

> VANBRUGH, *The False Friend*, 1702

Love, like fire, cannot survive without continual movement, and it ceases to live as soon as it ceases to hope or fear.

> LA ROCHEFOUCAULD, *Maxims*, 1665

There can be no peace of mind in love, since the advantage one has secured is never anything but a fresh starting-point for further desires.

> MARCEL PROUST, *Remembrance of Things Past* (*Within a Budding Grove*, 1919)

Habit is everything – even in love.

> VAUVENARGUES, *Reflections and Maxims*, 1746

Love as it exists in high society is a love of duelling or a love of gambling.

STENDHAL, *Love*, 1822

A *grande passion* is the privilege of people who have nothing to do. That is the one use of the idle classes of a country.

OSCAR WILDE, *The Picture of Dorian Gray*, 1891

Take away leisure and Cupid's bow is broken.

OVID, *Remedia Amoris*, early 1st century

Every day men sleep with women whom they do not love, and do not sleep with women whom they do love.

DIDEROT, *Jacques le fataliste*, 1773

Few romantic intrigues can be kept secret; many women are as well known by the names of their lovers as they are by those of their husbands.

LA BRUYÈRE, 'Of Women', *Characters*, 1688

Christianity has done a great deal for love by making a sin of it.

ANATOLE FRANCE, *The Garden of Epicurus*, 1894

Free love is sometimes love but never freedom.

ELIZABETH BIBESCO, *Haven*, 1951

As bees their sting, so the promiscuous leave behind them in each encounter something of themselves by which they are made to suffer.

CYRIL CONNOLLY, *The Unquiet Grave*, 1944

What we suppose to be our love or our jealousy is never a single, continuous and indivisible passion. It is composed of an infinity of successive loves, of different jealousies, each of which is ephemeral although by their uninterrupted multiplicity they give us the impression of continuity, the illusion of unity.

MARCEL PROUST, *Remembrance of Things Past* (*Swann's Way*, 1913)

The heart may think it knows better: the senses know that absence blots people out.

ELIZABETH BOWEN, *The Death of the Heart*, 1938

A short absence quickens love, a long absence kills it.

CHARLES DE SAINT-EVREMOND, letter, 1674

Sudden love takes the longest time to be cured.

LA BRUYÈRE, 'Of the Affections', *Characters*, 1688

We ought not to complain if someone we dearly love behaves now and then in ways we find distasteful, nerve-wracking or hurtful. Instead of grumbling we should avidly hoard up our feelings of irritation and bitterness: they will serve to alleviate our grief on the day when she has gone and we miss her.

CESARE PAVESE, *This Business of Living: Diaries 1935–50*

The most ardent lover holds yet a private court – and his love can never be so strong or ethereal that there will not be danger that judgment may be delivered against the beloved.

THOREAU, *Journal*, 1841

We grow tired of a single creature, and the whole world is repopulated!

JEAN ROSTAND, *Journal d'un Caractère*, 1931

Once a woman has given her heart you can never get rid of the rest of her.

VANBRUGH, *The Relapse*, 1697

It is very hard to be in love with someone who no longer loves you, but it is far worse to be loved by someone with whom you are no longer in love.

GEORGES COURTELINE, *La Philosophie de Georges Courteline*, 1917

It is seldom indeed that one parts on good terms, because if one were on good terms one would not part.

MARCEL PROUST, *Remembrance of Things Past* (*The Fugitive*, 1925)

Now hatred is by far the longest pleasure:
Men love in haste, but they detest at leisure.

LORD BYRON, *Don Juan*, 1819–24

Perhaps a great love is never returned.

DAG HAMMARSKJÖLD, *Markings*, 1964

If pure love exists, free from the dross of our other passions, it lies hidden in the depths of our hearts and unknown even to ourselves.

LA ROCHEFOUCAULD, *Maximes*, 1665

Happiness & Sorrow

The happiest people seem to be those who have no particular reason for being happy except that they are so.

W. R. INGE

There are men who seem to have started in life with a bottle or two of champagne inscribed to their credit.

WILLIAM JAMES, *Varieties of Religious Experience*, 1902

Well-being is attained by little and little, and nevertheless it is no little thing itself.

ZENO OF CITIUM (4th–3rd century BC), cit. Diogenes Laertius, *Lives and Opinions of Eminent Philosophers*

Human felicity is produced not so much by great pieces of good fortune that seldom happen, as by little advantages that occur every day.

BENJAMIN FRANKLIN, *Autobiography*, later 18th century

The sense of existence is the greatest happiness.

BENJAMIN DISRAELI, *Contarini Fleming*, 1832

Happiness is a how, not a what; a talent, not an object.

HERMANN HESSE, *Collected Letters*, I, 1895–1921

Whatever affection we have for our friends or our family, the happiness of others never suffices for our own.

VAUVENARGUES, *Reflections and Maxims*, 1746

What is more wonderful than the delight which the mind feels when it *knows*? This delight is not for anything beyond the knowing, but is in the act of knowing. It is the satisfaction of a primary instinct.

MARK RUTHERFORD, *Last Pages from a Journal*, 1915

Happiness and Beauty are by-products.

> BERNARD SHAW, 'Maxims for Revolutionists', *Man and Superman*, 1903

Happiness is a mystery like religion, and should never be rationalized.

> G. K. CHESTERTON, *Heretics*, 1905

Few men would be happy if others had the determining of their occupation and pleasures.

> VAUVENARGUES, *Reflections and Maxims*, 1746

The happiness of life is so nice a thing that, like the sensitive plant, it shrinks away, even upon thinking of it.

> JOSEPH SPENCE, *Anecdotes*, 1756

Mankind are always happy for having been happy; so that if you make them happy now, you make them happy twenty years hence by the memory of it.

> SYDNEY SMITH, *Elementary Sketches of Moral Philosophy*, 1804–6

Life admits not of delays; when pleasure is to be had, it is fit to catch it. Every hour takes away part of the things that please us, and perhaps part of our disposition to be pleased.

> DR JOHNSON in Boswell's *Life of Johnson*, 1777

The best way for a man to lead his life is to have been as cheerful as possible and to have suffered as little as possible. This could happen if one did not seek one's pleasures in mortal things.

> DEMOCRITUS OF ABDERA, 5th–4th century BC

What a foolish thing a man's heart is! Though we realize, for example, that fragrances are short-lived and the scent burnt into clothes lingers but briefly, how our hearts always leap when we catch a whiff of an exquisite perfume!

> YOSHIDA KENKO, *Essays in Idleness*, c.1340

There is no pleasure comparable to the not being captivated by any external thing whatever.

> THOMAS WILSON, *Sacra Privata*, early 18th century

To be able to throw oneself away for the sake of a moment, to be able to sacrifice years for a woman's smile – that is happiness.

HERMANN HESSE, *Diesseits*

What golden hour of life, what glittering moment will ever equal the pain its loss can cause?

VALÉRY, *Mauvaises pensées et autres*, 1942

The secret of happiness is to admire without desiring. And that is not happiness.

F. H. BRADLEY, *Aphorisms*, 1930

Felicity is a continual progress of the desire, from one object to another; the attaining of the former being still but the way to the latter.

HOBBES, *Leviathan*, 1651

The lustre of the present hour is always borrowed from the background of the possibilities it goes with.

WILLIAM JAMES, *Varieties of Religious Experience*, 1902

There is an hour wherein a man might be happy all his life, could he find it.

GEORGE HERBERT, *Jacula Prudentum*, 1651

A moment of time may make us unhappy for ever.

JOHN GAY, *The Beggar's Opera*, 1728

Golden dreams make men awake hungry.

THOMAS FULLER (II), *Gnomologia*, 1732

Hope is itself a species of happiness, and, perhaps, the chief happiness which this world affords.

DR JOHNSON in Boswell's *Life of Johnson*, 1762

The things we have most longed for do not happen; or if they do, it is never at the time nor under the circumstances when they could have made us happiest.

LA BRUYÈRE, 'Of the Affections', *Characters*, 1688

Pleasure is very seldom found where it is sought; our brightest blazes of gladness are commonly kindled by unexpected sparks.

DR JOHNSON, *The Idler*, 1758

A trifle consoles us because a trifle upsets us.

PASCAL, *Pensées*, 1670

One day's happiness makes a man forget his misfortune; and one day's misfortune makes him forget his past happiness.

ECCLESIASTICUS, *c.*170 BC

If we only wanted to be happy, it would be easy; but we want to be happier than other people, and that is almost always difficult, since we think them happier than they are.

MONTESQUIEU, *Mes pensées*, *c.*1722–55

Many things cause pain which would cause pleasure if you regarded their advantages.

GRACIÁN, *The Art of Worldly Wisdom*, 1647

When a man forgets his ideals he may hope for happiness, but not till then.

JOHN OLIVER HOBBES, *Some Emotions and a Moral*, 1891

There is no duty we so much underrate as the duty of being happy.

ROBERT LOUIS STEVENSON, *Virginibus Puerisque*, 1881

My theory is to enjoy life, but the practice is against it.

CHARLES LAMB, *Letters*, 1822

Human life is so tiresome a scene, and men generally are of such indolent dispositions, that whatever amuses them, though by a passion mixed with pain, does in the main give them a sensible pleasure.

HUME, *A Treatise of Human Nature*, 1739

How can there be laughter, how can there be pleasure, when the whole world is burning?

The Dhammapada, probably 3rd century BC

We humans are such limited creatures – how is it that there are so few
limits when it comes to human suffering?

> PIERRE MARIVAUX, *La Vie de Marianne*, 1731–41

Where life ranks highest, there it can suffer most. Human life has
among its privileges that of pre-eminence of pain.

> SIR CHARLES SHERRINGTON, *Man on his Nature*, 1940

'All is vanity', saith the Preacher. But if all were only vanity, who
would mind? Alas, it is too often worse than vanity: agony, darkness, death also.

> THOMAS HARDY in F. E. Hardy, *The Later Years of Thomas
> Hardy*, 1930

I can think of no state so insupportable and dreadful, as to have the
soul vivid and afflicted, without means to declare itself.

> MONTAIGNE, 'Use makes perfect', *Essays*, 1580–8

> Sorrow concealèd, like an oven stopp'd,
> Doth burn the heart to cinders where it is.

> > SHAKESPEARE, *Titus Andronicus*, 1593–4

Ah, how ghastly is a hurt from one of whom you daren't complain!

> PUBLILIUS SYRUS, *Sententiae*, 1st century BC

Our imaginary woes are conjured up by our passions, and are
fostered by passionate feeling; our real ones come of themselves, and
are opposed by an abstract exertion of mind. Real grievances are
displacers of passion.

> KEATS, letter, 1819

Beyond a certain pitch of suffering, men are overcome by a kind of
ghostly indifference.

> VICTOR HUGO, *Les Misérables*, 1865

Afflictions induce callosities.

> SIR THOMAS BROWNE, *Urn Burial*, 1658

Stolidity is more dreadful than sorrow, for it is the stubble of the soil where sorrow grew.

EMILY DICKINSON, notebook, *c*.1880

Is it only the mouth and belly which are injured by hunger and thirst? Men's minds are also injured by them.

MENCIUS, 4th century BC

Mental torture is more readily endured, alas, than physical pain; and if I were forced to choose between a bad conscience and an aching tooth, I would settle for the bad conscience.

HEINE, *Letters on the French Stage*, 1837

We think back with repugnance to that ancient biological pre-human scene whence we came; there *no* life was a sacred thing. There millions of years of pain went by without one moment of pity, not to speak of mercy.

SIR CHARLES SHERRINGTON, *Man on his Nature*, 1940

There are two things for which animals are to be envied: they know nothing of future evils, or of what people say about them.

VOLTAIRE, letter, 1739

In growing civilized has man really done anything more than complicate his barbarism and refine his misery?

PAUL BOURGET, *Essais de psychologie contemporaine*, 1883

The sole cause of man's unhappiness is that he does not know how to stay quietly in his room.

PASCAL, *Pensées*, 1670

Man is so unhappy that he would be bored even if he had no cause for boredom, by the very nature of his temperament, and he is so vain that, though he has a thousand and one basic reasons for being bored, the slightest thing, like pushing a ball with a billiard cue, will be enough to divert him.

PASCAL, *Pensées*, 1670

If troubles destroy happiness, pleasures disturb it.

JEAN SENAL, 19th century

Pleasure chews and grinds us.

> MONTAIGNE, 'That we taste nothing pure', *Essays*, 1580–8

Misfortune has a way of choosing some unprecedented means or other of impressing its power on those who might be said to have forgotten it.

> SENECA, *Epistles*, 1st century

Why did Hamlet trouble about ghosts after death, when life itself is haunted by ghosts so much more terrible?

> CHEKHOV, *Notebooks*, 1892–1904

A sigh can break a man in two.

> *The Talmud*

It is of no avail to weep for the loss of a loved one, which is why we weep.

> SOLON, cit. Diogenes Laertius, *Lives and Opinions of Eminent Philosophers*

In every country the universal faults and evils of mankind are set down as local peculiarities. Men are miserable by necessity, and determined to believe themselves miserable by accident.

> LEOPARDI, *Pensieri*, 1834–7

Despite the sight of all the miseries which affect us and hold us by the throat we have an irrepressible instinct which bears us up.

> PASCAL, *Pensées*, 1670

Ah! Those strange people who have the courage to be unhappy! *Are* they unhappy, by the way?

> ALICE JAMES, *Diary*, 1889

Query: Whether it be not delightful to complain? And whether there be not many who had rather utter their complaints than redress their evils?

> BISHOP BERKELEY, *The Querist*, 1735

There is a small dose of revenge in every complaint; one reproaches those who are different for one's feeling vile, sometimes even with one's being vile.

NIETZSCHE, *Twilight of the Idols*, 1888

Complainants are the greatest persecutors.

SAMUEL BUTLER (I), *Prose Observations*, 1660–80

Pessimism, when you get used to it, is just as agreeable as optimism. Indeed, I think it must be more agreeable, must have a more real savour than optimism – from the way in which pessimists abandon themselves to it.

ARNOLD BENNETT, *Things that have Interested Me*, 1921

Perhaps the most despairing cry of the pessimistic mind is that the world is never quite as bad as it ought and should be for intellectual purposes.

BERNARD BERENSON, letter, 1911

Consolation for unhappiness can often be found in a certain satisfaction we get from looking unhappy.

LA ROCHEFOUCAULD, *Maxims*, 1665

If you are foolish enough to be contented, don't show it, but grumble with the rest.

JEROME K. JEROME, *The Idle Thoughts of an Idle Fellow*, 1889

Is your cucumber bitter? Throw it away. Are there briars in your path? Turn aside. That is enough. Do not go on to say, 'Why were things of this sort ever brought into the world?'

MARCUS AURELIUS, *Meditations*, 2nd century

Nothing is more depressing than consolations based on the necessity of evil, the uselessness of remedies, the inevitability of fate, the order of Providence, or the misery of the human condition. It is ridiculous to try to alleviate misfortune by observing that we are born to be miserable.

MONTESQUIEU, *Persian Letters*, 1721

Good & Evil

●

'There is nothing good or bad but thinking makes it so'; and Nature
has in that sense no 'thinking' outside man's. He and his ethics stand
alone.

SIR CHARLES SHERRINGTON, Man on his Nature, 1940

Think not that morality is ambulatory; that vices in one age are not
vices in another; or that virtues, which are the everlasting seal of
right reason, may be stamped by opinion.

SIR THOMAS BROWNE, Christian Morals, mid 17th century

The laws of conscience, which we pretend to be derived from
nature, proceed from custom.

MONTAIGNE, 'Of custom', Essays, 1580–8

More men become good through practice than by nature.

DEMOCRITUS OF ABDERA (5th–4th century BC)

One must either be good, or imitate a good man.

DEMOCRITUS OF ABDERA

Of neighbourhoods benevolence is the most beautiful. How can the
man be considered wise who, when he has the choice, does not settle
in benevolence?

CONFUCIUS, Analects, 5th century BC

Whatever the world may say or do, my part is to keep myself good;
just as a gold piece, or an emerald, or a purple robe insists perpetually, 'Whatever the world may say or do, my part is to remain an
emerald and keep my colour true.'

MARCUS AURELIUS, Meditations, 2nd century

Virtue is not the absence of vice or the avoidance of moral dangers;
virtue is a vivid and separate thing, like pain or a particular smell.

G. K. CHESTERTON, Tremendous Trifles, 1909

It is not enough to do good; one must do it in the right way.
JOHN MORLEY, *Rousseau*, 1876

Innocence hath a very short style.
MARQUESS OF HALIFAX, *Moral thoughts and reflections*, late 17th century

He who wants to do good knocks at the gate; he who loves finds the gate open.
RABINDRANATH TAGORE, *Stray Birds*, 1916

For it is of great advantage to human nature that the most virtuous men can hardly ever fully say why they are virtuous, and while they believe they are preaching their faith they are not really preaching it at all.
LICHTENBERG, *Aphorisms*, 1764–99

I have often looked upon the conduct of fathers and mothers of the lower classes of society towards idiots as the great triumph of the human heart.
WORDSWORTH, letter, 1802

At the day of judgment we shall not be asked what we have read but what we have done.
THOMAS À KEMPIS, *The Imitation of Christ*, c.1420

Waste no more time arguing what a good man should be. Be one.
MARCUS AURELIUS, *Meditations*, 2nd century

We are no more responsible for the evil thoughts which pass through our minds, than a scarecrow for the birds which fly over the seed-plot he has to guard; the sole responsibility in each case is to prevent them from settling.
CHURTON COLLINS, aphorisms in the *English Review*, 1914

Since most crimes are committed in a state of somnambulism, one might say that the function of the moral sense consists in wakening the dreadful dreamer in the nick of time.
VALÉRY, *Tel Quel*, 1941–3

The best way to avoid a bad action is by doing a good one for there is no difficulty in the world like that of trying to do nothing.

> JOHN CLARE, *Fragments*, 1825–37

Many people would be much better if they would let themselves be as good as they really are. They seem to take delight in making themselves less.

> MARK RUTHERFORD, *More Pages from a Journal*, 1910

Man will only become better when you make him see what he is like.

> CHEKHOV, *Notebooks*, 1892–1904

How can we tell when a sin we have committed has been pardoned? By the fact that we no longer commit that sin.

> RABBI BUNAM OF PZYSHA, *c*.1800, cit. Martin Buber, *Tales of the Hasidim*

Saintly conduct would be the most perfect conduct conceivable in an environment where all were saints already.

> WILLIAM JAMES, *Varieties of Religious Experience*, 1902

In the life of saints, technically so called, the spiritual faculties are strong, but what gives the impression of extravagance proves usually on examination to be a relative deficiency of intellect.

> WILLIAM JAMES, *Varieties of Religious Experience*, 1902

I think it is Franklin who says that philosophers are sages in their maxims and fools in their conduct but this is an everyday fact consonant with maxims – that human nature is ever capable of improvement and never able of being made perfect.

> JOHN CLARE, *Fragments*, 1825–37

To act from pure benevolence is not possible for finite beings. Human benevolence is mingled with vanity, interest, or some other motive.

> DR JOHNSON in Boswell's *Life of Johnson*, 1776

There is nothing which human courage will not undertake, and little that human patience will not endure.

> DR JOHNSON, *Thoughts on the Late Transactions Respecting Falkland's Islands*, 1771

You cannot have power for good without having power for evil too. Even mother's milk nourishes murderers as well as heroes.

BERNARD SHAW, *Major Barbara*, 1905

What we all love is good touched up with evil –
Religion's self must have a spice of devil.

CLOUGH, *Dipsychus*, c.1850

Satan is inconsistent. He persuades a man not to go to synagogue on a cold morning; yet when the man does go, he follows him into it.

THE KORETSER RABBI (18th century), *Hasidic Anthology*, ed. Louis Newman

The Devil tempts men to be wicked that he may punish them for being so.

SAMUEL BUTLER (I), *Prose Observations*, 1660–80

In our holiest moment our devil with a leer stands close at hand. He is a very busy devil. It gains vice some respect, I must confess, thus to be reminded how indefatigable it is.

THOREAU, *Journal*, 1841

Evil comes at leisure like the disease; good comes in a hurry like the doctor.

G. K. CHESTERTON, *The Man who was Orthodox*, 1963

It often needs as much effort to yield as to resist, to do harm as to do good; as many struggles with oneself, no less arduous, and grimmer.

VALÉRY, *Tel Quel*, 1941–3

Many might go to heaven with half the labour they go to hell.

BEN JONSON, *Timber; or Discoveries*, 1640

We have neither the strength nor the opportunity to accomplish all the good and all the evil which we design.

VAUVENARGUES, *Reflections and Maxims*, 1746

Not only do men tend to forget kindnesses and wrongs alike, but they even hate those who have done them kindnesses and give up hating those who have wronged them. The effort needed to reward goodness and take revenge upon evil seems to them a tyranny to which they are loth to submit.

LA ROCHEFOUCAULD, *Maxims*, 1665

The multi-cellular organism stood for a change from conflict between cell and cell to harmony between cell and cell. It is surely more than mere analogy to liken to those small beginnings of multi-cellular life of millions of years ago the slender beginnings of altruism today.

SIR CHARLES SHERRINGTON, *Man on his Nature*, 1940

Altruism as passion; that would seem as yet Nature's noblest product; the greatest contribution made by man to Life. At first glance such altruism may strike the biologist as contrary to the broad trend and polity of life. That makes more notable the fact that evolution nevertheless has brought it about.

SIR CHARLES SHERRINGTON, *Man on his Nature*, 1940

Granted that some men have now developed an ethical outlook which enables them to criticize the cruelties they observe in nature, this does not, on the face of it, serve to demonstrate that man is bound steadily to improve himself, morally and intellectually. Perhaps it is just these morally sensitive men who are destined to die out.

JOHN PASSMORE, *The Perfectibility of Man*, 1970

Combinations of wickedness would overwhelm the world, did not those who have long practised perfidy grow faithless to each other.

DR JOHNSON, 'Waller', *Lives of the Poets*, 1779-81

Malicious men may die, but malice never.

MOLIÈRE, *Tartuffe*, 1664 (trans. Richard Wilbur)

Malice is the unprovoked desire of producing evil to another, in order to reap a pleasure from the comparison.

HUME, *A Treatise of Human Nature*, 1739

He who seeks happiness for himself by making others unhappy is bound in the chains of hate and from those he cannot be free.

The Dhammapada, probably 3rd century BC

Envy, malice, hatred are the qualities of Satan, close and dark like himself, and where such brands smoke the soul cannot be white.

SIR THOMAS BROWNE, *Christian Morals*, mid 17th century

Some men delight in things for no other reason but because they are ugly and infamous.

SAMUEL BUTLER (I), *Prose Observations*, 1660–80

Grief and disappointment give rise to anger, anger to envy, envy to malice, and malice to grief again, till the whole circle be completed.

HUME, *A Treatise of Human Nature*, 1739

The Devil himself is good when he is pleased.

THOMAS FULLER (II), *Gnomologia*, 1732

Wicked people sometimes perform good actions. I suppose they wish to see if this gives as great a feeling of pleasure as the virtuous claim for it.

CHAMFORT, *Maximes et pensées*, 1805

Upon the whole I dislike mankind: whatever people on the other side of the question may advance, they cannot deny that they are always surprised at hearing of a good action and never of a bad one.

KEATS, letter, 1820

Man is the only animal who causes pain to others with no other object than wanting to do so.

SCHOPENHAUER, 'On Ethics', *Parerga and Paralipomena*, 1851

The truest wild beasts live in the most populous places.

GRACIÁN, *The Art of Worldly Wisdom*, 1647

Pigs are not corrupted with the Higher Imperialism. Tigers have no spiritual pride. Whales never sneer. Crocodiles are not (despite a pleasing legend) in the least hypocritical. On examining their exterior, it is difficult to understand why anyone ever gave them credit for so vivacious and ingenious a quality. The worst sins of all are the purely human sins.

G. K. CHESTERTON, *The Man who was Orthodox*, 1963

I never wonder to see men wicked, but I often wonder to see them not ashamed.

SWIFT, *Thoughts on Various Subjects*, 1711

Power takes as ingratitude the writhings of its victims.

RABINDRANATH TAGORE, *Stray Birds*, 1916

It is a sin peculiar to man to hate his victim.

TACITUS, *Agricola*, early 2nd century

Cruelty isn't softened by tears, it feeds on them.

PUBLILIUS SYRUS, *Sententiae*, 1st century BC

Man is almost always as wicked as his needs require.

LEOPARDI, *Pensieri*, 1834–7

The belief in a supernatural source of evil is not necessary; men alone are quite capable of every wickedness.

JOSEPH CONRAD, *Under Western Eyes*, 1911

A situation in which the actor really suffers can only be found comic by children who see only the situation and are unaware of the suffering, as when a child laughs at a hunchback, or by human swine.

W. H. AUDEN, *The Dyer's Hand*, 1963

When the cruel fall into the hands of the cruel, we read their fate with horror, not with pity.

CHARLES CALEB COLTON, *Lacon*, 1825

Bad natures never lack an instructor.

PUBLILIUS SYRUS, *Sententiae*, 1st century BC

Malice is cunning.

CICERO, *De Natura Deorum*, 45 BC

A knave is a machine made up of materials which are joined together like Hebrew letters; to be read backwards, if you would understand him.

ANON., *Characters and Observations*, early 18th century

The wicked are always surprised to find that the good can be clever.

VAUVENARGUES, *Reflections and Maxims*, 1746

However evil men may be they dare not be openly hostile to virtue, and so when they want to attack it they pretend to find it spurious, or impute crimes to it.

LA ROCHEFOUCAULD, *Maxims*, 1665

The common excuse of those who bring misfortune on others is that they desire their good.

VAUVENARGUES, *Reflections and Maxims*, 1746

When one has once given Evil a lodging, it no longer demands that one believes it.

KAFKA, 'Aphorisms 1917–19', *The Great Wall of China*

Few men are sufficiently discerning to appreciate all the evil they do.

LA ROCHEFOUCAULD, *Maxims*, 1665

How many crimes are committed merely because their authors could not endure being wrong!

ALBERT CAMUS, Jean-Baptiste Clamance in *The Fall*, 1956

In a course of criminal conduct every fresh step that we make appears a justification of the one that preceded it, it seems to bring again the moment of liberty and choice.

WORDSWORTH, Preface to *The Borderers*, *c*.1796

Crime can be regarded as a relief, an exorcism, even a regeneration of the criminal – who, before the crime, may well have been far more criminal, more horrible, pregnant with the evil to be done.

VALÉRY, *Tel Quel*, 1941–3

Every crime has something of the dream about it. Crimes *determined* to take place engender all they need: victims, circumstances, pretexts, opportunities.

VALÉRY, *Tel Quel*, 1941–3

The remembrance of a crime committed in vain has been considered as the most painful of all reflections.

DR JOHNSON, 'Pope', *Lives of the Poets*, 1779–81

To commit murder is the mark of a moment, exceptional. To defend it is constant, and shows a more perverted conscience.

LORD ACTON, MSS notes, Cambridge, late 19th century

One may be driven to commit murder by love or hatred, but one can only advocate murder out of sheer wickedness.

ITALO SVEVO, *Confessions of Zeno*, 1923

Scarce anything awakens attention like a tale of cruelty.

DR JOHNSON, *The Idler*, 1758

With what pleasure we read newspaper reports of crime! A true criminal becomes a popular figure because he unburdens in no small degree the consciences of his fellow men, for now they know once more where evil is to be found.

JUNG, 'Archetypes of the Collective Unconscious', 1934

'If those two were sane they'd have gone mad long ago.'

ANON., comment on the Moors Murderers, quoted by Maurice Richardson, *Fits and Starts*, 1979

A wonder is often expressed that the greatest criminals look like other men. The reason is that *they are like other men in many respects*.

HAZLITT, 'On the Knowledge of Character', 1822

Bad men do what good men only dream.

GAVIN EWART, 'The Great Lines', *The Deceptive Grin of the Gravel Porters*, 1968

It is not enough to be exceptionally mad, licentious and fanatical in order to win a great reputation; it is still necessary to arrive on the scene at the right time.

VOLTAIRE, letter, 1776

The popularity of a bad man is as treacherous as he is himself.

PLINY THE YOUNGER, *Epistles*, early 2nd century

We imagine that it would be impossible to prevent our feeling some pleasure if we were present at the death of a wicked man, for then we could reap the harvest of our hatred, and get from him all that we could ever hope to get from him, namely, the delight his death causes us. But at last this man really dies, at a time when our interest will not allow us to rejoice; he dies either too soon or too late for us.

LA BRUYÈRE, 'Of the Affections', *Characters*, 1688

The search of an investigator for the Unpardonable Sin – he at last finds it in his own heart and practice.

NATHANIEL HAWTHORNE, *American Notebooks*, 1841–52

There is a passion for hunting something deeply implanted in the human breast.

DICKENS, *Oliver Twist*, 1837–8

The human lot would be unbearable if it were as common to carry out atrocities as it is to believe in them.

VOLTAIRE, *Essai sur les moeurs*, 1756

The lunatic's visions of horror are all drawn from the material of daily fact.

WILLIAM JAMES, *Varieties of Religious Experience*, 1902

Kill a man, and you are a murderer. Kill millions of men, and you are a conqueror. Kill everyone, and you are a god.

JEAN ROSTAND, *Pensées d'un biologiste*, 1955

Vices & Virtues

●

God created the world, but it is the Devil who keeps it going.

TRISTAN BERNARD (1866–1947), *Contes, Repliques et Bons Mots*

Virtues and vices are of a strange nature; for the more we have, the fewer we think we have.

ANON., *Characters and Observations*, early 18th century

If you want to be good, begin by assuming that you are bad.

EPICTETUS, *Fragments*, 1st century

Virtue, among other definitions, may thus be defined: an action against the will.

ANON., *Characters and Observations*, early 18th century

Good resolutions are useless attempts to interfere with scientific laws.

OSCAR WILDE, *The Picture of Dorian Gray*, 1891

Man's partial good resolutions that always succumb to ingrained habit are like the cleaning, scrubbing and adorning that we practice on Sundays and feast days. We always get dirty again, to be sure, but such a partial cleaning process has the advantage of upholding the principle of cleanliness.

GOETHE, conversation with Riemer, 1806

Virtue would hardly be distinguished from a kind of sensuality, if there were no labour, no opposition, no difficulty in doing our duty.

THOMAS WILSON, *Sacra Privata*, early 18th century

Adam was but human – this explains it all. He did not want the apple for the apple's sake; he wanted it only because it was forbidden. The mistake was in not forbidding the serpent; then he would have eaten the serpent.

MARK TWAIN, *Pudd'nhead Wilson*, 1894

Temptation laughs at the fool who takes it seriously.

THE CHOFETZ CHAIM, late 19th century

That which we call sin in others, is experiment for us.

EMERSON, 'Experience', *Essays, Second Series*, 1844

Virtue brings honour, and honour vanity.

THOMAS FULLER (II), *Gnomologia*, 1732

Am I blameable, if I do a good action, upon account of the happiness which that honest consciousness will give me? Surely not. On the contrary, that pleasing consciousness is a proof of my virtue.

LORD CHESTERFIELD, *Letters*, 1748

If our virtues are neither recognized nor appreciated by anyone, what is the point of having them since, humanly speaking, they only do us harm?

HENRY DE MONTHERLANT, *Notebooks*, 1930–44

An honest man, that cries up his own honesty, acts the honest man, but speaks like a rogue.

ANON., *Characters and Observations*, early 18th century

Virtue is so praiseworthy that wicked people practise it from self-interest.

VAUVENARGUES, *Reflections and Maxims*, 1746

It is not possible for everyone to have virtues of the same character; yet 'tis possible for everyone to be equally virtuous.

ANON., *Characters and Observations*, early 18th century

What to one man is the virtue which he has sunk below the possibility of aspiring to, is to another the backsliding by which he forfeits his spiritual crown.

GEORGE ELIOT, *Felix Holt*, 1866

Virtue itself needs limits.

MONTESQUIEU, *De l'esprit des lois*, 1748

Our virtues and vices couple with one another, and get children that resemble both their parents.

> MARQUESS OF HALIFAX, *Moral thoughts and reflections*, late 17th century

Virtues and vices are very near of kin and like the Austrian family beget one another.

> SAMUEL BUTLER (I), *Prose Observations*, 1660–80

Every vice you destroy has a corresponding virtue, which perishes along with it.

> ANATOLE FRANCE, *The Garden of Epicurus*, 1894

No vice exists which does not pretend to be more or less like some virtue and which does not take advantage of this assumed resemblance.

> LA BRUYÈRE, 'Of the Affections', *Characters*, 1688

There are some faults which bear witness to a good character more clearly than some virtues.

> CARDINAL DE RETZ, *Memoirs*, 1673–6

Fidelity to large truths often requires betrayal of small ones.

> PETER DE VRIES, *The Tents of Wickedness*, 1959

It is some kind of scandal not to bear with the faults of an honest man. It is not loving honesty enough to allow it distinguishing privileges.

> MARQUESS OF HALIFAX, *Miscellaneous thoughts and reflections*, late 17th century

Virtue is praised but hated. People run away from it, for it is ice-cold and in this world you must keep your feet warm.

> DIDEROT, *Rameau's Nephew*, 1761

Virtue is so near reduced to nothing that the very name is become pedantic.

> SAMUEL BUTLER (I), *Prose Observations*, 1660–80

Some people are thought well of in society whose only good points are the vices useful in social life.

LA ROCHEFOUCAULD, *Maxims*, 1665

The secret police arrest us all. I, who have been a well-mannered and amusing guest at your dinner parties these past ten years, betray you as soon as they show me the electrodes. That bore. Puling refuses, heroically.

If we ever all get out again, don't make the mistake of inviting him to your dinner parties instead of me!

MICHAEL FRAYN, *Constructions*, 1974

There must be a spice of mischief and wilfulness thrown into the cup of our existence to give it its sharp taste and sparkling colour.

HAZLITT, 'On Depth and Superficiality', 1826

When people are said to be good company, often the reason is simply that they have the more civilized kinds of vices; perhaps it is the same as with poisons, the subtlest of which are also the most dangerous.

MONTESQUIEU, *Persian Letters*, 1721

Vice would not be altogether vice if it did not hate virtue.

CHAMFORT, *Maximes et pensées*, 1805

What is it that reason demands of a man? Something very easy – that he live in accordance with his own nature. Yet this is turned into something difficult by the madness that is universal among men; we push one another into vices.

SENECA, *Epistles*, 1st century

Throughout our life, our worst weaknesses and meannesses are usually committed for the sake of the people whom we most despise.

DICKENS, *Great Expectations*, 1860–1

Who are next to knaves? Those that converse with them.

POPE, *Thoughts on Various Subjects*, 1727

When two or three rogues find themselves together for the first time, they easily, and as if by signs intelligible only to themselves, know each other for what they are, and at once fraternize; or if their interests will not allow this, at least respect and feel at home with each other.

LEOPARDI, *Pensieri*, 1834–7

Two starving men cannot be twice as hungry as one; but two rascals can be ten times as vicious as one.

BERNARD SHAW, 'Maxims for Revolutionists', *Man and Superman*, 1903

'We must do as others do' is a dangerous maxim, which nearly always means 'we must do wrong' if it is applied to any but external things of no consequence.

LA BRUYÈRE, 'Of Opinions', *Characters*, 1688

If someone tells you he is going to make 'a realistic decision', you immediately understand that he has resolved to do something bad.

MARY McCARTHY, *On the Contrary*, 1962

Want of principle is power. Truth and honesty set a limit to our efforts, which impudence and hypocrisy easily overleap.

HAZLITT, *Characteristics*, 1823

Injurious men brook no injuries.

THOMAS FULLER (II), *Gnomologia*, 1732

When a mean person plans to injure a gentleman, his heart is cruel, his plans are well laid out and his action is firm; therefore the gentleman can seldom escape. When a gentleman intends to punish a mean person, his heart is kind, his plans are incomplete, and he cannot quite go to the limit; therefore more often he himself is victimized by it.

'MR. TUT-TUT', *A Night's Talk*, Chinese, 17th century

That which is base does not have the power to debase; honour alone can inflict dishonour.

CHATEAUBRIAND, *Mémoires d'Outre-Tombe*, 1849–50

Men perish with whispering sins, nay with silent sins, sins that never tell the conscience they are sins, as often as with crying sins.

DONNE, sermon, 1624

We often pride ourselves on even the most criminal passions, but envy is a timid and shamefaced passion we never dare acknowledge.

LA ROCHEFOUCAULD, *Maxims*, 1665

Envy which talks and cries out is always maladroit; it is the envy which keeps silent that one ought to fear.

ANTOINE RIVAROL, *Pensées, traits et bons mots*, late 18th century

One of envy's favourite stratagems is the attempt to provoke envy in the envied one.

LESLIE FARBER, *The Ways of the Will*, 1966

Envy can scarcely hold back her tears, when she sees nothing to cry at.

OVID, *Metamorphoses*, c.AD 2–8

Envy honours the dead in order to insult the living.

HELVÉTIUS (1715–71), *Notes, maximes et pensées*

It is not given to everyone to find the right outlet for his envy.

JEAN ROSTAND, *De la vanité*, 1925

We spend our time envying people whom we wouldn't like to be.

JEAN ROSTAND, *De la vanité*, 1925

Whereas true admiration keeps its distance, respecting the discrepancy between the admirer and the admired one, envy's assault upon its object with a barrage of compliments serves not only its need to assert itself in the costume of admiration, but also the lust of the envier to possess the very quality that initially incited his envy.

LESLIE FARBER, *The Ways of the Will*, 1966

Covetousness often starves other vices.

THOMAS FULLER (II), *Gnomologia*, 1732

We call that a man's means, which he hath; but that is truly his means, what way he came by it.

DONNE, sermon, 1626

Even in a palace life may be lived well.

MARCUS AURELIUS, *Meditations*, 2nd century

The man who leaves money to charity in his will is only giving away what no longer belongs to him.

VOLTAIRE, letter, 1769

Coarseness, clownishness and brutality may be the vices of an intelligent man.

LA BRUYÈRE, 'Of Opinions', *Characters*, 1688

Pride is generally censured and decried, but mainly by those who have nothing to be proud of.

SCHOPENHAUER, 'What a man represents', *Parerga and Paralipomena*, 1851

Pride wants the best condition of vice; that is, concealment.

SAMUEL BUTLER (I), *Prose Observations*, 1660–80

Though pride is not a virtue, it is the parent of many virtues.

CHURTON COLLINS, aphorisms in the *English Review*, 1914

Endurance is frequently a form of indecision.

ELIZABETH BIBESCO, *Haven*, 1951

One can always be kind to people about whom one cares nothing.

OSCAR WILDE, *The Picture of Dorian Gray*, 1891

Self-sacrifice enables us to sacrifice other people without blushing.

BERNARD SHAW, 'Maxims for Revolutionists', *Man and Superman*, 1903

It's the imperfectly selfish souls that cause themselves and others so many heart-burnings. People who make half sacrifices for others always find that it's the unfinished half that's being looked at.

SAKI, *The Watched Pot*, 1924

Intemperate temperance injures the cause of temperance, while temperate temperance helps it in its fight against intemperate intemperance.

MARK TWAIN, *Notebooks*, later 19th century

Use, carried on according to reason, has in it more of difficulty than abstinence; moderation is a virtue that gives more work than suffering.

MONTAIGNE, 'The Story of Spurina', *Essays*, 1580–8

The path of duty lies in what is near, and man seeks for it in what is remote.

MENCIUS, 4th century BC

The highest panegyric that private virtue can receive is the praise of servants.

DR JOHNSON, *The Rambler*, 1750–2

I do not admire the excess of a virtue like courage unless I see at the same time an excess of the opposite virtue, as in Epaminondas, who possessed extreme courage and extreme kindness. We show greatness not by being at one extreme, but by touching both at once and occupying all the space in between.

PASCAL, *Pensées*, 1670

Magnanimity has no need to prove the prudence of its motives.

VAUVENARGUES, *Reflections and Maxims*, 1746

No man of honour ever quite lives up to his code, any more than a moral man manages to avoid sin.

H. L. MENCKEN, *Minority Report: Notebooks*, 1956

To do the best can seldom be the lot of man; it is sufficient if, when opportunities are presented, he is ready to do good. How little virtue could be practised if beneficence were to wait always for the most proper objects, and the noblest occasions – occasions that may never happen, and objects that may never be found!

DR JOHNSON, *Proceedings of the Committee for Clothing French Prisoners*, 1760

Do not ask me to be kind; just ask me to act as though I were.

JULES RENARD, *Journal*, 1898

There are cynicisms and cruelties which, when put to the test, prove no more genuine than certain apparent virtues and generosities.

MARCEL PROUST, *Remembrance of Things Past (Within a Budding Grove*, 1919)

The weak sometimes wish to be thought wicked, but the wicked wish to be thought virtuous.

VAUVENARGUES, *Reflections and Maxims*, 1746

Sin is like a mountain with two aspects according to whether it is viewed before or after it has been reached: yet both aspects are real.

SAMUEL BUTLER (II), *Notebooks*, 1912

If we escape punishment for our vices, why should we complain if we are not rewarded for our virtues?

CHURTON COLLINS, aphorisms in the *English Review*, 1914

As well as thoughts which are unworthy of us, we have thoughts of which we are unworthy.

JEAN ROSTAND, *Journal d'un caractère*, 1931

Alas, he cried at the mishap which had befallen him, if I had only done something agreeably wicked this morning, I would know why I am suffering now.

LICHTENBERG, *Aphorisms*, 1764–99

Shame operates most strongly in our earliest years.

DR JOHNSON, *Notes upon Shakespeare*, 1765

It is usurping life to do no more than simply avoid doing harm; the dead do as much, and exact nothing for it.

PRINCE DE LIGNE, *Mes écarts*, 1796

When the vices give us up we flatter ourselves that we are giving up them.

LA ROCHEFOUCAULD, *Maxims*, 1665

There are some vices which only keep hold on us through other ones, and if we take the trunk away they come off like the branches.

PASCAL, *Pensées*, 1670

Every reformation must have its victims. You can't expect the fatted calf to share the enthusiasm of the angels over the prodigal's return.

SAKI, 'Reginald on the Academy', *Reginald*, 1904

Repentance is not a free and fair highway to God. A wise man will dispense with repentance. It is shocking and passionate. God prefers that you approach him thoughtful, not penitent.

THOREAU, *Journal*, 1850

We as often repent the good we have done as the ill.

HAZLITT, *Characteristics*, 1823

True penitence condemns to silence. What a man is ready to recall he would be willing to repeat.

F. H. BRADLEY, *Aphorisms*, 1930

There is not, perhaps, to a mind well instructed, a more painful occurrence, than the death of one we have injured without reparation.

DR JOHNSON, *The Rambler*, 1750–2

Wretches are ungrateful; it is part of their wretchedness.

VICTOR HUGO, *Tas de pierres*, mid 19th century

O you who complain of ingratitude, have you not had the pleasure of doing good?

CHAMFORT, *Maximes et pensées*, 1805

Our gratitude to most benefactors is the same as our feeling for dentists who have pulled our teeth. We acknowledge the good they have done and the evil from which they have delivered us, but we remember the pain they occasioned and do not love them very much.

CHAMFORT, *Maximes et pensées*, 1805

Once you have done a man a service, what more would you have? Is it not enough to have obeyed the laws of your own nature, without expecting to be paid for it? That is like the eye demanding a reward for seeing, or the feet for walking.

MARCUS AURELIUS, *Meditations*, 2nd century

The greatest pleasure I have known is to do a good action by stealth, and to have it found out by accident.

CHARLES LAMB, 'Table Talk', 1834

Men imagine that they communicate their virtue or vice only by overt actions, and do not see that virtue or vice emit a breath every moment.

EMERSON, 'Self-Reliance', *Essays*, First Series, 1841

If better were within, better would come out.

THOMAS FULLER (II), *Gnomologia*, 1732

We may decorate a villain with graces and felicities for nine volumes, and hang him on the last page. This is not teaching virtue, but gilding the gallows, and raising up splendid associations in favour of being hanged.

SYDNEY SMITH, *Edinburgh Review*, 1803

Of the two, I prefer those who render vice lovable to those who degrade virtue.

JOUBERT, *Pensées*, 1842

No man is such a fool as not to have wit enough sometime to be a knave; nor any so cunning a knave, as not to have the weakness sometimes to play the fool.

MARQUESS OF HALIFAX, *Moral thoughts and reflections*, late 17th century

The utmost exertion of right is always invidious; and where claims are not easily determinable, is always dangerous.

DR JOHNSON, *Thoughts on the Late Transactions Respecting Falkland's Islands*, 1771

How many virtues and vices are unimportant!

VAUVENARGUES, *Reflections and Maxims*, 1746

The Moralist

●

If he sinned, the harm is his own. Yet perhaps, after all, he did not.
MARCUS AURELIUS, *Meditations*, 2nd century

Devotion to what is right is simple, devotion to what is wrong is complex and admits of infinite variations.
SENECA, *Epistles*, 1st century

We have, in fact, two kinds of morality side by side; one which we preach but do not practise, and another which we practise but seldom preach.
BERTRAND RUSSELL, *Sceptical Essays*, 1928

There is a certain list of vices committed in all ages, and declaimed against by all authors, which will last as long as human nature; or digested into commonplaces may serve for any theme, and never be out of date until Doomsday.
SIR THOMAS BROWNE, *Pseudodoxia Epidemica*, 1646

The world can ill spare any vice which has obtained long and large among civilized people. Such a vice must have some good along with its deformities.
SAMUEL BUTLER (II), *Notebooks*, 1912

The best moral virtues are those of which the vulgar are perhaps the best judges.
LORD CHESTERFIELD, *Detached Thoughts*, mid 18th century

If it was necessary to tolerate in other people everything that one permits oneself, life would be unbearable.
GEORGES COURTELINE, *La Philosophie de Georges Courteline*, 1917

Conscience warns us before it reproaches us.
COMTESSE DIANE, *Maximes de la vie*, 1908

I cannot love anyone if I hate myself. That is the reason why we feel
so extremely uncomfortable in the presence of people who are noted
for their special virtuousness, for they radiate an atmosphere of the
torture to which they subject themselves.

JUNG, *Psychological Reflections*, 1953, ed. Jolande Jacobi

Virtuous people often revenge themselves for the constraints to
which they submit by the boredom which they inspire.

GUSTAVE LE BON, *Aphorismes du temps présent*, 1913

It is well that there is no one without a fault, for he would not have
a friend in the world: he would seem to belong to a different
species.

HAZLITT, *Characteristics*, 1823

Men never forgive those in whom there is nothing to pardon.

EDWARD BULWER-LYTTON, *Weeds and Wild Flowers*, 1826

Reproof should not exhaust its power upon petty failings; let it
watch diligently against the incursion of vice, and leave foppery and
futility to die of themselves.

DR JOHNSON, *The Idler*, 1758

Wink at small faults; for thou hast great ones.

THOMAS FULLER (II), *Introductio ad Prudentiam*, 1731

To preach long, loud and damnation, is the way to be cried up. We
love a man that damns us, and we run after him again to save us.

JOHN SELDEN, *Table Talk*, mid 17th century

Denunciations do not affect
the culprit; nor blows, but it
is torture to him not to be spoken to.

MARIANNE MOORE, 'Spenser's Ireland', *Collected Poems*, 1941

Be not too hasty to trust or admire the teachers of virtue: they
discourse like angels but they live like men.

DR JOHNSON, *Rasselas*, 1759

Saints should always be judged guilty until they are proved innocent.

GEORGE ORWELL, 'Reflections on Gandhi', 1949

He who is too busy doing good finds no time to be good.

RABINDRANATH TAGORE, Stray Birds, 1916

Those who are fond of setting things to rights have no great objection to seeing them wrong. There is often a good deal of spleen at the bottom of benevolence.

HAZLITT, Characteristics, 1823

Many men mistake the love for the practice of virtue, and are not so much good men as the friends of goodness.

DR JOHNSON, Life of Savage, 1744

Who can bear to see a fellow-creature suffering pain and poverty when he can order other fellow-creatures to relieve them? Is it in human nature that A should see B in tears and misery and not order C to assist him?

SYDNEY SMITH

The passion for setting people right is in itself an afflictive disease. Distaste which takes no credit to itself is best.

MARIANNE MOORE, 'Snakes, Mongooses, Snake Charmers and the Like', Selected Poems, 1935

The name 'moralist' sounds like a perversion, one wouldn't be surprised at finding it suddenly in Krafft-Ebing.

ELIAS CANETTI, The Human Province, 1978

The word morality, if we met it in the Bible, would surprise us as much as the word telephone or motor car.

BERNARD SHAW, Preface to Fanny's First Play, 1911

Sometimes the knowledge that there is just one disapproving puritan in the world, looking out from his belfry, is enough to destroy our pleasure.

GERALD BRENAN, Thoughts in a Dry Season, 1978

Puritanism – The haunting fear that someone, somewhere, may be happy.

> H. L. MENCKEN, *A Book of Burlesques*, 1928

If your morals make you dreary, depend upon it, they are wrong.

> ROBERT LOUIS STEVENSON, *Across the Plains*, 1892

Don't be on the side of the angels, it's too lowering.

> D. H. LAWRENCE, letter, 1927

To enjoy yourself and make others enjoy themselves, without harming yourself or any other; that, to my mind, is the whole of ethics.

> CHAMFORT, *Maximes et pensées*, 1805

Perhaps there is not a more effectual key to the discovery of hypocrisy than a censorious temper. The man possessed of real virtue knows the difficulty of attaining it; and is, of course, more inclined to pity others, who happen to fail in the pursuit.

> WILLIAM SHENSTONE, *Essays on Men and Manners*, 1764

The propriety of some persons seems to consist in having improper thoughts about their neighbours.

> F. H. BRADLEY, *Aphorisms*, 1930

We confess our faults in the plural, and deny them in the singular.

> RICHARD FULKE GREVILLE, *Maxims, Characters and Reflections*, 1756

> Sin recognized – but that – may keep us humble,
> But oh, it keeps us nasty.
>> STEVIE SMITH, 'Recognition not Enough', *Selected Poems*, 1964

The error of a lively rake lies in his Passions, which may be reformed; but a dry rogue, who sets up for Judgment, is incorrigible.

> BISHOP BERKELEY, *Alciphron*, 1732

A man has generally the good or ill qualities which he attributes to mankind.

> WILLIAM SHENSTONE, *Essays on Men and Manners*, 1764

He who says there is no such thing as an honest man, you may be sure is himself a knave.

BISHOP BERKELEY, *Maxims Concerning Patriotism*, 1740

My great idea is that one must forgive the Pope. To begin with, he needs it more than anyone else. Secondly, that's the only way to set oneself above him.

ALBERT CAMUS, Jean-Baptiste Clamance in *The Fall*, 1956

God is tolerant, man is *not* tolerant; Omniscience pardons, frailty is inexorable.

SYDNEY SMITH, 'A Sermon on Toleration', 1807

Men are not sufficiently perfect to exercise justice in the name of virtue: the rule of life should be indulgence and kindness of heart.

ANATOLE FRANCE, *The Gods are Athirst*, 1912

A fastidious benefactor should reflect that there is a material side to his service, of which the beneficiary should be spared all thought. The idea of it must, as it were, be wrapped and hidden away in the sentiment which has prompted the benefit.

CHAMFORT, *Maximes et pensées*, 1805

Gratitude is a debt, 'tis true, but it differs from all other debts; for though it ought always to be paid, yet it is never to be demanded.

ANON., *Characters and Observations*, early 18th century

Don't use the impudence of a beggar as an excuse for not helping him.

RABBI SHMELKE OF NICOLSBURG, mid 18th century

A great deal may be done by severity, more by love, but most by clear discernment and impartial justice.

GOETHE, conversation with Eckermann, 1825

Where the generality are offenders, justice cometh to be cruelty.

MARQUESS OF HALIFAX, *Miscellaneous thoughts and reflections*, late 17th century

Men should bear with each other – there lives not the man who may
not be cut up, aye hashed to pieces on his weakest side.

KEATS, letter, 1818

As I know more of mankind I expect less of them, and am ready now
to call a man *a good man* upon easier terms than I was formerly.

DR JOHNSON in Boswell's *Life of Johnson*, 1783

No one gossips about other people's secret virtues.

BERTRAND RUSSELL, *On Education*, 1926

Praise & Blame

●

Praise is always pleasing, let it come from whom, or upon what account it will.

MONTAIGNE, 'Of vanity', *Essays*, 1580–8

The applause of a single human being is of great consequence.

DR JOHNSON in Boswell's *Life of Johnson*, 1780

What is the sign of a proud man? He never praises anyone.

The Zohar, 13th century

All panegyrics are mingled with infusion of poppy.

SWIFT, *Thoughts on Various Subjects*, 1711

Compliments were made for strangers, not for friends.

ANON., *Characters and Observations*, early 18th century

One needs a dash of satire to enliven a eulogy.

VOLTAIRE, letter, 1770

You must not pay a person a compliment, and then straightway follow it with a criticism.

MARK TWAIN, *Notebooks*, later 19th century

A man is sometimes extolled to the skies for the very thing which occasioned his misfortune.

ANON., *Characters and Observations*, early 18th century

I never knew a man so mean that I was not willing he should admire me.

E. W. HOWE, *Country Town Sayings*, 1911

It is not failure of others to appreciate your abilities that should trouble you, but rather your failure to appreciate theirs.

CONFUCIUS, *Analects*, 5th century BC

Merit unregarded is a very troublesome thing both to itself and others.

ANON., *Characters and Observations*, early 18th century

Praises of the unworthy are felt by ardent minds as robberies of the deserving.

COLERIDGE, *Biographia Literaria*, 1817

Some strictures can be compliments, and some compliments can be slanderous.

LA ROCHEFOUCAULD, *Maxims*, 1665

Do you want to injure someone's reputation? Don't speak ill of him, speak too well.

ANDRÉ SIEGFRIED, *Quelques maximes*, 1943

There is probably an element of malice in our readiness to over-estimate people – we are, as it were, laying up for ourselves the pleasure of later cutting them down to size.

ERIC HOFFER in Calvin Tomkins, *Eric Hoffer: An American Odyssey*, 1969

Praise undeserved is satire in disguise.

BROADHURST, 'To the Celebrated Beauties of the British Court', early 18th century

A flatterer is a man that tells you your opinion and not his own.

ANON., *Characters and Observations*, early 18th century

He who knows how to flatter also knows how to slander.

NAPOLEON, *Maxims*, early 19th century

We praise or blame according to whether the one or the other offers a greater opportunity for our power of judgment to shine out.

NIETZSCHE, *Human, All Too Human*, 1878

None are more apt to praise others extravagantly, than those who desire to be praised themselves.

> ANON., *Characters and Observations*, early 18th century

If the commending others well did not recommend ourselves, there would be few panegyrics.

> MARQUESS OF HALIFAX, *Moral thoughts and reflections*, late 17th century

A man seldom gives praise gratis. He commends a qualification in another, but then he would be thought himself to be master of that qualification.

> ANON., *Characters and Observations*, early 18th century

Be sparing in praise, and more so in blame.

> WILLIAM LANGLAND, *Piers Plowman*, later 14th century

Censure is willingly indulged, because it always implies some superiority. Men please themselves with imagining that they have made a deeper search, or wider survey than others, and detected faults and follies which escape vulgar observation.

> DR JOHNSON, *The Rambler*, 1750–2

It is well, when one is judging a friend, to remember that he is judging you with the same godlike and superior impartiality.

> ARNOLD BENNETT

To accuse requires less eloquence (such is man's nature) than to excuse.

> HOBBES, *Leviathan*, 1651

True genuine contempt remains entirely concealed and gives no hint of its existence. For whoever shows contempt, thereby gives a hint of some regard in so far as he wants to let the other man know how little he esteems him. In this way he betrays hatred which excludes and only feigns contempt.

> SCHOPENHAUER, 'Psychological Remarks', *Parerga and Paralipomena*, 1851

There are innumerable modes of insult and tokens of contempt for which it is not easy to find a name, which vanish to nothing in an attempt to describe them, and yet may, by continual repetition, make day pass after day in sorrow and in terror.

DR JOHNSON, *The Rambler*, 1750–2

Insults, sneers, and so forth are signs of impotence, not to say cowardice, being substitutes for murder, appeals to others to devalue or destroy. Insults to be effective need outside aid, for in the absence of a third party they lose their sting.

VALÉRY, *Mauvaises pensées et autres*, 1942

Young people do not perceive at once that the giver of wounds is the enemy and the quoted tattle merely the arrow.

SCOTT FITZGERALD, *The Crack-Up*, 1945

A man usually has no idea what is being said about him. The entire town may be slandering him, but if he has no friends he will never hear of it.

BALZAC

Heaven knows what would become of our sociality if we never visited people we speak ill of: we should live, like Egyptian hermits, in crowded solitude.

GEORGE ELIOT, *Scenes of Clerical Life*, 1858

There are always people in whose presence it is unsuitable to be over-modest, they are only too pleased to take you at your word.

LOUIS PASTEUR

If a friend tell thee a fault, imagine always that he telleth thee not the whole.

THOMAS FULLER (II), *Introductio ad Prudentiam*, 1731

Some sentences release their poisons only after years.

ELIAS CANETTI, *The Human Province*, 1978

The dead are indifferent to slander, but the living can die of it.

VOLTAIRE, letter, 1768

Genuine polemics approach a book as lovingly as a cannibal spices a baby.

WALTER BENJAMIN, *One-Way Street*, 1925–6

Against criticism a man can neither protest nor defend himself; he must act in spite of it, and then it will gradually yield to him.

GOETHE, *Maxims and Reflections*, early 19th century

There is nothing that so much gratifies an ill tongue as when it finds an angry heart.

THOMAS FULLER (II), *Introductio ad Prudentiam*, 1731

The art of reproving scandal is to take no notice of it.

GRACIÁN, *The Art of Worldly Wisdom*, 1647

Scandal is an importunate wasp, against which we must make no movement unless we are quite sure that we can kill it; otherwise it will return to the attack more furious than ever.

CHAMFORT, *Maximes et pensées*, 1805

It is a dangerous task to answer objections, because they are helped by the malice of mankind.

MARQUESS OF HALIFAX, *Moral thoughts and reflections*, late 17th century

Most expressions of contempt deserve to be treated with contempt.

MONTESQUIEU, *Mes pensées*, c.1722–55

To show resentment at a reproach is to acknowledge that one may have deserved it.

TACITUS, *Annals*, early 2nd century

If you hear that someone is speaking ill of you, instead of trying to defend yourself you should say: 'He obviously does not know me very well, since there are so many other faults he could have mentioned'.

EPICTETUS, *Enchiridion*, 2nd century

To deny undoubted merit in others is to deny its existence

altogether, and consequently our own. The example of illiberality
we set is easily turned against ourselves.

HAZLITT, *Characteristics*, 1823

He that hath a satirical vein, as he maketh others afraid of his wit, so
he need be afraid of other's memory.

SIR FRANCIS BACON, 'Of Discourse', *Essays*, 1597–1625

Take no part with scandalizers; thou knowest not thy turn among
them.

THOMAS FULLER (II), *Introductio ad Prudentiam*, 1731

He that speaks ill of another, commonly, before he is aware, makes
himself such a one as he speaks against; for if he had civility or
breeding, he would forbear such kind of language.

JOHN SELDEN, *Table Talk*, mid 17th century

Penetrate into their inmost minds, and you will see what manner of
critics you are afraid of, and how capable they are of criticizing
themselves.

MARCUS AURELIUS, *Meditations*, 2nd century

If the witty backbiter is blamed and condemned as obnoxious, he is
none the less absolved and praised as a clever fellow.

CERVANTES, *Persiles and Sigismunda*, 1617

People say ill-natured things without design, but not without having a pleasure in them.

HAZLITT, *Characteristics*, 1823

We criticize Virtue severely for her faults, while we are full of
indulgence for Vice.

BALZAC, *La vieille fille*, 1836

If we had no faults we should not find so much enjoyment in seeing
faults in others.

LA ROCHEFOUCAULD, *Maxims*, 1665

Do you wish to find out a person's weak points? Note the failings he has the quickest eye for in others. They may not be the very failings he is himself conscious of; but they will be their next-door neighbours.

JULIUS HARE, *Guesses at Truth*, 1827

Malice is a greater magnifying-glass than kindness.

MARQUESS OF HALIFAX, *Moral thoughts and reflections*, late 17th century

Those see nothing but faults that seek for nothing else.

THOMAS FULLER (II), *Gnomologia*, 1732

Our culture peculiarly honours the act of blaming, which it takes as the sign of virtue and intellect.

LIONEL TRILLING, *The Liberal Imagination*, 1950

This is an old saying, Atula, it is not a saying of today. 'They blame the man who is silent, they blame the man who speaks too much, and they blame the man who speaks too little.' No man can escape blame in this world.

The Dhammapada, probably 3rd century BC

Conversation & Manners

One always speaks badly when one has nothing to say.

VOLTAIRE, *Commentaries on Corneille*, 18th century

Never argue. In society nothing must be discussed; give only results.

BENJAMIN DISRAELI, *Contarini Fleming*, 1832

Imagination has more charms in writing than in speaking. It must fold its wings when it enters a salon.

PRINCE DE LIGNE, *Mes écarts*, 1796

A perpetual succession of good things puts an end to common conversation.

HAZLITT, 'On Wit and Humour', 1818

The Socratic manner is not a game at which two can play.

MAX BEERBOHM, *Zuleika Dobson*, 1911

The secret of being a bore is to tell everything.

VOLTAIRE, *Sept discours en vers sur l'homme*, 1738

It is not sufficiently considered, that men more frequently require to be reminded than informed.

DR JOHNSON, *The Rambler*, 1750–2

To do all the talking and not be willing to listen is a form of greed.

DEMOCRITUS OF ABDERA, 5th–4th century BC

There are people who instead of listening to what is being said to them are already listening to what they are going to say themselves.

ALBERT GUINON, *c*.1900

If to talk to oneself when alone is folly, it must be doubly unwise to listen to oneself in the presence of others.

GRACIÁN, *The Art of Worldly Wisdom*, 1647

No syren did ever so charm the ear of the listener, as the listening ear has charmed the soul of the syren.

SIR HENRY TAYLOR, *The Statesman*, 1836

If we would please in society, we must be prepared to be taught many things we know already by people who do not know them.

CHAMFORT, *Maximes et pensées*, 1805

We are almost always bored by the very people by whom it is vital not to be bored.

LA ROCHEFOUCAULD, *Maxims*, 1665

We often forgive those who bore us, but we cannot forgive those who find us boring.

LA ROCHEFOUCAULD, *Maxims*, 1665

When you talk to the half-wise, twaddle; when you talk to the ignorant, brag; when you talk to the sagacious, look very humble, and ask their opinion.

EDWARD BULWER-LYTTON, *Paul Clifford*, 1835

A timid question will always receive a confident answer.

MR JUSTICE DARLING, *Scintillae Juris*, 1889

Whoever wants his judgment to be believed, should express it coolly and dispassionately; for all vehemence springs from the will. And so the judgment might be attributed to the will and not to knowledge, which by its nature is cold.

SCHOPENHAUER, 'Counsels and Maxims', *Parerga and Paralipomena*, 1851

How much one has to say in order to be heard when silent.

ELIAS CANETTI, *The Human Province*, 1978

We make more enemies by what we say than friends by what we do.
CHURTON COLLINS, aphorisms in the *English Review*, 1914

As long as a word remains unspoken, you are its master; once you utter it, you are its slave.
SOLOMON IBN GABIROL, *The Choice of Pearls*, c.1050

Talk as if you were making your will: the fewer words the less litigation.
GRACIÁN, *The Art of Worldly Wisdom*, 1647

A genius for repartee is a gift for saying what a wise man thinks only.
THOMAS HARDY in F. E. Hardy, *The Later Years of Thomas Hardy*, 1930

If we are polite in manner and friendly in tone, we can without immediate risk be really rude to many a man.
SCHOPENHAUER, 'Counsels and Maxims', *Parerga and Paralipomena*, 1851

Silence is the most perfect expression of scorn.
BERNARD SHAW, *Back to Methuselah*, 1921

We often praise and dispraise in conversation, rather that the company should have a good opinion of our judgment, than for any love or hatred to the persons we mention.
ANON., *Characters and Observations*, early 18th century

When you are unwilling to sacrifice or conceal any of your abilities their reputation is generally diminished.
VAUVENARGUES, *Reflections and Maxims*, 1746

His whole nature fails to persuade; that is because he has never remained silent about any of his good deeds.
NIETZSCHE, *The Gay Science*, 1882–7

It is easier to confess a defect than to claim a quality.
MAX BEERBOHM, *And Even Now*, 1921

Good breeding consists in concealing how much we think of ourselves and how little we think of other persons.

MARK TWAIN, *Notebooks*, later 19th century

The need for society which springs from the emptiness and monotony of men's lives drives them together; but their many unpleasant and repulsive qualities once more drive them apart. The mean distance which they finally discover, and which enables them to endure being together, is politeness.

SCHOPENHAUER, 'Similes, Parables, and Fables', *Parerga and Paralipomena*, 1851

Good manners are the settled medium of social, as *specie* is of commercial, life; returns are equally expected from both; and people will no more advance their civility to a bear, than their money to a bankrupt.

LORD CHESTERFIELD, *Letters*, 1753

There is a natural good-breeding, which occurs to every man of common sense, and is practised by every man of common good nature.

LORD CHESTERFIELD, *Letters*, 1749

Manners rest on a twofold foundation: to show the other every attention yet not to obtrude upon him.

HUGO VON HOFMANNSTHAL, *The Book of Friends*, 1922

Good manners are made up of petty sacrifices.

EMERSON, *Letters and Social Aims*, 1876

Good manners is such a part of good sense that they cannot be divided; but that which a fool calleth good breeding is the most unmannerly thing in the world.

MARQUESS OF HALIFAX, *Miscellaneous thoughts and reflections*, late 17th century

It is possible for a man wholly to disappear and be merged in his manners.

THOREAU, *Journal*, 1850

I always treat fools and coxcombs with great ceremony; true good breeding not being a sufficient barrier against them.

LORD CHESTERFIELD, *Letters*, 1752

The test of good manners is to be patient with bad ones.

SOLOMON IBN GABIROL, *The Choice of Pearls*, c.1050

Honesty is no greater where elegance is less.

DR JOHNSON, *Journey to the Western Islands of Scotland*, 1775

When a man is positively rude, it is as if he had cast off all his clothes and stood before us naked. Of course, like most people in this condition, he cuts a poor figure.

SCHOPENHAUER, 'Counsels and Maxims', *Parerga and Paralipomena*, 1851

It is surely better to be arrogant than to look it. The arrogant character insults you only now and then; the arrogant look insults you continually.

DIDEROT, *Rameau's Nephew*, 1761

The man whose habitual expression is supercilious, or distrustful, or apologetic, is making a statement of belief about himself in relation to other people though he may not hold the belief in verbal form.

D. W. HARDING, *Experience into Words*, 1963

Haughty, silent faces should not deceive us: these are the timid ones.

JULES RENARD, *Journal*, 1887

A bad manner spoils everything, even reason and justice.

GRACIÁN, *The Art of Worldly Wisdom*, 1647

Affectation is recognized even before it is clear what a man really affects.

SCHOPENHAUER, 'Counsels and Maxims', *Parerga and Paralipomena*, 1851

When a man is known to have merit and intelligence, he is never ugly, however plain he may be; or even if he is ugly, it leaves no bad impression.

LA BRUYÈRE, 'Of Opinions', *Characters*, 1688

People of the greatest gaiety of manner are often the dullest company imaginable. Nothing is so dreary as the serious conversation or writing of a professional wag.

HAZLITT, *Characteristics*, 1823

Every man becomes, to a certain degree, what the people he generally converses with are.

LORD CHESTERFIELD, *Letters*, 1750

We often irritate others when we think we could not possibly do so.

LA ROCHEFOUCAULD, *Maxims*, 1665

Perfect behaviour is born of complete indifference.

CESARE PAVESE, *This Business of Living: Diaries 1935–50*

Secrets

A man's most open actions have a secret side to them.
JOSEPH CONRAD, *Under Western Eyes*, 1911

Could we but enter into the hearts of mankind, and see the motives and springs that prompt them to the undertaking of many illustrious actions, we should very probably see fewer of them performed.
ANON., *Characters and Observations*, early 18th century

If we knew each other's secrets, what comforts we should find!
CHURTON COLLINS, aphorisms in the *English Review*, 1914

There is more of fear than delight in a secret pleasure.
PUBLILIUS SYRUS, *Sententiae*, 1st century BC

There is an unseemly exposure of the mind, as well as of the body.
HAZLITT, 'On Disagreeable People', 1827

A nice man is a man of nasty ideas.
SWIFT, *Thoughts on Various Subjects*, 1711

All charming people have something to conceal, usually their total dependence on the appreciation of others.
CYRIL CONNOLLY, *Enemies of Promise*, 1938

If all hearts were open and all desires known – as they would be if people showed their souls – how many gapings, sighings, clenched fists, knotted brows, broad grins and red eyes should we see in the market-place!
THOMAS HARDY in F. E. Hardy, *The Later Years of Thomas Hardy*, 1930

Too much secrecy in our affairs and too little are equally indicative of
a weak spirit.

> VAUVENARGUES, *Reflections and Maxims*, 1746

Some are open, and to all men known;
Others so very close, they're hid from none.

> POPE, *Epistle to Lord Cobham*, 1734

That I, or any man, should tell everything of himself, I hold to be
impossible. Who could endure to own the doing of a mean thing?
Who is there that has done none?

> TROLLOPE, *An Autobiography*, 1883

Men intend sometimes to conceal their imperfections, or attenuate
the opinion of others about them, by frankly acknowledging them.
'I am very ignorant,' says some man who knows nothing; 'I am
getting old,' says a second above threescore; 'I am far from rich,'
says a third who is wretchedly poor.

> LA BRUYÈRE, 'Of Mankind', *Characters*, 1688

Qui s'accuse s'excuse.

> CHRISTOPHER RICKS, 'Great Expectations', *Dickens and the
> Twentieth Century*, 1962

Explaining is generally half confessing.

> MARQUESS OF HALIFAX, *Moral thoughts and reflections*, late 17th
> century

We often happen to blurt out something which might in some way
be dangerous to us; but we are not deserted by our reticence and
discretion in the case of those things that might make us ridiculous,
because here the effect follows close on the cause.

> SCHOPENHAUER, 'Psychological Remarks', *Parerga and
> Paralipomena*, 1851

The best way to find out if a man has done something is to advise
him to do it. He will not be able to resist boasting that he has done it
without being advised.

> COMTESSE DIANE, *Maximes de la vie*, 1908

You can take better care of your secret than another can.

EMERSON, *Journals*, 1863

When a man comes into possession of some chance secrets now and then – some one or two – he is tempted to parade them to this friend or that. But when he is known to be trusted to all manner of secrets, his vanity is interested, not to show them, but to show that he can keep them.

SIR HENRY TAYLOR, *The Statesman*, 1836

Nothing is easier than to keep a secret: there needs no more but to shut one's mouth.

ANON., *Characters and Observations*, early 18th century

If you want to keep something concealed from your enemy, do not disclose it to your friend.

SOLOMON IBN GABIROL, *The Choice of Pearls*, c.1050

Nobody will keep the thing he hears to himself, and nobody will repeat just what he hears and no more.

SENECA, *Epistles*, 1st century

Confidant, confidante, *n.* One entrusted by A with the secrets of B confided to himself by C.

AMBROSE BIERCE, *The Devil's Dictionary*, 1906

A secret may be sometimes best kept by keeping the secret of its being a secret.

SIR HENRY TAYLOR, *The Statesman*, 1836

There is something about a cupboard that makes a skeleton terribly restless.

ANON.

Conversation has a kind of charm about it, an insinuating and insidious something that elicits secrets from us just like love or liquor.

SENECA, *Epistles*, 1st century

Secrets are so seldom kept, that it may be with some reason doubted whether a secret has not some subtle volatility by which it escapes, imperceptibly, at the smallest vent; or some power of fermentation, by which it expands itself, so as to burst the heart that will not give it way.

DR JOHNSON, *The Rambler*, 1750–2

There are no secrets except the secrets that keep themselves.

BERNARD SHAW, *Back to Methuselah*, 1921

True & False

The truth is generally seen, rarely heard.
GRACIÁN, *The Art of Worldly Wisdom*, 1647

During a carnival men put cardboard faces over their masks.
XAVIER FORNERET, *Sans titre, par un homme noir, blanc de visage*, 1838

When in doubt, tell the truth.
MARK TWAIN, *Following the Equator*, 1897

A liar is a man who does not know how to deceive, a flatterer one who only deceives fools: he alone can pride himself on his cleverness who knows how to make skilful use of the truth.
VAUVENARGUES, *Reflections and Maxims*, 1746

Much truth is spoken, that more may be concealed.
MR JUSTICE DARLING, *Scintillae Juris*, 1889

It often happens that, if a lie be believed only for an hour, it has done its work, and there is no further occasion for it.
SWIFT, *The Examiner*, 1715

The best liar is he who makes the smallest amount of lying go the longest way.
SAMUEL BUTLER (II), *The Way of All Flesh*, 1903

The accomplished hypocrite does not exercise his skill upon every possible occasion. In all unimportant matters, who is more just, more upright, more candid, more honourable?
SIR ARTHUR HELPS, *Thoughts in the Cloister and the Crowd*, 1835

Liars are commonly very good natured and do their feats as well to please others as themselves, and require no more of any man but his belief; for which they will return real courtesies.

> SAMUEL BUTLER (1), *Prose Observations*, 1660–80

Malice must go under the disguise of plainness, or else it is exposed.

> MARQUESS OF HALIFAX, *Moral thoughts and reflections*, late 17th century

Perjury is often bold and open. It is truth that is shamefaced – as, indeed, in many cases is no more than decent.

> MR JUSTICE DARLING, *Scintillae Juris*, 1889

The fact of a man's having proclaimed (as leader of a political party, or in any other capacity) that it is wicked to lie obliges him as a rule to lie more than other people.

> MARCEL PROUST, *Remembrance of Things Past* (*The Captive*, 1923)

How hollow and insincere it sounds when someone says, 'I am determined to be perfectly straightforward with you.' The thing needs no prologue; it will declare itself.

> MARCUS AURELIUS, *Meditations*, 2nd century

As universal a practice as lying is, and as easy a one as it seems, I do not remember to have heard three good lies in any conversation, even from those who were most celebrated in that faculty.

> SWIFT, *Thoughts on Various Subjects*, 1711

Cunning has effect from the credulity of others rather than from the abilities of those who are cunning. It requires no extraordinary talents to lie and deceive.

> DR JOHNSON in Boswell's *Life of Johnson*, 1781

There is so much wit necessary to make a skilful hypocrite that the faculty is fallen among bunglers, who make it ridiculous.

> MARQUESS OF HALIFAX, *Miscellaneous thoughts and reflections*, late 17th century

Be a hypocrite, if you like, but don't talk like one!

> DIDEROT, *Rameau's Nephew*, 1761

Nothing seems to me to be rarer today than genuine hypocrisy. I greatly suspect that this plant finds the mild atmosphere of our culture unendurable. Hypocrisy has its place in the ages of strong belief: in which even when one is compelled to exhibit a different belief one does not abandon the belief one already has.

NIETZSCHE, *Twilight of the Idols*, 1888

Hypocrisy is the most difficult and nerve-racking vice that any man can pursue; it needs an unceasing vigilance and a rare detachment of spirit. It cannot, like adultery or gluttony, be practised at spare moments; it is a whole-time job.

SOMERSET MAUGHAM, *Cakes and Ale*, 1930

With all great deceivers there is a noteworthy occurrence to which they owe their power. In the actual act of deception they are over-come by *belief in themselves*: it is this which then speaks so miracu-lously and compellingly to those who surround them.

NIETZSCHE, *Human, All Too Human*, 1878

It is not in human nature to deceive others, for any long time, without, in a measure, deceiving ourselves.

J. H. NEWMAN, *Parochial and Plain Sermons*, 1837–42

We ought to see far enough into a hypocrite to see even his sincerity.

G. K. CHESTERTON, *Heretics*, 1905

The hypocrite who always plays one and the same role finally ceases to be a hypocrite.

NIETZSCHE, *Human, All Too Human*, 1878

If you run through the streets, saying you imitate a lunatic, you are in fact a lunatic. If you kill a man, saying you imitate a criminal, you are a criminal yourself. A man who studies wisdom, even insin-cerely, should be called wise.

YOSHIDA KENKO, *Essays in Idleness*, c.1340

Some disguised deceits counterfeit truth so perfectly that not to be taken in by them would be an error of judgment.

LA ROCHEFOUCAULD, *Maxims*, 1665

We are inclined to believe those whom we do not know because they have never deceived us.

> DR JOHNSON, *The Idler*, 1758

Is a man not superior who, without anticipating attempts at deception or presuming acts of bad faith, is, nevertheless, the first to be aware of such behaviour?

> CONFUCIUS, *Analects*, 5th century BC

If we suspect that a man is lying, we should pretend to believe him; for then he becomes bold and assured, lies more vigorously, and is unmasked.

> SCHOPENHAUER, 'Counsels and Maxims', *Parerga and Paralipomena*, 1851

It is not only the difficulty and labour which men take in finding out of truth that doth bring lies in favour; but a natural though corrupt love of the lie itself.

> SIR FRANCIS BACON, 'Of Truth', *Essays*, 1597–1625

Most of the lies and stories that fly about town every day are not owing so much to the immediate authors of them, as to the curiosity and inquisitiveness of other people. We are forced to lie (I had almost said) rather than not say somewhat to please.

> ANON., *Characters and Observations*, early 18th century

One of the most striking differences between a cat and a lie is that a cat has only nine lives.

> MARK TWAIN, *Pudd'nhead Wilson*, 1894

Large offers and sturdy rejections are among the most common topics of falsehood.

> DR JOHNSON, 'Milton', *Lives of the Poets*, 1779–81

How badly a woman lies when you know that she is lying!

> ROBERT DE FLERS and FRANCIS DE CROISSET, *Les nouveaux Messieurs*, 1926

Hypocrisy delights in the most sublime speculations; for, never intending to go beyond speculation, it costs nothing to have it magnificent.

EDMUND BURKE, *Reflections on the Revolution in France*, 1790

Difficulty is a coin the learned make use of, like jugglers, to conceal the inanity of their art; and which human sottishness easily takes for current pay.

MONTAIGNE, 'Apology for Raimond de Sebonde', *Essays*, 1580–8

One is not bound to believe that all the water is deep that is muddy.

THOMAS FULLER (I), *The Holy State and the Profane State*, 1642

Many are content to wear the mask of foolishness, in order to carry on their vicious schemes; and not a few are willing to shelter their folly behind the respectability of downright vice.

SIR ARTHUR HELPS, *Thoughts in the Cloister and the Crowd*, 1835

The cruellest lies are often told in silence.

ROBERT LOUIS STEVENSON, *Virginibus Puerisque*, 1881

I have always considered it as treason against the great republic of human nature to make any man's virtues the means of deceiving him, whether on great or little occasions. All imposture weakens confidence and chills benevolence.

DR JOHNSON, *Rasselas*, 1759

Some degree of affectation is as necessary to the mind as dress is to the body; we must overact our part in some measure, in order to produce an effect at all.

HAZLITT, 'On Cant and Hypocrisy', 1828

There is an honest unwillingness to pass off another's observations for our own, which makes a man appear pedantic.

AUGUSTUS HARE, *Guesses at Truth*, 1827

We remember the truth because it has a name, is rooted in the past, but a makeshift lie is quickly forgotten.

MARCEL PROUST, *Remembrance of Things Past* (*The Captive*, 1923)

Sincerity has to do with the connexion between our words and thoughts, and not between our belief and actions.

HAZLITT, 'Of Cant and Hypocrisy', 1828

You never speak to God; you address a fellow-man, full of his own tempers; and to tell truth, rightly understood, is not to state the true facts, but to convey a true impression.

ROBERT LOUIS STEVENSON, *Virginibus Puerisque*, 1881

A man who will show every knave or fool that he thinks him such, will engage in a most ruinous war against numbers much superior to those that he and his allies can bring into the field.

LORD CHESTERFIELD, *Letters*, 1748

We find it easy to believe that praise is sincere: why should anyone lie in telling us the truth?

JEAN ROSTAND, *De la vanité*, 1925

> Praise, of course, is best: plain speech breeds hate.
> But ah the Attic honey
> Of telling a man exactly what you think of him!
>
> PALLADAS (4th–5th century), *The Greek Anthology* (trans. Dudley Fitts)

The great consolation in life is to say what one thinks.

VOLTAIRE, letter, 1765

He who does not need to lie is proud of not being a liar.

NIETZSCHE, *Nachgelassene Fragmente*, 1882–9

Truth is such a rare thing, it is delightful to tell it.

EMILY DICKINSON, letter, 1870

All truths that are kept silent become poisonous.

NIETZSCHE, *Thus Spake Zarathustra*, 1883–5

What is bad in the candid friend is simply that he is not candid. He is keeping something back – his own gloomy pleasure in saying unpleasant things.

G. K. CHESTERTON, *Orthodoxy*, 1909

A man had rather have a hundred lies told of him, than one truth which he does not wish should be told.

DR JOHNSON in Boswell's Life of Johnson, 1773

If we seek real rather than technical truth, it is more true to be considerately untruthful within limits than to be inconsiderately truthful without them.

SAMUEL BUTLER (II), Notebooks, 1912

Good manners to those one does not love are no more a breach of truth than 'your humble servant' at the bottom of a challenge is; they are universally agreed upon, and understood to be matters of course.

LORD CHESTERFIELD, Letters, 1752

Politeness is a false coin; to be niggardly with it shows a want of intelligence.

SCHOPENHAUER, 'Counsels and Maxims', Parerga and Paralipomena, 1851

There are times when lying is the most sacred of duties.

EUGÈNE LABICHE, Les Vivacités du Capitaine Tic, 1861

A hypocrite is a person who – but who isn't?

DON MARQUIS (1878–1937)

Illusion & Reality

●

The chief use to which we put our love of the truth is in persuading ourselves that what we love is true.

PIERRE NICOLE, *Essais de morale*, 1671–8

What probably distorts everything in life is that one is convinced that one is speaking the truth because one says what one thinks.

SACHA GUITRY, *Toutes réflexions faites*, 1947

Consciousness may be set down as one of the most mendacious witnesses that ever was questioned. But it is the only witness there is; and all we can do is to put it in the sweat-box and torture the truth out of it, with such judgment as we can command.

C. S. PEIRCE, *Collected Papers*, I, late 19th–early 20th century

Appearances are not held to be a clue to the truth. But we seem to have no other.

IVY COMPTON-BURNETT, *Manservant and Maidservant*, 1947

Anyone who can handle a needle convincingly can make us see a thread which is not there.

E. H. GOMBRICH, *Art and Illusion*, 1960

The world wants to be deceived.

SEBASTIAN BRANT, *Ship of Fools*, 1494

Truth is more of a stranger than fiction.

MARK TWAIN, *Notebooks*, later 19th century

Wonders are willingly told and willingly heard.

DR JOHNSON, 'Pope', *Lives of the Poets*, 1779–81

Truth is too naked; she does not inflame men.

JEAN COCTEAU, *Cock and Harlequin*, 1918

Seldom any splendid story is wholly true.

DR JOHNSON

As in Rome there is, apart from the Romans, a population of statues, so apart from this real world there is a world of illusion, almost more potent, in which most men live.

GOETHE, Maxims and Reflections, early 19th century

Doth any man doubt, that if there were taken out of men's minds, vain opinions, flattering hopes, false valuations, imaginations as one would, and the like; but it would leave the minds of a number of men poor shrunken things, full of melancholy, and indisposition, and unpleasing to themselves?

SIR FRANCIS BACON, 'Of Truth', Essays, 1597–1625

That lies should be necessary to life is part and parcel of the terrible and questionable character of existence.

NIETZSCHE, The Will to Power, c.1885

If things were seen as they truly are, the beauty of bodies would be much abridged. And therefore the wise Contriver hath drawn the pictures and outsides of things softly and amiably unto the natural edge of our eyes, not leaving them to discover those uncomely asperities which make oyster-shells in good faces, and hedgehogs even in Venus's moles.

SIR THOMAS BROWNE, Christian Morals, mid 17th century

Life is barren enough surely with all her trappings; let us therefore be cautious how we strip her.

DR JOHNSON in Mrs Piozzi, Anecdotes, mid 18th century

There is no living in the world without a complaisant indulgence for people's weaknesses, and innocent, though ridiculous vanities. If a man has a mind to be thought wiser, and a woman handsomer than they really are, their error is a comfortable one to themselves, and an innocent one with regard to other people; and I would rather make them my friends, by indulging them in it, than my enemies, by endeavouring (and that to no purpose) to undeceive them.

LORD CHESTERFIELD, Letters, 1747

Nature rejoices in illusion. If a man destroys the power of illusion, either in himself or in others, she punishes him like the harshest tyrant.

GOETHE, *Maxims and Reflections*, early 19th century

The most terrible reality brings us, at the same time as suffering, the joy of a great discovery, because it merely gives a new and clear form to what we have long been ruminating without suspecting it.

MARCEL PROUST, *Remembrance of Things Past* (*Cities of the Plain*, 1921–2)

In the affairs of this world men are saved, not by faith, but by the want of it.

BENJAMIN FRANKLIN, *Poor Richard's Almanack*, 1754

Truth is the cry of all, but the game of the few.

BISHOP BERKELEY, *Siris*, 1744

He who does not know Truth at Sight is unworthy of Her Notice.

BLAKE, Notes on Reynolds's *Discourses*, c.1808

In vino, possibly, '*veritas*', but in a sober symposium '*verum*'.

J. L. AUSTIN, 'Truth', *Philosophical Papers*, 1961

God forbid that Truth should be confined to Mathematical Demonstration!

BLAKE, Notes on Reynolds's *Discourses*, c.1808

The ordinary man only knows one kind of truth, in the ordinary sense of the word. He cannot imagine what a higher or a highest truth may be. Truth seems to him no more capable of comparative degrees than death; and he cannot join in the leap from the beautiful to the true. Perhaps you will think as I do that he is right in this.

FREUD, 'A Weltanschauung', *New Introductory Lectures on Psychoanalysis*, 1933

If you shut your door to all errors truth will be shut out.

RABINDRANATH TAGORE, *Stray Birds*, 1916

The truth is too simple: one must always get there by a complicated route.

GEORGE SAND, letter to Armand Barbes, 1867

Clearness is so eminently one of the characteristics of truth that often it even passes for truth itself.

JOUBERT, *Pensées*, 1842

What is told in the fullest and most accurate annals bears an infinitely small proportion to what is suppressed. The difference between the copious work of Clarendon and the account of the civil wars in the abridgment of Goldsmith vanishes when compared with the immense amount of facts respecting which both are equally silent.

LORD MACAULAY, 'History', 1828

Truth in her dress finds facts too tight. In fiction she moves with ease.

RABINDRANATH TAGORE, *Stray Birds*, 1916

The great trick of regarding small departures from the truth as the truth itself – on which is founded the entire integral calculus – is also the basis of our witty speculations, where the whole thing would often collapse if we considered the departures with philosophical rigour.

LICHTENBERG, *Aphorisms*, 1764–99

A striking expression, with the aid of a small amount of truth, can surprise us into accepting a falsehood.

VAUVENARGUES, *Reflections and Maxims*, 1746

Ours is an age in which partial truths are tirelessly transformed into total falsehoods and then acclaimed as revolutionary revelations.

THOMAS SZASZ, *The Second Sin*, 1974

As scarce as truth is, the supply has always been in excess of the demand.

JOSH BILLINGS, *Affurisms*, 1865

Thinking & Reasoning

●

We are thinking beings, and we cannot exclude the intellect from participating in any of our functions.

WILLIAM JAMES, *Varieties of Religious Experience*, 1902

When the torrent sweeps a man against a boulder, you must expect him to scream, and you need not be surprised if the scream is sometimes a theory.

ROBERT LOUIS STEVENSON, *Virginibus Puerisque*, 1881

Through space the universe grasps me and swallows me up like a speck; through thought I grasp it.

PASCAL, *Pensées*, 1670

All the arts and sciences have their roots in the struggle against death.

ST GREGORY OF NYSSA, 4th century

The true scientific investigator completely loses sight of the utility of what he is about. Do you think that the physiologist who cuts up a dog reflects, while doing so, that he may be saving a human life? Nonsense. If he did, it would spoil him for a scientific man; and then vivisection would become a crime.

C. S. PEIRCE, *Collected Papers*, I, late 19th–early 20th century

He is a fool that has nothing of philosophy in him, but not so much as he that has nothing else but philosophy in him.

SAMUEL BUTLER (I), *Prose Observations*, 1660–80

Curiosity is, in great and generous minds, the first passion and the last.

DR JOHNSON, *The Rambler*, 1750–2

Curiosity will conquer fear even more than bravery will.

JAMES STEPHENS, *The Crock of Gold*, 1912

Thoughts are the shadows of our feelings – always darker, emptier, and simpler.

NIETZSCHE, *The Gay Science*, 1882–7

Faith and philosophy are air, but events are brass.

HERMAN MELVILLE, *Pierre*, 1852

It is easier to say new things than to reconcile those which have already been said.

VAUVENARGUES, *Reflections and Maxims*, 1746

Perception of the strange is hindered by strangeness; recognition of the familiar is prevented by familiarity.

HUGO VON HOFMANNSTHAL, *The Book of Friends*, 1922

Original thoughts can be understood only in virtue of the unoriginal elements which they contain.

STANISLAV ANDRESKI, *Social Sciences as Sorcery*, 1972

Did we but compare the miserable scantiness of our capacities with the vast profundity of things, both truth and modesty would teach us a *dialect*, more becoming short-sighted mortality.

JOSEPH GLANVILL, *The Vanity of Dogmatizing*, 1661

There are no new truths, but only truths that have not been recognized by those who have perceived them without noticing.

MARY McCARTHY, *On the Contrary*, 1962

A thought is often original, though you have uttered it a hundred times.

OLIVER WENDELL HOLMES sen., *The Autocrat at the Breakfast Table*, 1858

An artificial novelty is never as effective as a repetition that manages to suggest a fresh truth.

MARCEL PROUST, *Remembrance of Things Past* (*Within a Budding Grove*, 1919)

One keeps saying the same thing, but the fact that one *has* to say it is eery.

ELIAS CANETTI, *The Human Province*, 1978

Many ideas grow better when transplanted into another mind than in the one where they sprang up.

OLIVER WENDELL HOLMES jun.

We rarely fathom another person's thoughts, and if a similar reflection subsequently occurs to us it presents so many aspects which have escaped us that we are easily persuaded it is new.

VAUVENARGUES, *Reflections and Maxims*, 1746

All culture and all communication depend on the interplay between expectation and observation, the waves of fulfilment, disappointment, right guesses, and wrong moves that make up our daily life.

E. H. GOMBRICH, *Art and Illusion*, 1960

If we were not provided with the knack of being wrong, we could never get anything useful done. We think our way along by choosing between right and wrong alternatives, and the wrong choices have to be made as frequently as the right ones.

LEWIS THOMAS, *The Medusa and the Snail*, 1979

A proof tells us where to concentrate our doubts.

ANON., cit. W. H. Auden, *A Certain World*, 1971

There is in my mind a standing opposition party which subsequently attacks everything I have done or decided, even after mature consideration, yet without its always being right on that account. It is, I suppose, only a corrective form of the spirit of investigation; but it often casts an unmerited slur on me.

SCHOPENHAUER, 'Psychological Remarks', *Parerga and Paralipomena*, 1851

To probe a hole we first use a straight stick to see how far it takes us. To probe the visible world we use the assumption that things are simple until they prove to be otherwise.

E. H. GOMBRICH, *Art and Illusion*, 1960

Thought must be divided against itself before it can come to any knowledge of itself.

ALDOUS HUXLEY, *Do What You Will*, 1929

How many ideas hover dispersed in my head of which many a pair, if they should come together, could bring about the greatest of discoveries!

LICHTENBERG, *Aphorisms*, 1764–99

There are infinitely more ideas impressed on our minds than we can possibly attend to or perceive.

JOHN NORRIS, *Practical Discourses*, 1691–3

Man's great misfortune is that he has no organ, no kind of eyelid or brake, to mask or block a thought, or all thought, when he wants to.

VALÉRY, *Tel Quel*, 1941–3

A man's thoughts must be going. Whilst he is awake, the working of his mind is as constant as the beating of his pulse. He can no more stop the one than the other. Hence, if our thoughts have nothing to act upon, they act upon themselves. They acquire a corrosive quality; they become in the last degree irksome and tormenting.

WILLIAM PALEY, 'Reasons for Contentment', 1792

It is desirable at times for ideas to possess a certain roughness, like drawings on heavy-grain paper. Thoughts having this quality are most likely to match the texture of actual experience.

HAROLD ROSENBERG, *Discovering the Present*, 1973

Part of thinking is its cruelty, aside from its contents. It is the process of detachment from everything else, the ripping, the wrenching, the sharpness of cutting.

ELIAS CANETTI, *The Human Province*, 1978

A hard intellect is a hammer that can do nothing but crush. Hardness of intellect is sometimes no less harmful and hateful than hardness of heart.

JOUBERT, *Pensées*, 1842

There are some thoughts that are luminous of themselves; others
there are that owe their lustre to the place they occupy; to remove
them would be to extinguish them.

JOUBERT, *Pensées*, 1842

Along with thoughts which are unworthy of us, we have ones of
which we are not worthy.

JEAN ROSTAND, *Journal d'un Caractère*, 1931

Fully to understand a grand and beautiful thought requires, perhaps,
as much time as to conceive it.

JOUBERT, *Pensées*, 1842

In vain sedate reflections we would make,
When half our knowledge we must snatch, not take.

POPE, *Epistle to Lord Cobham*, 1734

To think is not enough; you must think of something.

JULES RENARD, *Journal*, 1899

Speculative reasonings, which cost so much pains to philosophers,
are often formed by the world naturally and without reflection.

HUME, *A Treatise of Human Nature*, 1739

Many who have not learnt Reason, nevertheless live according to
reason.

DEMOCRITUS OF ABDERA (5th–4th century BC)

I could never think of the study of wisdom confined only to the
philosopher; or of piety to the divine; or of state to the politic.

BEN JONSON, *Timber; or Discoveries*, 1640

In our society the simplest person is involved with ideas. Every
person we meet in the course of our daily life, no matter how
unlettered he may be, is groping with sentences toward a sense of his
life and his position in it; and he has what almost always goes with an
impulse to ideology, a good deal of animus and anger.

LIONEL TRILLING, *The Liberal Imagination*, 1950

Many have original minds who do not think it – they are led away by Custom.

KEATS, letter, 1818

A society made up of individuals who were all capable of original thought would probably be unendurable. The pressure of ideas would simply drive it frantic.

H. L. MENCKEN, *Minority Report: Notebooks*, 1956

Stupidity does not consist in being without ideas. Such stupidity would be the sweet, blissful stupidity of animals, molluscs and the gods. Human Stupidity consists in having lots of ideas, but stupid ones. Stupid ideas, with banners, hymns, loudspeakers and even tanks and flame-throwers as their instruments of persuasion, constitute the refined and the only really terrifying form of Stupidity.

HENRY DE MONTHERLANT, *Notebooks*, 1930–44

A prohibition whose reason we do not understand or admit is not only for the obstinate man but also for the man thirsty for knowledge almost the injunction: let us put it to the test, so as to learn *why* this prohibition exists.

NIETZSCHE, *The Wanderer and His Shadow*, 1880

Man is a cause-seeking creature, in the order of spirits he might be called the 'Cause-seeker'. Other spirits perhaps conceive of things in relations different from ours and incomprehensible to us.

LICHTENBERG, *Aphorisms*, 1764–99

Philosophy, hoping and promising at first to cure all our ills, is at last reduced to desiring in vain to remedy itself.

LEOPARDI, 'Timander and Eleander', *Essays and Dialogues*, 1824–32

For a long time now I have thought that philosophy will one day devour itself. Metaphysics has partly done so already.

LICHTENBERG, *Aphorisms*, 1764–99

I would say of metaphysicians what Scaliger said of the Basques: they are supposed to understand each other, but I do not believe it.

CHAMFORT, *Maximes et pensées*, 1805

As for the philosophers, they make imaginary laws for imaginary commonwealths, and their discourses are as the stars, which give little light because they are so high.

SIR FRANCIS BACON, *The Advancement of Learning*, 1605

As all Feats of Activity are the more admired, the nearer they come to Danger, so is all Speculative wit the nearer it comes to Nonsense.

SAMUEL BUTLER (I), *Prose Observations*, 1660–80

For hundreds of pages the closely-reasoned arguments unroll, axioms and theorems interlock. And what remains with us in the end? A general sense that the world can be expressed in closely-reasoned arguments, in interlocking axioms and theorems.

MICHAEL FRAYN, *Constructions*, 1974

This whole theory is good for nothing except disputing about.

LICHTENBERG, *Aphorisms*, 1764–99

In philosophy, there are many mistakes that it is no disgrace to have made: to make a first-water, ground-floor mistake, so far from being easy, takes one (*one*) form of philosophical genius.

J. L. AUSTIN, 'Ifs and Cans', *Philosophical Papers*, 1961

Almost all rich veins of original and striking speculation have been opened by systematic half-thinkers.

JOHN STUART MILL, 'Bentham', 1838

I doubt if the philosopher lives, or ever has lived, who could know himself to be heartily despised by a street boy without some irritation.

T. H. HUXLEY, *Evolution and Ethics*, 1893

The province of philosophy is not so much to prevent calamities befalling as to demonstrate that they are blessings when they have taken place.

ERNEST BRAMAH, *Kai Lung Unrolls his Mat*, 1928

One philosopher thinks he is dived to the bottom, when he says, he knows nothing but this, that he knows nothing; and yet another thinks he hath expressed more knowledge than he, in saying, that he knows not so much as that, that he knows nothing.

DONNE, sermon, 1626

Let us not pretend to doubt in philosophy what we do not doubt in our hearts.

C. S. PEIRCE, *Collected Papers*, V, late 19th–early 20th century

Philosophers never balance between profit and honesty, because their decisions are general, and neither their passions nor imaginations are interested in the objects.

HUME, *A Treatise of Human Nature*, 1739

Conscious thinking, especially that of the philosopher, is the least vigorous and therefore also the relatively mildest and calmest form of thinking; and thus precisely philosophers are the most apt to be led astray about the nature of knowledge.

NIETZSCHE, *The Gay Science*, 1882–7

If we fall into the error of believing that vitally important questions are to be decided by reasoning, the only hope of salvation lies in formal logic, which demonstrates in the clearest manner that reasoning itself testifies to its own ultimate subordination to sentiment. It is like a Pope who should declare *ex cathedra* and call upon all the faithful to implicitly believe on pain of damnation by the power of the keys that he was *not* the supreme authority.

C. S. PEIRCE, *Collected Papers*, I, late 19th–early 20th century

You can only find truth with logic if you have already found truth without it.

G. K. CHESTERTON, *The Man who was Orthodox*, 1963

The irrational is not necessarily unreasonable.

SIR LEWIS NAMIER, *Personalities and Powers*, 1955

Do you really believe that the sciences would ever have originated and grown if the way had not been prepared by magicians, alchemists, astrologers and witches whose promises and pretensions first had to create a thirst, a hunger, a taste for *hidden* and *forbidden* powers? Indeed, infinitely more had to be *promised* than could ever be fulfilled in order that anything at all might be fulfilled in the realms of knowledge.

NIETZSCHE, *The Gay Science*, 1882–7

It is not too much to say that next after the passion to learn there is no quality so indispensable to the successful prosecution of science as imagination. Find me a people whose early medicine is not mixed up with magic and incantations, and I will find you a people devoid of all scientific ability.

C. S. PEIRCE, *Collected Papers*, I, late 19th–early 20th century

It not seldom happens that in the purposeless rovings and wanderings of the imagination we hunt down such game as can be put to use by our purposeful philosophy in its well-ordered household.

LICHTENBERG, *Aphorisms*, 1764–99

The function of the imagination is not to make strange things settled, so much as to make settled things strange.

G. K. CHESTERTON, *The Defendant*, 1901

What is now proved was once only imagin'd.

BLAKE, *The Marriage of Heaven and Hell*, 1790–3

Imagination depends mainly upon memory, but there is a small percentage of creation of something out of nothing with it. We can invent a trifle more than can be got at by mere combination of remembered things.

SAMUEL BUTLER (II), *Notebooks*, 1912

In the realms of the unconscious mental life there is no such thing as exhaustion.

C. G. CARUS, *Psyche*, 1846

If it is for mind that we are searching the brain, then we are supposing the brain to be much more than a telephone-exchange. We are supposing it a telephone-exchange along with the subscribers as well.

SIR CHARLES SHERRINGTON, *Man on his Nature*, 1940

There is a road from the eye to the heart that does not go through the intellect.

G. K. CHESTERTON, *The Defendant*, 1901

If the doors of perception were cleansed every thing would appear to man as it is, infinite.

For man has closed himself up, till he sees all things thro' narrow chinks of his cavern.

BLAKE, *The Marriage of Heaven and Hell*, 1790–3

Vision is the art of seeing things invisible.

SWIFT, *Thoughts on Various Subjects*, 1711

Put the world's greatest philosopher on a plank that is wider than need be; if there is a precipice below, although his reason may convince him that he is safe, his imagination will prevail.

PASCAL, *Pensées*, 1670

In the philosopher there is nothing whatever impersonal; and, above all, his morality bears decided and decisive testimony to *who he is* – that is to say, to the order of rank in which the innermost drives of his nature stand in relation to one another.

NIETZSCHE, *Beyond Good and Evil*, 1886

There is only one thing a philosopher can be relied on to do, and that is to contradict other philosophers.

WILLIAM JAMES

Every philosopher knows that his own system rests on no surer foundations than the rest, but he maintains it because it is his own. There is not one of them who, if he chanced to discover the difference between truth and falsehood, would not prefer his own lie to the truth which another had discovered.

ROUSSEAU, *Emile*, 1762

Any philosopher who wants to keep his contact with mankind should pervert his own system in advance to see how it will really look a few decades after adoption.

SAUL BELLOW, Moses Herzog in *Herzog*, 1964

We must fight hard against the unreasonable temptations to turn against our most cherished ideas, when we see them vulgarized and degraded by belated success. Lost causes are betrayed through cowardice, and victorious ones through fastidiousness.

HENRY DE MONTHERLANT, *Notebooks*, 1930–44

All sensible talk about vitally important topics must be commonplace, all reasoning about them unsound, and all study of them narrow and sordid.

, C. S. PEIRCE, *Collected Papers*, I, late 19th–early 20th century

The voice of the intellect is a soft one, but it does not rest till it has gained a hearing.

FREUD, *The Future of an Illusion*, 1927

Wisdom & Folly

❀

The art of being wise is the art of knowing what to overlook.

WILLIAM JAMES, *Principles of Psychology*, 1890

Great wisdom is generous; petty wisdom is contentious. Great speech is impassioned, small speech cantankerous.

CHUANG-TZU, *On Levelling All Things*, 4th century BC

The steadfastness of the wise is but the art of keeping their agitation locked in their hearts.

LA ROCHEFOUCAULD, *Maxims*, 1665

You must not think me necessarily foolish because I am facetious, nor will I consider you necessarily wise because you are grave.

SYDNEY SMITH, letter to Bishop Blomfield, 1840

A wise man laughs at a fool; a fool does the same by a wise man; both are equally diverted.

ANON., *Characters and Observations*, early 18th century

A wise man's question contains half the answer.

SOLOMON IBN GABIROL, *The Choice of Pearls*, c.1050

A fool sees not the same tree that a wise man sees.

BLAKE, *The Marriage of Heaven and Hell*, 1790–3

To a great experience one thing is essential, an experiencing nature. It is not enough to have opportunity, it is essential to feel it.

WALTER BAGEHOT, *Literary Studies*, 1879

If a mean person uses a wise maxim, I bethink me how it can be interpreted so as to commend itself to his meanness; but if a wise

man makes a commonplace remark, I consider what wiser construc-
tion it will admit.

THOREAU, Journal, 1840

A fool's paradise is a wise man's hell.

THOMAS FULLER (I), The Holy State and the Profane State, 1642

When the human mind is left to itself, it invariably lapses into the
stupidity of childhood. Men will always prefer toys to objects
worthy of their admiration.

DELACROIX, Journal, 1847

Why want to exchange a child's wise incomprehension for defensiveness and disdain, since incomprehension is after all being alone,
while defensiveness and disdain are a sharing in that from which one
wants by these means to keep apart.

RILKE, Letters to a Young Poet, 1903

It's bad taste to be wise all the time, like being at a perpetual funeral.

D. H. LAWRENCE, 'Peace and War', Pansies, 1929

You look wise. Pray correct that error.

CHARLES LAMB, 'All Fools' Day', Essays of Elia, 1820–3

Nature meant there to be illusions for the wise as well as the foolish,
so that the wise should not be made too unhappy by their wisdom.

CHAMFORT, Maximes et pensées, 1805

The subtlest wisdom can produce the subtlest folly.

LA ROCHEFOUCAULD, Maxims, 1665

If the follies of fools were all set down like those of the wise, the wise
(who seem at present only a better sort of fool), would appear almost
intelligent.

BYRON, Detached Thoughts, 1821–2

The Arab who builds himself a hut out of the marble fragments of a
temple in Palmyra is more philosophical than all the curators of the
museums in London, Munich or Paris.

ANATOLE FRANCE, The Crime of Sylvestre Bonnard, 1881

There are well turned-out follies, just as there are smartly-dressed fools.

> CHAMFORT, *Maximes et pensées*, 1805

Subtlety is not a proof of wisdom. Fools and even madmen are at times extraordinarily subtle.

> PUSHKIN in 'Notes', *Pushkin on Literature*, trans. and ed. Tatiana Wolff

Many have been the wise speeches of fools, though not so many as the foolish speeches of wise men.

> THOMAS FULLER (I), *The Holy State and the Profane State*, 1642

The talk of a fool is like a heavy pack on a journey.

> ECCLESIASTICUS, *c.*170 BC

Silence is the wit of fools.

> LA BRUYÈRE, 'Conversation', *Characters*, 1688

A fool does not enter a room, or leave it, or sit down, or rise, or remain silent, or stand on his feet like a man of sense.

> LA BRUYÈRE, 'Of Personal Merit', *Characters*, 1688

Stupidity consists in wanting to reach conclusions. We are a thread, and we want to know the whole cloth.

> FLAUBERT, letter, 1850

Most fools think they are only ignorant.

> BENJAMIN FRANKLIN, *Poor Richard's Almanack*, 1748

There is a freemasonry among the dull by which they recognize and are sociable with the dull, as surely as a correspondent tact in men of genius.

> EMERSON, *Journals*, 1827

Who knows a fool must know his brother;
One fop will recommend another.

> JOHN GAY, *Fables*, 1727

A fool always finds someone more foolish than he is to admire him.
>   BOILEAU, *L'Art Poétique*, 1674

Perhaps there are not as many stupid things said as there are set down in print.
>   GONCOURT BROTHERS, *Journal*, 1866

A fool who has a moment's flash of wit is both astonishing and shocking, like cab horses at a gallop.
>   CHAMFORT, *Maximes et pensées*, 1805

Some people display a talent for pretending to be silly, even before they become intelligent. Girls have this talent very often.
>   LICHTENBERG, *Aphorisms*, 1764–99

If the fool would persist in his folly he would become wise.
>   BLAKE, *The Marriage of Heaven and Hell*, 1790–3

He must be a thorough fool, who can learn nothing from his own folly.
>   JULIUS HARE, *Guesses at Truth*, 1827

A fool hath no dialogue with himself, the first thought carrieth him, without the reply of a second.
>   MARQUESS OF HALIFAX, *Moral thoughts and reflections*, late 17th century

No precepts will profit a fool.
>   BEN JONSON, *Timber; or Discoveries*, 1640

I have seen wicked men and fools, a great many of them; and I believe they both get paid in the end; but the fools first.
>   ROBERT LOUIS STEVENSON, *Kidnapped*, 1886

If wicked actions are atoned for only in the next world, stupid ones are only atoned for in this.
>   SCHOPENHAUER, 'Counsels and Maxims', *Parerga and Paralipomena*, 1851

Some men are destined to be fools, and they do foolish things not from choice but because fate herself compels them to.

LA ROCHEFOUCAULD, *Maxims*, 1665

We do not commiserate with a man for being a fool, and perhaps rightly; but it is very agreeable to imagine that it is his fault.

VAUVENARGUES, *Reflections and Maxims*, 1746

If poverty is the mother of crime, stupidity is its father.

LA BRUYÈRE, 'Of Mankind', *Characters*, 1688

Folly is often more cruel in the consequence than malice can be in the intent.

MARQUESS OF HALIFAX, *Moral thoughts and reflections*, late 17th century

The faults of blockheads are sometimes so great and so difficult to foresee, that wise men are puzzled by them; they are only of use to those who commit them.

LA BRUYÈRE, 'Of Mankind', *Characters*, 1688

Idiots have always been exploited, and this is only right. The day they cease to be, they will triumph, and the world will be lost.

ALFRED CAPUS (1858–1922), *Mariage bourgeois*

The dulness of the fool is the whetstone of the wits.

SHAKESPEARE, *As You Like It*, 1599–1600

Strong and sharp as our wit may be, it is not so strong as the memory of fools, nor so keen as their resentment.

CHARLES CALEB COLTON, *Lacon*, 1825

A man must be a fool indeed, if I think him one at the time he is applauding me.

RICHARD FULKE GREVILLE, *Maxims, Characters and Reflections*, 1756

A man had as soon go to bed with a razor as to be intimate with a foolish friend.

> MARQUESS OF HALIFAX, *Moral thoughts and reflections*, late 17th century

When a book and a head collide and there is a hollow sound, is it always in the book?

> LICHTENBERG, *Aphorisms*, 1764–99

It is the property of fools, to be always judging.

> THOMAS FULLER (II), *Gnomologia*, 1732

I prefer rogues to imbeciles, because they sometimes take a rest.

> ALEXANDRE DUMAS *fils* (1824–95)

When dealing with the insane, the best method is to pretend to be sane.

> HERMANN HESSE, *Prosa und Feuilletons*

If others had not been foolish, we should be so.

> BLAKE, *The Marriage of Heaven and Hell*, 1790–3

We must know how to commit such foolishness as our character demands.

> CHAMFORT, *Maximes et pensées*, 1805

Every age and every condition indulges some darling fallacy; every man amuses himself with projects which he knows to be improbable, and which, therefore, he resolves to pursue without daring to examine them.

> DR JOHNSON, *The Adventurer*, 1753

How often we should stop in the pursuit of folly, if it were not for the difficulties that continually beckon us onwards.

> SIR ARTHUR HELPS, *Thoughts in the Cloister and the Crowd*, 1835

It is a self-flattering contradiction, that wise men despise the opinion of fools, and yet are proud of having their esteem.

> MARQUESS OF HALIFAX, *Miscellaneous thoughts and reflections*, late 17th century

Unless men have the prudence not to appear touched with the sarcasms of a jester, they subject themselves to his power, and the wise man will have his folly anatomized by a fool.

DR JOHNSON, *Notes upon Shakespeare*, 1765

The best lesson we can learn from witnessing the folly of mankind is not to irritate ourselves against it.

HAZLITT, *Characteristics*, 1823

The great thing to know is whether, after all, the imbecilities that time has consecrated do not form the best investment a man can make of his stupidity.

ANATOLE FRANCE, *The Garden of Epicurus*, 1894

A man can believe a considerable deal of rubbish, and yet go about his daily work in a rational and cheerful manner.

NORMAN DOUGLAS, *An Almanac*, 1945

Wise men are more dependent on fools than fools on wise men.

CHURTON COLLINS, aphorisms in the *English Review*, 1914

What we opprobriously call stupidity, though not an enlivening quality in common society, is Nature's favourite resource for preserving steadiness of conduct and consistency of opinion.

WALTER BAGEHOT, *Literary Studies*, 1879

Stupid sons don't ruin a family; it is the clever ones who do.

'MR TUT-TUT', *A Night's Talk*, Chinese, 17th century

He who hath not a dram of folly in his mixture hath pounds of much worse matter in his composition.

CHARLES LAMB, 'All Fools' Day', *Essays of Elia*, 1820–3

There is something the poor know that the rich do not know, something the sick know that people in good health do not know, something the stupid know that the intelligent do not know.

GERALD BRENAN, *Thoughts in a Dry Season*, 1978

The first step towards madness is to think oneself wise.

FERNANDO DE ROJAS, *La Celestina*, 1499–1502

Intelligence & Insight

✿

Wisdom is only a comparative quality, it will not bear a single definition.

MARQUESS OF HALIFAX, *Miscellaneous thoughts and reflections*, late 17th century

The more intelligent one is, the more men of originality one finds. Ordinary people find no difference between men.

PASCAL, *Pensées*, 1670

Wisdom cannot create materials; they are the gifts of nature or of chance; her pride is in the use.

EDMUND BURKE, *Reflections on the Revolution in France*, 1790

It is not enough to have a good mind. The main thing is to use it well.

DESCARTES, *Discourse on Method*, 1637

The wise man would rather see men needing him than thanking him.

GRACIÁN, *The Art of Worldly Wisdom*, 1647

Wit without employment is a disease.

ROBERT BURTON, *Anatomy of Melancholy*, 1621

You should never be clever but when you cannot help it.

RICHARD FULKE GREVILLE, *Maxims, Characters and Reflections*, 1756

A man is not necessarily intelligent because he has plenty of ideas, any more than he is a good general because he has plenty of soldiers.

CHAMFORT, *Maximes et pensées*, 1805

There are some men who are so intelligent that you wonder whether anything can still interest them.

MAURICE MARTIN DU GARD, *Petite suite de maximes et de caractères*, 1944

A really intelligent man feels what other men only know.

MONTESQUIEU, *Essai sur les causes qui peuvent affecter les esprits et les caractères*, 1736

An intelligent person often talks with his eyes; a shallow man often swallows with his ears.

'MR TUT-TUT', *A Night's Talk*, Chinese, 17th century

Certain good qualities are like the senses: people entirely lacking in them can neither perceive nor comprehend them.

LA ROCHEFOUCAULD, *Maxims*, 1665

There is a kinship, a kind of freemasonry, between all persons of intelligence, however antagonistic their moral outlook.

NORMAN DOUGLAS

Mere imagination would indeed be mere trifling; only no imagination is *mere*.

C. S. PEIRCE, *Collected Papers*, VI, late 19th–early 20th century

Extensive reflection and knowledge without much experience resemble one of those editions with two lines of text on a page and forty lines of commentary. Extensive experience without much reflection and knowledge is like an edition without notes which is often unintelligible.

SCHOPENHAUER, 'Counsels and Maxims', *Parerga and Paralipomena*, 1851

A moment's insight is sometimes worth a life's experience.

OLIVER WENDELL HOLMES sen., *The Professor at the Breakfast Table*, 1859

The wisest of critics is an altering being, subject to the better insight of the morrow, and right at any moment, only 'up to date' and 'on the whole'.

WILLIAM JAMES, *Varieties of Religious Experience*, 1902

A man should never be ashamed to own that he has been in the wrong, which is but saying, in other words, that he is wiser today than he was yesterday.

SWIFT, *Thoughts on Various Subjects*, 1711

Few people even scratch the surface, much less exhaust the contemplation of their own experience.

RANDOLPH BOURNE, *Youth and Life*, 1913

We do not receive wisdom, we must discover it for ourselves, after a journey through the wilderness which no-one else can make for us, which no-one can spare us, for our wisdom is the point of view from which we come at last to regard the world.

MARCEL PROUST, *Remembrance of Things Past* (*Within a Budding Grove*, 1919)

An ounce of a man's own wit is worth a ton of other people's.

STERNE, *Tristram Shandy*, 1759–67

'Tis commonly said that the justest portion nature has given us of her favours, is that of sense; for there is no-one who is not contented with his share.

MONTAIGNE, 'Of presumption', *Essays*, 1580–8

Many would be wise if they did not think themselves wise.

GRACIÁN, *The Art of Worldly Wisdom*, 1647

Some people will never learn anything, for this reason, because they understand everything too soon.

POPE, *Thoughts on Various Subjects*, 1727

The ever-alert, the conscientiously wakeful – how many fine things they fail to see!

NORMAN DOUGLAS, *An Almanac*, 1945

Some men's behaviour is like a verse, wherein every syllable is measured: how can a man comprehend great matters, that breaketh his mind too much to small observations?

SIR FRANCIS BACON, 'Of Ceremonies and Respects', *Essays*, 1597–1625

Chi Wen Tzu always thought three times before taking action. Twice would have been quite enough.

CONFUCIUS, *Analects*, 5th century BC

Next to knowing when to seize an opportunity, the most important thing in life is to know when to forego an advantage.

BENJAMIN DISRAELI, *The Infernal Marriage*, 1834

Sometimes it proves the highest understanding not to understand.

GRACIÁN, *The Art of Worldly Wisdom*, 1647

Curiosity is one of the permanent and certain characteristics of a vigorous intellect.

DR JOHNSON, *The Rambler*, 1750–2

Men do mightily wrong themselves when they refuse to be present in all ages and neglect to see the beauty of all kingdoms.

TRAHERNE, *Centuries of Meditation*, c.1665

Experience offers proof on every hand that vigorous mental life may be but one side of a personality, of which the other is moral barbarism.

GEORGE GISSING, *The Private Papers of Henry Ryecroft*, 1903

Simplicity of character is no hindrance to subtlety of intellect.

JOHN MORLEY, *Life of Gladstone*, 1903

One defeats the fanatic precisely by *not* being a fanatic oneself, but on the contrary by using one's intelligence.

GEORGE ORWELL, letter to Richard Rees, 1949

There is in us something wiser than our head.

SCHOPENHAUER, 'Counsels and Maxims', *Parerga and Paralipomena*, 1851

The metaphor is far more intelligent than its author, and this is the case with many things. Everything has its depths. He who has eyes sees something in everything.

LICHTENBERG, *Aphorisms*, 1764–99

Reason's last step is the recognition that there are an infinite number of things which are beyond it.

PASCAL, *Pensées*, 1670

Seeing through is rarely seeing into.

ELIZABETH BIBESCO, *Haven*, 1951

It is better not to reflect at all than not to reflect enough.

TRISTAN BERNARD, *Triplepatte*, 1905

Only the shallow know themselves.

OSCAR WILDE, 'Phrases and Philosophies for the Use of the Young', 1894

Even those who do not display any acuteness and acumen in other respects are experts in the algebra of other people's affairs.

SCHOPENHAUER, 'Counsels and Maxims', *Parerga and Paralipomena*, 1851

Fine sense and exalted sense are not half so useful as common sense. There are forty men of wit for one of sense; and he that will carry nothing about him but gold, will be every day at a loss for want of readier change.

POPE, *Thoughts on Various Subjects*, 1727

Prudence is of more frequent use than any other intellectual quality; it is exerted on slight occasions, and called into act by the cursory business of common life.

DR JOHNSON, *The Idler*, 1758

Never say anything remarkable. It is sure to be wrong.

MARK RUTHERFORD, *Last Pages from a Journal*, 1915

Anyone who has looked deeply into the world may guess how much wisdom lies in the superficiality of men. The instinct that preserves them teaches them to be flighty, light, and false.

NIETZSCHE, *Beyond Good and Evil*, 1886

Few have reason, most have eyes.

CHARLES CHURCHILL, *The Ghost*, 1762

The world may not be particularly wise – still, we know of nothing wiser.

SAMUEL BUTLER (II), *Notebooks*, 1912

All this worldly wisdom was once the unamiable heresy of some wise man.

THOREAU, *Journals*, 1840

Beliefs & Opinions

●

There is no such thing as absolute certainty, but there is assurance sufficient for the purposes of human life.

JOHN STUART MILL, *On Liberty*, 1859

We may despair of knowing, we must not despair of judging.

ANATOLE FRANCE, *Crainquebille*, 1901

The best ideas are common property.

SENECA, *Epistles*, 1st century

The mind of man, when its daily maxims are put before it, revolts from anything so stupid, so mean, so poor. It requires a consummate art to reconcile men in print to that moderate and insidious philosophy which creeps into all hearts, colours all speech, influences all action. We may not stiffen common sense into a creed; our very ambition forbids.

WALTER BAGEHOT, *Literary Studies*, 1879

The brute necessity of believing something so long as life lasts does not justify any belief in particular.

SANTAYANA, *Scepticism and Animal Faith*, 1923

The union of scepticism and yearning begets mysticism.

NIETZSCHE

There are infinite possibilities of error, and more cranks take up unfashionable untruths than unfashionable truths.

BERTRAND RUSSELL, *Unpopular Essays*, 1950

It is very easy upon granted foundations to build whatever we please: for according to the law and ordering of this beginning, the other parts are easily carried on.

MONTAIGNE, 'Apology for Raimond de Sebonde', *Essays*, 1580–8

The firmest line that can be drawn upon the smoothest paper is still jagged edges if seen through a microscope. This does not matter until important deductions are made on the supposition that there are no jagged edges.

SAMUEL BUTLER (II), *Notebooks*, 1912

The weakness of all Utopias is this, that they take the greatest difficulty of man and assume it to be overcome, and then give an elaborate account of the overcoming of the smaller ones.

G. K. CHESTERTON, *Heretics*, 1905

Irrationally held truths may be more harmful than reasoned errors.

T. H. HUXLEY, 'The Coming of Age of the *Origin of Species*', 1880

Prejudice may be trusted to guard the outworks for a short space of time, while Reason slumbers in the citadel; but if the latter sink into a lethargy, the former will quickly erect a standard for herself.

WILLIAM DRUMMOND, *Academical Questions*, 1805

It is a very curious thing about superstition. One would expect that the man who had once seen that his morbid dreams were not fulfilled would abandon them for the future; but on the contrary they grow even stronger just as the love of gambling increases in a man who has once lost in a lottery.

KIERKEGAARD, *Journal*, 1836

The most gross and childish ravings are most found in those authors who treat of the most elevated subjects.

MONTAIGNE, 'Apology for Raimond de Sebonde', *Essays*, 1580–8

It is easier to square the circle than to get round a mathematician.

AUGUSTUS DE MORGAN, *A Budget of Paradoxes*, 1872

Superstition is part of the very being of humanity; and when we imagine that we have banished it for good, it takes refuge in strange corners, and then suddenly ventures forth again, as soon as it sees its opportunity.

GOETHE, *Maxims and Reflections*, early 19th century

The only people who are *never* converted to spiritualism are conjurers.

GEORGE ORWELL, 'As I Please', 1944

Unless we *see* our object, how shall we know how to place or prize it, in our understanding, our imagination, our affections?

CARLYLE, 'Burns', 1828

Every truth has two faces, every rule two surfaces, every precept two applications.

JOUBERT, *Pensées*, 1842

Nothing is more dangerous than an idea, when a man has only one idea.

ALAIN, *Propos sur la religion*, 1938

I dreamt a line that would make a motto for a sober philosophy: *Neither a be-all nor an end-all be.*

J. L. AUSTIN, 'Pretending', *Philosophical Papers*, 1961

To accept an orthodoxy is always to inherit unresolved contradictions.

GEORGE ORWELL, 'Writers and Leviathan', 1948

The river of truth is always splitting up into arms which reunite. Islanded between them the inhabitants argue for a lifetime as to which is the mainstream.

CYRIL CONNOLLY, *The Unquiet Grave*, 1944

No perverseness equals that which is supported by system, no errors are so difficult to root out as those which the understanding has pledged its credit to uphold.

WORDSWORTH, Preface to *Poems*, 1815 (Supplementary Essay)

Convictions are more dangerous enemies of truth than lies.

NIETZSCHE, *Human, All Too Human*, 1878–86

The idea wants changelessness and eternity. Whoever lives under the

supremacy of the idea strives for permanence; hence everything that
pushes towards change must be against it.

JUNG, *Psychological Types*, 1921

Faith makes many of the mountains which it has to remove.

W. R. INGE, *More Lay Thoughts of a Dean*, 1931

We may cheerfully use, and with weight, terms which are not so
much head-on incompatible as simply disparate, which just do not
fit in or even on. Just as we cheerfully subscribe to, or have the grace
to be torn between, simply disparate ideals – why *must* there be a
conceivable amalgam, the Good Life for Man?

J. L. AUSTIN, 'A Plea for Excuses', *Philosophical Papers*, 1961

The miseries of life would be increased beyond all human power of
endurance, if we were to enter the world with the same opinions we
carry from it.

DR JOHNSON, *The Rambler*, 1750-2

Consistency requires you to be as ignorant today as you were a year
ago.

BERNARD BERENSON, notebook, 1892

Nothing is more ridiculous than to make an author a dictator, as the
Schools have done Aristotle. The damage is infinite knowledge
receives by it. For to many things a man should owe but temporary
belief, and a suspension of his own judgment, not an absolute
resignation of himself, or a perpetual captivity.

BEN JONSON, *Timber; or Discoveries*, 1640

In relation to their systems most systematizers are like a man who
builds an enormous castle and lives in a shack close by; they do not
live in their own enormous systematic buildings.

KIERKEGAARD, *Journal*, 1846

It is easier to fight for one's principles than to live up to them.

ALFRED ADLER, cit. Phyllis Bottome, *Alfred Adler*, 1939

What a man believes may be ascertained, not from his creed, but
from the assumptions on which he habitually acts.

> BERNARD SHAW, 'Maxims for Revolutionists', *Man and
> Superman*, 1903

A good life is a main argument.

> BEN JONSON, *Timber; or Discoveries*, 1640

In our ideals we unwittingly reveal our vices.

> JEAN ROSTAND, *Julien ou une conscience*, 1928

Opinions which justify cruelty are inspired by cruel impulses.

> BERTRAND RUSSELL, *Unpopular Essays*, 1950

There never was a cause yet, right or wrong, that ever wanted an
advocate to defend it.

> ANON., *Characters and Observations*, early 18th century

To praise oneself is considered improper, immodest; to praise one's
own sect, one's own philosophy, is considered the highest duty.

> LEO SHESTOV, *All Things are Possible*, 1905

Ideas are not always the mere signs and effects of social circumstances, they are themselves a power in history.

> JOHN STUART MILL, 'Tocqueville on Democracy in America',
> 1835

I doubt not, but if it had been a thing contrary to any man's right of
dominion, *That the three angles of a triangle should be equal to two angles
of a square*, that the doctrine should have been, if not disputed, yet by
the burning of all books of geometry suppressed, as far as he whom
it concerned was able.

> HOBBES, *Leviathan*, 1651

We mustn't forget how quickly the visions of genius become the
canned goods of intellectuals. The canned sauerkraut of Spengler's
'Prussian Socialism', the commonplaces of the Wasteland outlook,
the cheap mental stimulants of Alienation, the cant and rant of

pipsqueaks about Inauthenticity and Forlornness. I can't accept this foolish dreariness. We are talking about the whole life of mankind.

SAUL BELLOW, Moses Herzog in *Herzog*, 1964

The word 'orthodoxy' not only no longer means being right; it practically means being wrong.

G. K. CHESTERTON, *Heretics*, 1905

Man is used to having convictions, so there we are. We can none of us do without our hangers-on, though we despise them at the bottom of our souls.

LEO SHESTOV, *All Things are Possible*, 1905

The facts of life do not penetrate to the sphere in which our beliefs are cherished; they did not engender those beliefs, and they are powerless to destroy them.

MARCEL PROUST, *Remembrance of Things Past* (*Swann's Way*, 1913)

It is probable that a given opinion, as held by several individuals, even when of the most congenial views, is as distinct from itself as are their faces.

J. H. NEWMAN, *Oxford University Sermons*, 1843

Altered opinions do not alter a man's character (or very little); but they do illuminate individual aspects of the constellation of his personality which with a different constellation of opinions had hitherto remained dark and unrecognizable.

NIETZSCHE, *Assorted Opinions and Maxims*, 1886

Men who borrow their opinions can never repay their debts.

MARQUESS OF HALIFAX, *Miscellaneous thoughts and reflections*, late 17th century

He who knows only his own side of the case knows little of that.

JOHN STUART MILL, *On Liberty*, 1859

The desire for a strong faith is *not* the proof of a strong faith, rather the opposite. *If one has it* one may permit oneself the beautiful luxury of scepticism: one is secure enough, firm enough, fixed enough for it.

NIETZSCHE, *Twilight of the Idols*, 1888

Violent men reel from one extremity to another.

THOMAS FULLER (1), *The Holy State and the Profane State*, 1642

Prejudice is never easy unless it can pass itself off for reason.

HAZLITT, 'On Prejudice'

As soon as I have asserted a proposition: where can more examples be found?

LICHTENBERG, *Aphorisms*, 1764–99

Fanaticism consists in redoubling your effort when you have forgotten your aim.

SANTAYANA, *The Life of Reason*, 1905–6

A fanatic is a man that does what he thinks th' Lord wud do if He knew th' facts iv th' case.

FINLEY PETER DUNNE, *Mr. Dooley's Philosophy*, 1900

Heretics were often most bitterly persecuted for their least deviation from accepted belief. It was precisely their obstinacy about trifles that irritated the righteous to madness. 'Why can they not yield on so trifling a matter?'

LEO SHESTOV, *All Things are Possible*, 1905

Martyrs create faith more than faith creates martyrs.

UNAMUNO, *The Tragic Sense of Life*, 1913

To become properly acquainted with a truth we must first have disbelieved it, and disputed against it.

NOVALIS, *Fragments* (trans. Carlyle), late 18th century

Where it is a duty to worship the sun it is pretty sure to be a crime to examine the laws of heat.

JOHN MORLEY, *Voltaire*, 1872

We are usually convinced more easily by reasons we have found ourselves than by those which have occurred to others.

PASCAL, *Pensées*, 1670

A powerful idea communicates some of its power to the man who contradicts it.

MARCEL PROUST, *Remembrance of Things Past* (*Within a Budding Grove*, 1919)

To make arguments in my study and confute them is easy, where I answer myself, not an adversary.

BEN JONSON, *Timber; or Discoveries*, 1640

The most savage controversies are those about matters as to which there is no good evidence either way.

BERTRAND RUSSELL, *Unpopular Essays*, 1950

When myth meets myth, the collision is very real.

STANISLAW LEC, *Unkempt Thoughts*, 1962

Opponents fancy they refute us when they repeat their own opinion and pay no attention to ours.

GOETHE, *Maxims and Reflections*, early 19th century

Nothing was ever learned by either side in a dispute.

HAZLITT, 'On the Conversation of Authors', 1820

Theories and schools, like microbes and corpuscles, devour one another and by their warfare ensure the continuity of life.

MARCEL PROUST, *Remembrance of Things Past* (*Cities of the Plain*, 1921)

It is labour in vain to dispute with a man, unless somebody be in company, to whose judgment you would both submit.

ANON., *Characters and Observations*, early 18th century

Nothing hath an uglier look to us than reason, when it is not on our side.

MARQUESS OF HALIFAX, *Miscellaneous thoughts and reflections*, late 17th century

Every man will dispute with great good humour upon a subject in which he is not interested.

DR JOHNSON in Boswell's *Life of Johnson*, 1781

Some have wondered that disputes about opinions should so often end in personalities; but the fact is, that such disputes *begin* with personalities; for our opinions are a part of ourselves. Besides, after the first contradiction it is ourselves, and not the thing, we maintain.

EDWARD FITZGERALD, *Polonius*, 1852

Your judgment 'this is right' has a pre-history in your instincts, likes, dislikes, experiences, and lack of experiences. '*How* did it originate there?' you must ask, and then also: 'What is it that impels me to listen to it?'

NIETZSCHE, *The Gay Science*, 1882–7

Those who never retract their opinions love themselves more than they love the truth.

JOUBERT, *Pensées*, 1842

People often manifest a diseased desire to express their will. A theory is adopted, not because the facts force it upon them, but because its adoption shows their power.

MARK RUTHERFORD, *More Pages from a Journal*, 1910

Those who obstinately oppose the most widely-held opinions more often do so because of pride than lack of intelligence. They find the best places in the right set already taken, and they do not want back seats.

LA ROCHEFOUCAULD, *Maxims*, 1665

They who would combat general authority with particular opinion, must first establish themselves a reputation of understanding better than other men.

DRYDEN, 'Heroic Poetry and Heroic Licence', 1677

When everyone is against you, it means that you are absolutely wrong – or absolutely right.

ALBERT GUINON, *c.*1900

Intolerance is natural and logical, for in every dissenting opinion lies an assumption of superior wisdom.

AMBROSE BIERCE, *The Devil's Dictionary*, 1906

A bigot delights in public ridicule, for he begins to think he is a martyr.

SYDNEY SMITH, *The Letters of Peter Plymley*, 1808

Every word that we utter rouses its contrary.

GOETHE, *Maxims and Reflections*, early 19th century

Somebody has to have the last word. Otherwise, every reason can be met with another one and there would never be an end to it.

ALBERT CAMUS, Jean-Baptiste Clamance in *The Fall*, 1956

It were endless to dispute upon everything that is disputable.

WILLIAM PENN, *Some Fruits of Solitude*, 1693

Think before you think!

STANISLAW LEC, *Unkempt Thoughts*, 1962

Nothing is more conducive to peace of mind than not having any opinion at all.

LICHTENBERG, *Aphorisms*, 1764–99

Knowledge & Ignorance

All knowledge is of itself of some value. There is nothing so minute or inconsiderable, that I would not rather know it than not.

DR JOHNSON in Boswell's *Life of Johnson*, 1775

Ignorance is the necessary condition of life itself. If we knew everything, we could not endure existence for a single hour.

ANATOLE FRANCE, *The Garden of Epicurus*, 1894

All that we know is nothing, we are merely crammed waste-paper baskets, unless we are in touch with that which laughs at all our knowing.

D. H. LAWRENCE, 'All-Knowing', *Pansies*, 1929

Human life is limited, but knowledge is limitless. To drive the limited in pursuit of the limitless is fatal; and to presume that one really knows is fatal indeed!

CHUANG-TZU, *The Preservation of Life*, 4th century BC

Ole man Know-All died las' year.

JOEL CHANDLER HARRIS, 'Plantation Proverbs', *Uncle Remus*, 1880

The Sceptics that affirmed they knew nothing, even in that opinion confuted themselves, and thought they knew more than all the world beside.

SIR THOMAS BROWNE, *Religio Medici*, 1643

Ignorance is ignorance; no right to believe anything can be derived from it.

FREUD, *The Future of an Illusion*, 1927

Uncultivated minds are not full of wild flowers, like uncultivated fields. Villainous weeds grow in them, and they are full of toads.

LOGAN PEARSALL SMITH, *Afterthoughts*, 1931

There is nothing makes a man suspect much, more than to know little.

SIR FRANCIS BACON, 'Of Suspicion', *Essays*, 1597–1625

Admissions are mostly made by those who do not know their importance.

MR JUSTICE DARLING, *Scintillae Juris*, 1889

Few men make themselves masters of the things they write or speak.

JOHN SELDEN, *Table Talk*, mid 17th century

It distresses me, this failure to keep pace with the leaders of thought, as they pass into oblivion.

MAX BEERBOHM

The most certain way to hide from others the limits of our knowledge is not to go beyond them.

LEOPARDI, *Pensieri*, 1834–7

What truly indicates excellent knowledge, is the habit of constant, sudden, and almost unconscious allusion, which implies familiarity, for it can arise from that alone.

WALTER BAGEHOT, *Literary Studies*, 1879

Ignorance cannot always be inferred from inaccuracy, knowledge is not always present.

DR JOHNSON, *Notes upon Shakespeare*, 1765

He that knows little often repeats it.

THOMAS FULLER (II), *Gnomologia*, 1732

A weak man had rather be thought to know than not know, and that maketh him so impatient to be told of a mistake.

MARQUESS OF HALIFAX, *Miscellaneous thoughts and reflections*, late 17th century

Men are not to be judged by what they do not know, but by what they do know, and the manner in which they know it.

VAUVENARGUES, *Reflections and Maxims*, 1746

We should rather examine, who is better learned, than who is more learned.

MONTAIGNE, 'Of pedantry', *Essays*, 1580–8

Knowledge is little; to know the right context is much, to know the right spot is everything.

HUGO VON HOFMANNSTHAL, *The Book of Friends*, 1922

No man is the wiser for his learning; it may administer matter to work in, or objects to work upon, but wit and wisdom are born with a man.

JOHN SELDEN, *Table Talk*, mid 17th century

A silly remark can be made in Latin as well as in Spanish.

CERVANTES, *The Dialogue of the Dogs*, 1613

The end of all knowledge is to understand what is fit to be done; for to know what has been, and what is, and what may be, does but tend to that.

SAMUEL BUTLER (I), *Prose Observations*, 1660–80

There is an ABC ignorance which precedes knowledge and a doctoral ignorance that comes after it.

MONTAIGNE, 'Of vain subtleties', *Essays*, 1580–8

Whether learning has made more proud men or good men, may be a question.

ANON., *Characters and Observations*, early 18th century

The more scholastically educated a man is generally, the more he is an emotional boor.

D. H. LAWRENCE, 'John Galsworthy', 1927

How we hate this solemn Ego that accompanies the learned, like a double, wherever he goes.

EMERSON, *Journals*, 1839

A great deal of learning can be packed into an empty head.

KARL KRAUS, *Aphorisms and More Aphorisms*, 1909

People who have taken no intellectual food for ten years, except a few tiny crumbs from the journals, are found even among professors; they aren't rare at all.

LICHTENBERG, *Aphorisms*, 1764–99

The cherubim know most; the seraphim love most.

EMERSON, 'Intellect', *Essays*, First Series, 1841

Learning & Teaching

✿

Who is wise? He who learns from all men, as it is said, From all my teachers have I gotten understanding.

BEN ZOMA (1st century AD), *Ethics of the Fathers*

According as each has been educated, so he repents of or glories in his actions.

SPINOZA, *Ethics*, 1677

Doctrine should be such as should make men in love with the lesson, and not with the teacher.

SIR FRANCIS BACON, *The Advancement of Learning*, 1605

Precepts, like fomentations, must be rubbed into us – and with a rough hand too.

MARQUESS OF HALIFAX, *Political thoughts and reflections*, late 17th century

Education does not consist merely in adorning the memory and enlightening the understanding. Its main business should be to direct the will.

JOUBERT, *Pensées*, 1842

Whatever is preached to us, whatever we learn, we should still remember that it is man that gives and man that receives; 'tis a mortal hand that presents it to us, 'tis a mortal hand that accepts it.

MONTAIGNE, 'Apology for Raimond de Sebonde', *Essays*, 1580–8

The things we know best are the things we haven't been taught.

VAUVENARGUES, *Reflections and Maxims*, 1746

Books we want to have young people read should not be recommended to them but praised in their presence. Afterwards they will find them themselves.

LICHTENBERG, *Aphorisms*, 1764–99

Men must be taught as if you taught them not,
And things unknown proposed as things forgot.

POPE, *An Essay on Criticism*, 1711

The wisest of the Ancients considered what is not too Explicit as the fittest for Instruction, because it rouses the faculties to act.

BLAKE, letter, 1799

The self-educated are marked by stubborn peculiarities.

ISAAC D'ISRAELI, *The Literary Character*, 1795

It would be worth the trouble to investigate whether it is not harmful to refine too much on the business of bringing up children. We do not yet know human beings well enough to take this whole process, so to speak, out of the hands of chance.

LICHTENBERG, *Aphorisms*, 1764–99

Those who are slow to know suppose that slowness is the essence of knowledge.

NIETZSCHE, *The Gay Science*, 1882–7

No Pestalozzian pedagogics can turn a born simpleton into a thinker: never!

SCHOPENHAUER, 'On the Different Periods of Life', *Parerga and Paralipomena*, 1851

Headmasters have powers at their disposal with which Prime Ministers have never yet been invested.

SIR WINSTON CHURCHILL, *My Early Life*, 1930

I pay the schoolmaster, but 'tis the schoolboys that educate my son.

EMERSON, *Journal*, 1849

You can't expect a boy to be vicious till he's been to a good school.

SAKI, 'The Baker's Dozen', *Reginald in Russia*, 1910

We receive three educations, one from our parents, one from our schoolmasters, and one from the world. The third contradicts all that the first two teach us.

MONTESQUIEU

A young man who desires to know all that in all ages and in all lands has been thought by the best minds, and wishes to make a synthesis of those thoughts for the future benefit of mankind, is laying up for himself a very miserable old age.

MAX BEERBOHM, 'Music Halls of My Youth', 1942

That which anyone has been long learning unwillingly, he unlearns with proportional eagerness and haste.

HAZLITT, 'On Personal Character', 1821

Ye can lade a man up to th'university, but ye can't make him think.

FINLEY PETER DUNNE, Mr. Dooley's Opinions, 1900

The University brings out all abilities, including stupidity.

CHEKHOV, Notebooks, 1892–1904

Undergraduates are like decimals: they recur.

WARDEN SPOONER (1844–1930)

In examinations the foolish ask questions that the wise cannot answer.

OSCAR WILDE, 'Phrases and Philosophies for the Use of the Young', 1894

No instrument smaller than the world is fit to measure men and women: Examinations measures Examinees.

SIR WALTER RALEIGH (II), Laughter through a Cloud, 1923

Colleges hate geniuses, just as convents hate saints.

EMERSON, 'Public and Private Education'

Learning is like a great house that requires a great charge to keep it in constant repair.

SAMUEL BUTLER (I), Prose Observations, 1660–80

To teach is to learn twice.

JOUBERT, Pensées, 1842

If a little knowledge is dangerous, where is the man who has so much as to be out of danger?

T. H. HUXLEY, 'On Elemental Instruction in Physiology', 1877

In completing one discovery we never fail to get an imperfect knowledge of others of which we could have no idea before, so that we cannot solve one doubt without creating several new ones.

JOSEPH PRIESTLEY, Experiments and Observations on Different Kinds of Air, 1775–86

That some books are so valuable and so royal that whole generations of scholars are well employed if their labours preserve these books in a state that is pure and intelligible – philology exists in order to fortify this faith again and again. It presupposes that there is no lack of those rare human beings (even if one does not see them) who really know how to use such valuable books – presumably those who write, or could write, books of the same type.

NIETZSCHE, The Gay Science, 1882–7

Learning hath gained most by those books by which the printers have lost.

THOMAS FULLER (I), The Holy State and the Profane State, 1642

Scholars are men of peace, they bear no arms, but their tongues are sharper than Actius his razor, their pens carry farther and give a louder report than thunder; I had rather stand in the shock of a basilico [a large cannon] than in the fury of a merciless pen.

SIR THOMAS BROWNE, Religio Medici, 1643

Almost always the books of scholars are somehow oppressive, oppressed; the 'specialist' emerges somewhere – his zeal, his furiousness, his fury, his overestimation of the nook in which he sits and spins, his hunched back; every specialist has a hunched back.

NIETZSCHE, The Gay Science, 1882–7

A thorough-paced antiquarian not only remembers what all other people have thought proper to forget, but he also forgets what all other people think it proper to remember.

CHARLES CALEB COLTON, *Lacon*, 1825

To spend too much time in studies is sloth.

SIR FRANCIS BACON, 'Of Studies', *Essays*, 1597–1625

If I had read as much as other men, I should know no more than they.

HOBBES reported by Aubrey, *Brief Lives*

Experience is a good teacher, but she sends in terrific bills.

MINNA ANTRIM, *Naked Truth and Veiled Allusions*, 1902

This is what they all come to who exclusively harp on experience. They do not stop to consider that experience is only one half of experience.

GOETHE, *Maxims and Reflections*, early 19th century

> a man who is so dull
> that he can learn only by personal experience
> is too dull to learn
> anything important by experience.

DON MARQUIS, 'archy on this and that', *Archy Does His Part*, 1935

The world itself is a volume larger than all the libraries in it. Learning is a sacred deposit from the experience of ages; but it has not put all future experience on the shelf, or debarred the common herd of mankind from the use of their hands, tongues, eyes, ears or understandings.

HAZLITT, 'On the Conversation of Authors', 1820

Memories, Dreams, Expectations

●

The richness of life lies in memories we have forgotten.

CESARE PAVESE, *This Business of Living: Diaries 1935–50*

There is a concealed strength in men's memories which they take no notice of.

THOMAS FULLER (1), *The Holy State and the Profane State*, 1642

The memory is sometimes so retentive, so serviceable, so obedient; at others, so bewildered and so weak; and at others again, so tyrannic, so beyond control! We are, to be sure, a miracle every way; but our powers of recollecting and forgetting do seem peculiarly past finding out.

JANE AUSTEN, *Mansfield Park*, 1814

As Habit weakens everything, what best reminds us of a person is precisely what we had forgotten (because it was of no importance, and we therefore left it in full possession of its strength).

MARCEL PROUST, *Remembrance of Things Past* (*Within a Budding Grove*, 1919)

In plucking the fruit of memory one runs the risk of spoiling its bloom.

JOSEPH CONRAD, *The Arrow of Gold*, 1919

To endeavour to forget anyone is a certain way of thinking of nothing else.

LA BRUYÈRE, 'Of the Affections', *Characters*, 1688

The presence of an idea is like that of a loved one. We imagine that we shall never forget it, and that the beloved can never become indifferent to us; but out of sight, out of mind! The finest thought runs the risk of being irretrievably forgotten if it is not written down.

SCHOPENHAUER, 'On Thinking for Oneself', *Parerga and Paralipomena*, 1851

The things we remember best are those better forgotten.

GRACIÁN, *The Art of Worldly Wisdom*, 1647

The past is our mortal mother, no dead thing. Our future constantly reflects her to the soul. Nor is it ever the new man of today which grasps his fortune, good or ill. We are pushed to it by the hundreds of days we have buried, eager ghosts.

MEREDITH, *The Adventures of Harry Richmond*, 1871

When we are tired, we are attacked by ideas we conquered long ago.

NIETZSCHE

All the things one has forgotten scream for help in dreams.

ELIAS CANETTI, *The Human Province*, 1978

How odd is the world of dreams! Thoughts, inner speech crowd and swarm – a little world hastening to live before the awakening that is its end, its particular death.

JULES RENARD, *Journal*, 1887

> I get out of bed
> and say goodbye to people
> I won't meet again.

PETER PORTER, 'Japanese Jokes', *The Last of England*, 1970

In sleep we receive confirmation – I cannot find another, more fitting word. We receive confirmation that we must go on living.

ANDREY SINYAVKSY, *A Voice from the Chorus*, 1973

The future enters into us, in order to transform itself in us, long before it happens.

RILKE, *Letters to a Young Poet*, 1903

He who asks fortune-tellers the future unwittingly forfeits an inner intimation of coming events that is a thousand times more exact than anything they may say.

WALTER BENJAMIN, *One-Way Street*, 1925–6

There are some such very great foreseers, that they grow into the vanity of pretending to see where nothing is to be seen.

> MARQUESS OF HALIFAX, *Miscellaneous thoughts and reflections*, late 17th century

The best qualification of a prophet is to have a good memory.

> MARQUESS OF HALIFAX, *Miscellaneous thoughts and reflections*, late 17th century

Study prophecies when they are become histories.

> SIR THOMAS BROWNE, *Christian Morals*, mid 17th century

Events play cat-and-mouse with our ideas. They belong to a quite different species and even when seeming to bear out our preconceptions are never quite as we expected. Foresight is a dream from which the event awakes us.

> VALÉRY, *Mauvaises pensées et autres*, 1942

One never knows what will happen if things are suddenly changed. But do we know what will happen if they are *not* changed?

> ELIAS CANETTI, *The Human Province*, 1978

The future is a mirror without any glass in it.

> XAVIER FORNERET, *Sans titre, par un homme noir, blanc de visage*, 1838

One should never place one's trust in the future. It doesn't deserve it.

> ANDRÉ CHAMSON (b. 1900), *On ne voit pas les coeurs*

I am in no hurry to see the society of the future: ours is helpful to writers. By its absurdities, its injustices, its vices, its stupidities, it feeds a writer's observations. The better men will become, the more colourless man will be.

> JULES RENARD, *Journal*, 1906

I cannot like posterity. With all their accomplishments, they seem to me a little crude.

> ROSE MACAULAY, *A Casual Commentary*, 1925

The Future is something which everyone reaches at the rate of sixty minutes an hour, whatever he does, whoever he is.

C. S. LEWIS, *The Screwtape Letters*, 1942

All expectation hath something of torment.

BENJAMIN WHICHCOTE, *Moral and Religious Aphorisms*, 1703

Tomorrow is an old deceiver, and his cheat never grows stale.

DR JOHNSON, letter, 1773

The Human Comedy

❀

'Tis a good thing to laugh at any rate; and if a straw can tickle a man, it is an instrument of happiness.

DRYDEN, *A Parallel of Poetry and Painting*, 1695

Of all days, the day on which one has not laughed is surely the most wasted.

CHAMFORT, *Maximes et pensées*, 1805

Freedom produces jokes and jokes produce freedom.

JEAN PAUL RICHTER, *Introduction to Aesthetics*, 1804

Humour brings insight and tolerance. Irony brings a deeper and less friendly understanding.

AGNES REPPLIER, *In Pursuit of Laughter*, 1936

Both laughter and weeping are sudden motions, custom taking them both away. For no man laughs at old jests; or weeps for an old calamity.

HOBBES, *Leviathan*, 1651

Anything we must not think of makes us laugh, by its coming upon us by stealth and unawares, and from the very efforts we make to exclude it.

HAZLITT, 'On Wit and Humour', 1818

Two faces are alike; neither is funny by itself, but side by side their likeness makes us laugh.

PASCAL, *Pensées*, 1670

Wit consists in seeing the resemblance between things which differ, and the difference between things which are alike.

MADAME DE STAËL, *De l'Allemagne*, 1813

You can pretend to be serious; you can't pretend to be witty.

SACHA GUITRY

If you run after wit you will succeed in catching folly.

MONTESQUIEU, *Mes pensées*, *c*.1722–55

Nothing was ever said with uncommon felicity but by the co-operation of chance; and therefore wit as well as valour must be content to share its honours with fortune.

DR JOHNSON, *The Idler*, 1758

A witticism is a minor work that does not merit a second edition.

ANTOINE RIVAROL, *Pensées, traits et bon mots*, late 18th century

Of all failures, to fail in a witticism is the worst, and the mishap is the more calamitous in a drawn-out and detailed one.

LANDOR, 'Chesterfield and Chatham', *Imaginary Conversations*, 1824–9

It is not enough to possess wit. One must have enough of it to avoid having too much.

ANDRÉ MAUROIS, *De la conversation*, 1921

The task of every other slave has an end. The rower in time reaches the port; the lexicographer at last finds the conclusion of his alphabet; only the hapless wit has his labour always to begin, the call for novelty is never satisfied, and one jest only raises expectations of another.

DR JOHNSON, *The Rambler*, 1750–2

There is a great difference between seeking how to raise a laugh from everything, and seeking in everything what may justly be laughed at.

LORD SHAFTESBURY, *Sensus Communis: An Essay on the Freedom of Wit and Humour*, 1709

Look for the ridiculous in everything and you will find it.

JULES RENARD, *Journal*, 1890

You can parody and make fun of almost anything, but that does not turn the universe into a caricature.

BERNARD BERENSON, notebook, 1893

He is as great a fool that laughs at all as he that weeps at all.

GRACIÁN, *The Art of Worldly Wisdom*, 1647

One must destroy one's adversaries' seriousness with laughter, and their laughter with seriousness.

GORGIAS OF LEONTINI (5th century BC)

We are always more disposed to laugh at nonsense than at genuine wit; because the nonsense is more agreeable to us, being more conformable to our natures.

MARGUERITE DE VALOIS (1553–1615)

I am thankful that my name is obnoxious to no pun.

WILLIAM SHENSTONE, *Essays on Men and Manners*, 1764

'Tis the loud laugh bespeaks the vacant mind.

JAMES JOYCE, *Ulysses*, 1922 (echoing Goldsmith)

As a wry face without pain moves laughter, or a deformed vizard, or a rude clown, dressed in a lady's habit and using her actions, we dislike and scorn such representations; which made the ancient philosophers ever to think laughter unfitting in a wise man.

BEN JONSON, *Timber; or Discoveries*, 1640

Much laughter at the defects of others is a sign of pusillanimity.

HOBBES, *Leviathan*, 1651

Far less envy in America than in France, and far less wit.

STENDHAL, *Love*, 1822

Some one is generally sure to be the sufferer by a joke.

HAZLITT, 'On Wit and Humour', 1818

Better lose a jest than a friend.

THOMAS FULLER (II), *Gnomologia*, 1732

Every day produces some new wonders; jests are turned into earnest and those who were planning to laugh at others find that they are laughed at themselves.

CERVANTES, *Don Quixote*, 1605–15

There's no such sport as sport by sport o'erthrown.

SHAKESPEARE, *Love's Labour's Lost*, 1594–5

The aim of a joke is not to degrade the human being but to remind him that he is already degraded.

GEORGE ORWELL, 'Funny, But Not Vulgar', 1944

In comedy, reconcilement with life comes at the point when to the tragic sense only an inalienable difference or dissension with life appears.

CONSTANCE ROURKE, *American Humor*, 1931

The common saying of life being a farce is true in every sense but the most important one, for it is a ridiculous tragedy, which is the worst kind of composition.

SWIFT, letter, 1731

Life does not cease to be funny when people die any more than it ceases to be serious when people laugh.

BERNARD SHAW, *The Doctor's Dilemma*, 1911

Everything human is pathetic. The secret source of Humour itself is not joy but sorrow. There is no humour in heaven.

MARK TWAIN, *Following the Equator*, 1897

To laugh is proper to man.

RABELAIS, *Gargantua and Pantagruel*, 1532

Language

Syllables govern the world.

JOHN SELDEN, *Table Talk*, mid 17th century

Words – so innocent and powerless as they are, as standing in a dictionary, how potent for good and evil they become, in the hands of one who knows how to combine them!

NATHANIEL HAWTHORNE, *American Notebooks*, 1841–52

Thanks to words, we have been able to rise above the brutes; and thanks to words, we have often sunk to the level of the demons.

ALDOUS HUXLEY, *Adonis and the Alphabet*, 1956

Ceremony forbids us to express by words things that are lawful and natural, and we obey it: reason forbids us to do things unlawful and ill, and nobody obeys it.

MONTAIGNE, 'Of Presumption', *Essays*, 1580

Language most shows a man: Speak, that I may see thee.

BEN JONSON, *Timber; or Discoveries*, 1640

Expression is the act of the whole man, that our speech may be vascular. The intellect is powerless to express thought without the aid of the heart and liver and of every member.

THOREAU, *Journal*, 1851

Language is by its very nature a communal thing; that is, it expresses never the exact thing but a compromise – that which is common to you, me, and everybody.

T. E. HULME, *Speculations*, 1924

The coldest word was once a glowing new metaphor.

CARLYLE, *Past and Present*, 1843

A word never – well, hardly ever – shakes off its etymology and its formation. In spite of all changes in and extensions of and additions to its meanings, and indeed rather pervading and governing them, there will persist the old idea.

J. L. AUSTIN, 'A Plea for Excuses', *Philosophical Papers*, 1961

Most of our expressions are metaphorical – the philosophy of our forefathers lies hidden in them.

LICHTENBERG, *Aphorisms*, 1764–99

Our common stock of words embodies all the distinctions men have found worth drawing, and the connexions they have found worth marking, in the lifetimes of many generations; these surely are likely to be more numerous, more sound, since they have stood up to the long test of the survival of the fittest, and more subtle, at least in all ordinary and reasonably practical matters, than any that you or I are likely to think up in our arm-chairs of an afternoon – the most favoured alternative method.

J. L. AUSTIN, 'A Plea for Excuses', *Philosophical Papers*, 1961

The immense profundity of thought contained in commonplace turns of phrase – holes burrowed by generations of ants.

BAUDELAIRE, *Fusées*, 1862

All speech, even the commonest speech, has something of song in it: not a parish in the world but has its parish-accent – the rhythm or *tune* to which the people there *sing* what they have to say.

CARLYLE, *On Heroes and Hero-Worship*, 1841

Languages happily restrict the mind to what is of its own native growth and fitted for it, as rivers and mountains bound countries; or the empire of learning, as well as states, would become unwieldy and overgrown.

HAZLITT, 'On Old English Writers and Speakers', 1825

A foreign tongue is spread not by fire and the sword but by its own richness and superiority.

ALEXANDER PUSHKIN, on a translation of Krylov's *Fables*, cit. *Pushkin on Literature*, trans. and ed. Tatiana Wolff

A language is a dialect that has an army and navy.

MAX WEINREICH (1894–1969)

It has always been lawful, and always will be, to issue words stamped with the mint-mark of the day.

HORACE, *Ars Poetica*, *c.*8 BC

As any custom is disused, the words that expressed it must perish with it; as any opinion grows popular, it will innovate speech in the same proportion as it alters practice.

DR JOHNSON, Preface, *Dictionary of the English Language*, 1755

The smashers of language are looking for a new justice among words. It does not exist. Words are unequal and unjust.

ELIAS CANETTI, *The Human Province*, 1978

Every age has a language of its own; and the difference in the words is often far greater than in the thoughts. The main employment of authors, in their collective capacity, is to translate the thoughts of other ages into the language of their own.

AUGUSTUS HARE, *Guesses at Truth*, 1827

Wheresoever manners and fashions are corrupted, language is. It imitates the public riot.

BEN JONSON, *Timber; or Discoveries*, 1640

The one stream of poetry which is continually flowing is slang.

G. K. CHESTERTON, *The Defendant*, 1901

The mass of men are very unpoetic, yet that Adam that names things is always a poet.

THOREAU, *Journal*, 1853

What is originality? *To see* something that has no name as yet and hence cannot be mentioned although it stares us all in the face. The way men usually are, it takes a name to make something visible for them. Those with originality have for the most part also assigned names.

NIETZSCHE, *The Gay Science*, 1882–7

Certainly ordinary language is *not* the last word: in principle it can everywhere be supplemented and improved upon and superseded. Only remember, it *is* the *first* word.

J. L. AUSTIN, 'A Plea for Excuses', *Philosophical Papers*, 1961

That the vulgar express their thoughts clearly is far from true; and what perspicuity can be found among them proceeds not from the easiness of their language, but the shallowness of their thoughts.

DR JOHNSON, *The Idler*, 1758

As men abound in copiousness of language, so they become more wise, or more mad than ordinary.

HOBBES, *Leviathan*, 1651

Loquacity storms the ear, but modesty takes the heart.

ROBERT SOUTH, *A Discourse Against Long and Extempore Prayers*, 1661

Before using a fine word, make a place for it!

JOUBERT, *Pensées*, 1842

A simile committing suicide is always a depressing spectacle.

OSCAR WILDE, 'Sententiae', *A Critic in Pall Mall*, 1919

For every man there is something in the vocabulary that would stick to him like a second skin. His enemies have only to find it.

AMBROSE BIERCE, *The Devil's Dictionary*, 1906

A nickname is a mode of insinuating a prejudice against another under some general designation, which, as it offers no proof, admits of no reply.

HAZLITT, *Characteristics*, 1823

As soon as I hear a name I feel convinced I can guess what the owner looks like, but it never happens, when I actually meet the man, that his face is as I had supposed.

YOSHIDA KENKO, *Essays in Idleness*, c.1340

Words do not change their meaning as much in centuries as names do for us in the space of a few years.

MARCEL PROUST, *Remembrance of Things Past* (*The Guermantes Way*, 1920–1)

The appropriately beautiful or ugly sound of any word is an illusion wrought on us by what the word connotes. *Beauty* sounds as ugly as *ugliness* sounds beautiful.

MAX BEERBOHM, *Yet Again*, 1909

I and *me*. *I* feel *me* – that makes two objects. Our false philosophy is embodied in the language as a whole: one might say that we can't reason without reasoning wrong.

LICHTENBERG, *Aphorisms*, 1764–99

Philosophy lives in words, but truth and fact well up into our lives in ways that exceed verbal formulation. There is in the living act of perception always something that glimmers and twinkles and will not be caught, and for which reflection comes too late.

WILLIAM JAMES, *Varieties of Religious Experience*, 1902

The Written Word

⬤

They do most by books, who could much without them.
SIR THOMAS BROWNE, *Christian Morals*, mid 17th century

Books will speak plain when counsellors blanch.
SIR FRANCIS BACON, 'Of Counsel', *Essays*, 1597–1625

Weak men are the worse for the good sense they read in books because it furnisheth them only with more matter to mistake.
MARQUESS OF HALIFAX, *Moral thoughts and reflections*, late 17th century

There are more books upon books than upon any other subject.
MONTAIGNE, 'Of experience', *Essays*, 1580–8

Wherever they burn books they will also, in the end, burn human beings.
HEINE, *Almansor: A Tragedy*, 1823

There can hardly be a stranger commodity in the world than books. Printed by people who don't understand them; sold by people who don't understand them; bound, criticized and read by people who don't understand them; and now even written by people who don't understand them.
LICHTENBERG, *Aphorisms*, 1764–99

Never disregard a book because the author of it is a foolish fellow.
LORD MELBOURNE

Some books are undeservedly forgotten, none are undeservedly remembered.
W. H. AUDEN, *The Dyer's Hand*, 1963

A classic is something that everyone wants to have read and nobody wants to read.

> MARK TWAIN, speech, 'The Disappearance of Literature', 1900

Big book, big bore.

> CALLIMACHUS (3rd century BC), *The Greek Anthology* (trans. Peter Jay)

Books do not teach the use of books.

> ANON.

We find little in a book but what we put there. But in great books, the mind finds room to put many things.

> JOUBERT, *Pensées*, 1842

A well-written Life is almost as rare as a well-spent one.

> CARLYLE, 'Richter', 1827

Autobiography is an unrivalled vehicle for telling the truth about other people.

> PHILIP GUEDALLA

The books one reads in childhood, and perhaps most of all the bad and good bad books, create in one's mind a sort of false map of the world, a series of fabulous countries into which one can retreat at odd moments throughout the rest of life, and which in some cases can even survive a visit to the real countries which they are supposed to represent.

> GEORGE ORWELL, 'Riding Down from Bangor', 1946

Before a child of our time finds his way clear to opening a book, his eyes have been exposed to such a blizzard of changing, colourful, conflicting letters that his chances of penetrating the archaic stillness of the book are slight.

> WALTER BENJAMIN, *One-Way Street*, 1925–6

The Classics! it is the Classics, and not the Goths nor Monks, that Desolate Europe with Wars.

> BLAKE, 'On Homer's Poetry and On Virgil', *c.*1820

Some books seem to have been written, not to teach us anything, but to let us know that the author has known something.

GOETHE, *Maxims and Reflections*, early 19th century

The better the book the more room for the reader.

HOLBROOK JACKSON, *Maxims of Books and Reading*, 1934

There is no surer way to make oneself a name than by writing about things which have a semblance of importance but which a reasonable man is not likely to take the time to investigate for himself.

LICHTENBERG, *Aphorisms*, 1764–99

The number of lunatic books is as finite as the number of lunatics.

LEWIS CARROLL

Manuscript: something submitted in haste and returned at leisure.

OLIVER HERFORD (1863–1935)

Literature is the art of writing something that will be read twice; journalism what will be grasped at once.

CYRIL CONNOLLY, *Enemies of Promise*, 1938

Literature is news that *stays* news.

EZRA POUND, *ABC of Reading*, 1934

Journalism largely consists in saying 'Lord Jones Dead' to people who never knew Lord Jones was alive.

G. K. CHESTERTON, *The Wisdom of Father Brown*, 1914

There is much to be said in favour of modern journalism. By giving us the opinions of the uneducated, it keeps us in touch with the ignorance of the community.

OSCAR WILDE, 'The Critic as Artist', 1891

If an editor can only make people angry enough, they will write half his newspaper for him for nothing.

G. K. CHESTERTON, *Heretics*, 1905

Once a newspaper touches a story, the facts are lost forever, even to the protagonists.

NORMAN MAILER, *The Presidential Papers*, 1964

The newspaper is the natural enemy of the book, as the whore is of the decent woman.

GONCOURT BROTHERS, *Journal*, 1858

If there's one major cause for the spread of mass illiteracy, it's the fact that everybody can read and write.

PETER DE VRIES, *The Tents of Wickedness*, 1959

One of the conditions for reading what is good is that we must not read what is bad; for life is short and time and energy are limited.

SCHOPENHAUER, 'On Reading and Books', *Parerga and Paralipomena*, 1851

There are no bad books, any more than there are ugly women.

ANATOLE FRANCE

The art of *not* reading is extremely important. It consists in our not taking up whatever happens to be occupying the larger public at the time.

SCHOPENHAUER, 'On Reading and Books', *Parerga and Paralipomena*, 1851

Read at whim! Read at whim!

RANDALL JARRELL, *A Sad Heart at the Supermarket*, 1965

The pedantic decisions and definable readjustments of man may be found in scrolls and statute books and scriptures: but men's basic assumptions and everlasting energies are to be found in penny dreadfuls and halfpenny novelettes.

G. K. CHESTERTON, *Heretics*, 1905

It is no more necessary that a man should remember the different dinners and suppers which have made him healthy, than the different books which have made him wise. Let us see the result of good food in a strong body, and the result of great reading in a full and powerful mind.

SYDNEY SMITH, *Elementary Sketches of Moral Philosophy*, 1806

To expect a man to retain everything that he has ever read is like expecting him to carry about in his body everything that he has ever eaten.

SCHOPENHAUER, 'On Reading and Books', *Parerga and Paralipomena*, 1851

Superficial the reading of grown men in some sort must ever be; it is only once in a lifetime that we can know the passionate reading of youth.

WALTER BAGEHOT, *Literary Studies*, 1879

It is one of the oddest things in the world that you can read a page or more and think of something utterly different.

CHRISTIAN MORGENSTERN, *Aphorisms*, c.1900

There is hardly any grief that an hour's reading will not dissipate.

MONTESQUIEU, *Mes pensées*, c.1722–55

Books cannot always please, however good;
Minds are not ever craving for their food.

GEORGE CRABBE, *The Borough*, 1810

To buy books would be a good thing if we could also buy the time to read them; as it is, the mere act of purchasing them is often mistaken for the assimilation and mastering of their contents.

SCHOPENHAUER, 'On Reading and Books', *Parerga and Paralipomena*, 1851

No furniture so charming as books.

SYDNEY SMITH in Lady Holland, *Memoir*, 1855

Thank God, Achilles and Don Quixote are well enough known so that we can dispense with reading Homer and Cervantes.

JULES RENARD, *Journal*, 1895

Where do I find all the time for not reading so many books?

KARL KRAUS, *Aphorisms and More Aphorisms*, 1909

Sometimes I read a book with pleasure, and detest the author.

SWIFT, *Thoughts on Various Subjects*, 1711

When we see a natural style we are quite amazed and delighted, because we expected to see an author and find a man.

PASCAL, *Pensées*, 1670

Nothing goes by luck in composition. It allows of no tricks. The best you can write will be the best you are. Every sentence is the result of a long probation. The author's character is read from title-page to end. Of this he never corrects the proofs.

THOREAU, *Journal*, 1841

When some passion or effect is described in a natural style, we find within ourselves the truth of what we hear, without knowing it was there.

PASCAL, *Pensées*, 1670

An excellent precept for writers: have a clear idea of all the phrases and expressions you need, and you will find them.

XIMÉNÈS DOUDAN, *Pensées et fragments*, 1880

Those who write as they speak, even though they speak well, write badly.

COMTE DE BUFFON, *Discours sur le style*, 1753

Neither Christ nor Buddha nor Socrates wrote a book, for to do that is to exchange life for a logical process.

W. B. YEATS, 'Estrangement', *Autobiography*, 1936

Everything one *records* contains a grain of hope, no matter how deeply it may come from despair.

ELIAS CANETTI, *The Human Province*, 1978

The deepest concerns of the heart and the mind should be discussed only by word of mouth.

GOETHE, *Maxims and Reflections*, early 19th century

Artists & Authors

●

The great artists are those who impose their personal vision upon humanity.

MAUPASSANT, Preface to *Pierre et Jean*, 1887

What there was in the world to be done in Shakespearean has largely been done by Shakespeare.

LICHTENBERG, *Aphorisms*, 1764–99

An artist is a person who has invented an artist.

HAROLD ROSENBERG, *Discovering the Present*, 1973

When a true genius appears in the world, you may know him by this sign, that the dunces are all in confederacy against him.

SWIFT, *Thoughts on Various Subjects*, 1711

I am afraid humility to genius is as an extinguisher to a candle.

WILLIAM SHENSTONE, *Essays on Men and Manners*, 1764

Art is constitutive – the artist determines beauty. He does not take it over.

GOETHE, *Notes for Publications on Art*, 1798

The painter should not paint what he sees, but what will be seen.

VALÉRY, *Mauvaises pensées et autres*, 1942

The writer cannot afford to question his own essential nature.

RANDALL JARRELL, *A Sad Heart at the Supermarket*, 1965

To do easily what is difficult for others is the mark of talent. To do what is impossible for talent is the mark of genius.

AMIEL, *Journal*, 1856

Only a born artist can endure the labour of becoming one.
>COMTESSE DIANE, *Maximes de la vie*, 1908

At what expense any valuable work is performed! At the expense of a life! If you do one thing well, what else are you good for in the meanwhile?
>THOREAU, *Journal*, 1852

True genius walks along a line, and, perhaps, our greatest pleasure is in seeing it so often near falling, without being ever actually down.
>OLIVER GOLDSMITH, 'The Characteristics of Greatness', *The Bee*, 1759

What moves men of genius, or rather, what inspires their work, is not new ideas, but their obsession with the idea that what has already been said is still not enough.
>DELACROIX, *Journal*, 1824

Every writer creates his own precursors.
>JORGE LUIS BORGES, *Other Inquisitions*, 1952

Immature poets imitate; mature poets steal.
>T. S. ELIOT, 'Philip Massinger', 1920

The mind conceives with pain, but brings forth with joy.
>JOUBERT, *Pensées*, 1842

It is as easy to dream a book as it is hard to write one.
>BALZAC, *Le Cabinet des antiques*, 1836

Whoever is able to write a book and does not, it is as if he has lost a child.
>NACHMAN OF BRATSLAV (*c.*1800)

The book I am writing will not be good unless my first thought, my involuntary thought on awakening, is for it.
>ANDRÉ GIDE, *Pretexts*, 1903

Persons devoted to mere literature commonly become devoted to mere idleness.

WALTER BAGEHOT, *Literary Studies*, 1879

The artistic temperament is a disease that afflicts amateurs.

G. K. CHESTERTON, *Heretics*, 1905

To commence author is to claim praise, and no man can justly aspire to honour, but at the hazard of disgrace.

DR JOHNSON, *The Rambler*, 1750–2

It is taken for granted that, on every publication, there is at least a seeming violation of modesty; a presumption, on the writer's side, that he is able to entertain or instruct the world; which implies a supposition that he can communicate, what they cannot draw from their own reflections.

WILLIAM SHENSTONE, *Essays on Men and Manners*, 1764

There is nothing more dreadful to an author than neglect, compared with which, reproach, hatred and opposition are names of happiness.

DR JOHNSON, *The Rambler*, 1750–2

Only a person with a Best Seller mind can write Best Sellers.

ALDOUS HUXLEY

The profession of letters is, after all, the only one in which one can make no money without being ridiculous.

JULES RENARD, *Journal*, 1906

There is no amount of praise which a man and an author cannot bear with equanimity. Some authors can even stand flattery.

MAURICE BARING, *Dead Letters*, 1910

Every author, however modest, keeps a most outrageous vanity chained like a madman in the padded cell of his breast.

LOGAN PEARSALL SMITH, *Afterthoughts*, 1931

No writer goes the whole length with any other. Each of them shivers at the lapses of the rest, and is blind to his own. And the youngest shiver the most. And the greatest writers have them.

IVY COMPTON-BURNETT, Zillah in *A God and his Gifts*, 1963

I cannot think that Real Poets have any competition. None are greatest in the Kingdom of Heaven; it is so in Poetry.

BLAKE, Annotations to Wordsworth's *Poems*, 1826

The Poison of the Honey Bee
Is the Artist's Jealousy.

BLAKE, *Auguries of Innocence*, *c.*1803

Nothing more abnormal than the poet who approximates to the normal man: Hugo or Goethe. This is the madman at large. The madman who does not appear mad.

JEAN COCTEAU, *Opium*, 1930

The poet dreams being awake. He is not possessed by his subject but has dominion over it.

CHARLES LAMB, 'Sanity of True Genius', *Essays of Elia*, 1820–3

A poet looks at the world as a man looks at a woman.

WALLACE STEVENS, 'Adagia', *Opus Posthumous*, 1957

Every poem is in a sense a kiss bestowed upon the world, but mere kisses do not produce children.

GOETHE, conversation with Ortlepp, 1825

The poet is a man who lives at last by watching his moods. An old poet comes at last to watch his moods as narrowly as a cat does a mouse.

THOREAU, *Journal*, 1851

A writer who lives long enough becomes an academic subject and almost qualified to teach it himself.

HAROLD ROSENBERG, *Discovering the Present*, 1973

An author's works are his esoteric biography.
> SIR ARTHUR HELPS, *Thoughts in the Cloister and the Crowd*, 1835

The artist is present in every page of every book from which he sought so assiduously to eliminate himself.
> HENRY JAMES

The artist must work with indifferency – too great interest vitiates his work.
> THOREAU, *Journal*, 1842

No tears in the writer, no tears in the reader.
> ROBERT FROST, Preface to *Collected Poems*, 1939

Literature: proclaiming in front of everyone what one is careful to conceal from one's immediate circle.
> JEAN ROSTAND, *Journal d'un caractère*, 1931

The crying of a nice child is ugly: so in bad verses you may recognize that the author is a nice man.
> CHEKHOV, *Notebooks*, 1892–1904

The Weak Man may be Virtuous Enough, but will Never be an Artist.
> BLAKE, Annotations to Reynolds's *Discourses*, *c.*1808

The writer who cannot sometimes throw away a thought about which another man would have written dissertations, without worrying whether or not the reader will find it, will never become a great writer.
> LICHTENBERG, *Aphorisms*, 1764–99

It perpetually happens that one writer tells less truth than another, merely because he tells more truths.
> LORD MACAULAY, 'History', 1828

There is no method except to be very intelligent.
> T. S. ELIOT, 'The Perfect Critic', *The Sacred Wood*, 1920

The perfect man has no method; or rather the best of methods, which is the method of no-method.

> SHIH-T'AO (17th century), cit. Lin Yutang, *The Chinese Theory of Art*

I never practise; I always play.

> WANDA LANDOWSKA, cit. Nat Shapiro, *An Encyclopaedia of Quotations about Music*

It is the role of the poet to look at what is happening in the world and to know that quite other things are happening.

> V. S. PRITCHETT, *The Myth Makers*, 1979

There was far more imagination in the head of Archimedes than in that of Homer.

> VOLTAIRE, *Philosophical Dictionary*, 1764

In order to compose, all you need to do is to remember a tune that no one else has thought of.

> attrib. ROBERT SCHUMANN

Only God can create.

> STRAVINSKY, *Memories and Commentaries* (with Robert Craft), 1959

The Arts

❀

Art happens – no hovel is safe from it, no prince may depend upon it, the vastest intelligence cannot bring it about.

J. M. WHISTLER, 'Ten O'Clock', 1885

Poetry heals the wounds inflicted by reason.

NOVALIS, *Detached Thoughts*, late 18th century

The creative mind plays with the objects it loves.

JUNG, *Psychological Types*, 1921

In a work of art it is the accident which *charms*, not the intention; *that* we only like and admire.

THOMAS HARDY in F. E. Hardy, *The Early Life of Thomas Hardy*, 1928

Art is in love with luck, and luck with art.

AGATHON (5th century BC) quoted by Aristotle, *Nicomachean Ethics*

Real books should be the offspring not of daylight and casual talk but of darkness and silence.

MARCEL PROUST, *Remembrance of Things Past* (*Time Regained*, 1927)

For art to exist, for any sort of aesthetic activity or perception to exist, a certain physiological precondition is indispensable: intoxication.

NIETZSCHE, *Twilight of the Idols*, 1889

The important thing is not what the author, or any artist, had in mind to begin with but at what point he decided to stop.

D. W. HARDING, *Experience into Words*, 1963

How many good books suffer neglect through the inefficiency of their beginnings!

EDGAR ALAN POE, *Marginalia*, 1844–9

The most beautiful things are those that madness prompts and reason writes.

ANDRÉ GIDE, *Journal*, 1894

The Genius of Poetry must work out its own salvation in a man: it cannot be matured by law and precept, but by watchfulness in itself. That which is creative must create itself.

KEATS, letter, 1818

There are two kinds of obscurity; one arises from a lack of feelings and thoughts, which have been replaced by words; the other from an abundance of feelings and thoughts, and the inadequacy of words to express them.

ALEXANDER PUSHKIN in 'Notes', *Pushkin on Literature*, trans. and ed. Tatiana Wolff

One of the marks of a great poet is that he creates his own family of words and teaches them to live together in harmony and to help one another.

GERALD BRENAN, *Thoughts in a Dry Season*, 1978

I know nothing in the world but poetry that is not acquired by application and care.

LORD CHESTERFIELD, *Letters*, 1750

Poetry has no golden mean; mediocrity is here of another metal.

LANDOR

Instead of whining complaints concerning the imagined cruelty of their mistresses, if poets would address the same to their Muse, they would act more agreeably to nature and to truth.

WILLIAM SHENSTONE, *Essays on Men and Manners*, 1764

A true poet does not bother to be poetical. Nor does a nursery gardener scent his roses.

JEAN COCTEAU, *Professional Secrets*, 1922

In a man's work there is a gravity which he himself does not possess.
DELACROIX, *Journal*, 1852

You may know a new utterance by the element of danger in it.
D. H. LAWRENCE, review of 'A Second Contemporary Verse Anthology', 1923

In every work of genius we recognize our own rejected thoughts; they come back to us with a certain alienated majesty.
EMERSON, 'Self-Reliance', *Essays*, 1841

True revolutions in art restore more than they destroy.
LOUISE BOGAN, 'Reading Contemporary Poetry', 1953

Abandoning rhyme and fixed rules in favour of other intuitive rules brings us back to fixed rules and to rhyme with renewed respect.
JEAN COCTEAU, *Professional Secrets*, 1922

Every work of art adheres to some system of morality. But if it be really a work of art, it must contain the essential criticism of the morality to which it adheres.
D. H. LAWRENCE, 'Study of Thomas Hardy', *Phoenix*, 1936

A work in which there are theories is like an object which still has its price-tag on it.
MARCEL PROUST, *Remembrance of Things Past* (*Time Regained*, 1927)

Realism is a corruption of reality.
WALLACE STEVENS, 'Adagia , *Opus Posthumous*, 1957

It takes a sound realist to make a convincing symbolist.
D. J. ENRIGHT, *The Apothecary's Shop*, 1957

The copy of a beautiful thing is always an ugly thing. It is an act of cowardice in admiration of an act of energy.
RÉMY DE GOURMONT, *The Problem of Style*, 1902

There is no neutral naturalism. The artist, no less than the writer, needs a vocabulary before he can embark on a 'copy' of reality.

E. H. GOMBRICH, *Art and Illusion*, 1960

Photography is unreal; it alters value and perspective. Its cowlike eye stupidly registers everything that our eye first has to correct and distribute according to the needs of the case.

JEAN COCTEAU, *Professional Secrets*, 1922

The cinema has thawed out people's brains.

JEAN COCTEAU, *Opium*, 1930

When I hear music, I flutter, and am the scene of life, as a fleet of merchantmen when the wind rises.

THOREAU, *Journal*, 1841

Music is a thing which delighteth all ages, and beseemeth all states; a thing as seasonable in grief as in joy.

RICHARD HOOKER, *The Laws of Ecclesiastical Polity*, 1594

The things that act through the ears are said to make a noise, discord or harmony, and this last has caused men to lose their heads to such a degree that they have believed God himself is delighted with it.

SPINOZA, *Ethics*, 1677

Preposterous ass! that never read so far
To know the cause why music was ordained!

SHAKESPEARE, *The Taming of the Shrew*, c.1593

Music – makes a people's disposition more gentle; e.g. 'The Marseillaise'.

FLAUBERT, *Dictionary of Received Ideas*, mid 19th century

Classical music is the kind we keep thinking will turn into a tune.

KIN HUBBARD, *Abe Martin's Sayings*, 1915

In music the dignity of art seems to find supreme expression. There is no subject-matter to be discounted.

GOETHE, *Maxims and Reflections*, early 19th century

It is the honourable characteristic of poetry that its materials are to be found in every subject which can interest the human mind.

WORDSWORTH, 'Advertisement to Lyrical Ballads', 1798

There is no sixth commandment in art. The poet is entitled to lay his hands on whatever material he finds necessary for his work.

HEINE, *Letters on the French Stage*, 1837

It is a feature of the artistic imagination that it should be able to reconstitute everything on the basis of very limited data. When Delacroix wanted to paint a tiger, he used his cat as a model.

HENRY DE MONTHERLANT, 'The Goddess Cypris', 1944

Of all lies, art is the least untrue.

FLAUBERT, letter, 1846

The main difference between living people and fictitious characters is that the writer takes great pains to give the characters coherence and inner unity, whereas the living people may go to extremes of incoherence because their physical existence holds them together.

HUGO VON HOFMANNSTHAL, *The Book of Friends*, 1922

Truth must necessarily be stranger than fiction; for fiction is the creation of the human mind and therefore congenial to it.

G. K. CHESTERTON, *The Club of Queer Trades*, 1905

Fiction, imaginative work that is, is not dropped like a pebble upon the ground, as science may be; fiction is like a spider's web, attached ever so lightly perhaps, but still attached to life at all four corners.

VIRGINIA WOOLF, *A Room of One's Own*, 1929

Everything one invents is true, you can be sure of that. Beyond a doubt my poor Bovary is suffering and weeping in twenty French villages at this very moment.

FLAUBERT, letter, 1853

Literature is a luxury; fiction is a necessity.

G. K. CHESTERTON, *The Defendant*, 1901

We may, without offending any laws of good taste, require of an architect, as we do of a novelist, that he should be not only correct, but entertaining.

RUSKIN, *The Stones of Venice*, 1851–3

If only, in aesthetics, we could forget for a while about the beautiful and get down instead to the dainty and the dumpy.

J. L. AUSTIN, 'A Plea for Excuses', *Philosophical Papers*, 1961

Farce is nearer tragedy in its essence than comedy is.

COLERIDGE, *Table Talk*, 1833

In the theatre the audience want to be surprised – but by things that they expect.

TRISTAN BERNARD (1866–1947), *Contes, Repliques et Bon Mots*

The People's Theatre, what nonsense! Call it the Aristocrats' Theatre and the people will come.

JULES RENARD, *Journal*, 1903

A nation which lives a pastoral and innocent life never decorates the shepherd's staff or the plough-handle; but races who live by depredation and slaughter nearly always bestow exquisite ornaments on the quiver, the helmet, and the spear.

RUSKIN, *The Two Paths*, 1859

Pride, victory over weight and gravity, the will to power, seek to render themselves visible in a building; architecture is a kind of rhetoric of power.

NIETZSCHE, *Twilight of the Idols*, 1889

No architecture is so haughty as that which is simple.

RUSKIN, *The Stones of Venice*, 1851–3

The function of literature, through all its mutations, has been to make us aware of the particularity of selves, and the high authority of the self in its quarrel with its society and its culture. Literature is in that sense subversive.

LIONEL TRILLING, *Beyond Culture*, 1966

Have you ever remarked how all *authority* is stupid concerning Art?
Our wonderful governments (kings or republics) imagine that they
have only to order work to be done, and it will be forthcoming.
They set up prizes, encouragements, academies, and they forget
only one thing, one little thing, without which nothing can live: the
atmosphere.

FLAUBERT, letter, 1853

If Galileo had said in verse that the world moved, the Inquisition
might have let him alone.

THOMAS HARDY in F. E. Hardy, *The Later Years of Thomas
Hardy*, 1930

'Burn the museums!' This old revolutionary slogan can now be
realized by the museums themselves. A museum set on fire would
today attract the usual crowd that visits its exhibitions. 'Burn the
museums,' it turns out, calls not for the end of art but for the
expansion of art institutions to include the medium of combustion.

HAROLD ROSENBERG, *Discovering the Present*, 1973

The earliest poets and authors made fools wise. Modern authors try
to make wise men fools.

JOUBERT, *Pensées*, 1842

Literature has soared up like an eagle to the skies. And has fallen
down. Now it is quite clear that literature is not the 'sought-after
invisible city'.

V. V. ROZANOV, *Solitaria*, 1912

Less disappointing than life, great works of art do not begin by
giving us all their best.

MARCEL PROUST, *Remembrance of Things Past* (*Within a Budding
Grove*, 1919)

Literature is a fragment of fragments. How small a part of what has
happened and been spoken has been written; and of those things that
have been written very few have been preserved.
And yet, with all the fragmentary nature of literature, we find

things repeated a thousand times; which shows how limited is man's mind and his destiny.

GOETHE, *Maxims and Reflections*, early 19th century

Art is man's nature.

EDMUND BURKE, *An Appeal from the New to the Old Whigs*, 1791

Criticism, Judgement, Taste

❀

Criticism talks a good deal of nonsense, but even its nonsense is a useful force. It keeps the question of art before the world, insists upon its importance, and makes it always in order.
HENRY JAMES, 'On Some Pictures Lately Exhibited', 1875

Think before you speak is criticism's motto; speak before you think creation's.
E. M. FORSTER, *Two Cheers for Democracy*, 1951

A man's mind is hidden in his writings; criticism brings it to light.
SOLOMON IBN GABIROL, *The Choice of Pearls*, c.1050

No degree of dullness can safeguard a work against the determination of critics to find it fascinating.
HAROLD ROSENBERG, *Discovering the Present*, 1973

Sometimes an admirer spends more talent extolling a work than the author did in creating it.
JEAN ROSTAND, *De la vanité*, 1925

The work of criticism is rooted in the unconscious of the critic just as the poem is rooted in the unconscious of the poet.
RANDALL JARRELL, *A Sad Heart at the Supermarket*, 1965

A critic knows more than the author he criticizes, or just as much, or at least somewhat less.
CARDINAL MANNING, *Pastime Papers*, 1892

Criticism is powerless to reach art. Art proceeds itself in a region quite beyond the reach of other expression save itself.
JOHN JAY CHAPMAN, *Memories and Milestones*, 1915

The critic who over the close texture of a finished work shall pretend to trace a geography of items will mark some frontiers as artificial, I fear, as any that have been known to history.

HENRY JAMES, 'The Art of Fiction', 1884

Rules may obviate faults, but can never confer beauties.

DR JOHNSON, *The Idler*, 1758

Genuine works of art carry their own aesthetic theory implicit within them and suggest the standards according to which they are to be judged.

GOETHE, letter, 1808

Artistic enthusiasm is alien to the critic. In his hand the art-work is the shining sword in the battle of minds.

WALTER BENJAMIN, *One-Way Street*, 1925-6

Tedious polemic writers are more severe to their readers than those they contend with.

SAMUEL BUTLER (I), *Prose Observations*, 1660-80

Intolerance respecting other people's religion is toleration itself in comparison with intolerance respecting other people's art.

WALLACE STEVENS, 'Adagia', *Opus Posthumous*, 1957

Real culture lives by sympathies and admirations, not by dislikes and disdains; under all misleading wrappings it pounces unerringly upon the human core.

WILLIAM JAMES, *Memories and Studies*, 1911

A condescending disdainful tone towards little people, only because they are little, does no credit to the human heart. In literature low ranks are as indispensable as in the army – thus speaks the head, and the heart must say it even more emphatically.

CHEKHOV, letter, 1887

In some cases taking up the trade of critic is only an embittered form of renunciation.

ALBERT GUINON, *c*.1900

A critic enjoys a tremendous advantage if he has done nothing himself; but it is one that should not be abused.

ANTOINE RIVAROL, *Notes, pensées et maximes*, late 18th century

In literature young men usually begin their careers by being judges, and as wisdom and old experience arrive they reach the dignity of standing as culprits at the bar before new young bloods who have in their turn sprung up in the judgment-seat.

THOMAS HARDY in F. E. Hardy, *The Early Life of Thomas Hardy*, 1928

Criticism is necessary, I suppose; I know. Yet criticism to the poet is no necessity, but a luxury he can ill afford.

RANDALL JARRELL, *A Sad Heart at the Supermarket*, 1965

There is a certain race of men that either imagine it their duty, or make it their amusement, to hinder the reception of every work of learning or genius, who stand as sentinels in the avenues of fame, and value themselves upon giving Ignorance and Envy the first notice of a prey.

DR JOHNSON, *The Rambler*, 1750–2

Insects sting, not from malice, but because they want to live. It is the same with critics – they desire our blood, not our pain.

NIETZSCHE, *Miscellaneous Maxims and Reflections*, 1880

As small tyrants are always found to be the most severe, so are all little critics the most unmerciful, and never give quarter for the least mistake.

SAMUEL BUTLER (1), *Prose Observations*, 1660–80

True judgment in Poetry takes a view of the whole together; 'tis a sign that malice is hard driven, when 'tis forced to lay hold on a word or syllable.

DRYDEN, Preface to *Sylvae*, 1685

A critic is a creature without a spiritual home, and it is his point of honour never to seek one.

DESMOND MacCARTHY, *Criticism*, 1932

Prolonged, indiscriminate reviewing of books involves constantly *inventing* reactions towards books about which one has no spontaneous feelings whatever.

GEORGE ORWELL, 'Confessions of a Book Reviewer', 1946

Even reviewers read a preface.

PHILIP GUEDALLA, *The Missing Muse*, 1929

I suspect that the only books that influence us are those for which we are ready, and which have gone a little further down our particular path than we have yet gone ourselves.

E. M. FORSTER, *Two Cheers for Democracy*, 1951

Readers, real readers, are almost as wild a species as writers; most critics are so domesticated as to seem institutions.

RANDALL JARRELL, *Poetry and the Age*, 1953

Every man ought to be a judge of pictures, and every man is so who has not been connoisseured out of his senses.

BLAKE, letter, 1806

The number of those who undergo the fatigue of judging for themselves is very small indeed.

SHERIDAN, *The Critic*, 1781

While watching the ups and downs of reputations, I have often found myself exclaiming, 'Ah! the rats are leaving the floating ship.'

DESMOND MacCARTHY, *Criticism*, 1932

The multitude commend writers, as they do fencers, or wrestlers; who if they come in robustiously, and put for it, with a deal of violence, are received for the braver fellows.

BEN JONSON, *Timber; or Discoveries*, 1640

People do not deserve to have good writing, they are so pleased with bad.

EMERSON, *Journals*, 1841

Next to sound judgment, diamonds and pearls are the rarest things in the world.

> LA BRUYÈRE, 'Of Opinions', *Characters*, 1688

We easily enough confess to others an advantage of courage, strength, experience, activity and beauty; but an advantage in judgment we yield to none.

> MONTAIGNE, 'Of presumption', *Essays*, 1580–8

Criticism is not just a question of taste, but of whose taste.

> JAMES GRAND, *c*.1980

Good taste is better than bad taste, but bad taste is better than no taste at all.

> ARNOLD BENNETT

The only impeccable writers are those that never wrote.

> HAZLITT, *Table Talk*, 1821–2

Taste ripens at the expense of happiness.

> JULES RENARD, *Journal*, 1908

A monk need not abstain from wine, he need only abstain from vulgarity; a red petticoat need not understand literature, she need only understand what is artistically interesting.

> CHANG CH'AO, *Sweet Dream Shadows*, mid 17th century

Good taste is much more a matter of discrimination than of exclusion, and when good taste feels compelled to exclude, it is with regret, not with pleasure.

> W. H. AUDEN, *The Dyer's Hand*, 1963

Look twice, if you want a just conception; look once, if what you want is a sense of beauty.

> AMIEL, *Journal*, 1852

To the aristocratic pleasure of displeasing other people, the conscious offender against good taste can add the still more aristocratic pleasure of displeasing himself.

> ALDOUS HUXLEY, *Music at Night*, 1931

What I detest most of all in the arts, what sets me on edge, is the *ingenious*, the clever. That is not at all the same as bad taste, which is a good quality gone astray.

FLAUBERT, letter, 1853

Style is nothing, but nothing is without its style.

ANTOINE RIVAROL, *Notes, pensées et maximes*, late 18th century

It is easy to be heavy; hard to be light.

G. K. CHESTERTON, *Orthodoxy*, 1909

Some men have a peculiar taste for bad words. They will pick you out of a thousand the still-born words, the falsettos, the wing-clipped and lame words, as if only the false notes caught their ears.

THOREAU, *Journal*, 1858

The greatest grossness sometimes accompanies the greatest refinement, as a natural relief.

HAZLITT, 'On the Knowledge of Character', 1822

When the mirror meets with an ugly woman, when a rare ink-stone finds a vulgar owner, and when a good sword is in the hands of a common general, there is utterly nothing to be done about it.

CHANG CH'AO, *Sweet Dream Shadows*, mid 17th century

There is no use in reproving vulgarity, for it never changes.

GOETHE, *Maxims and Reflections*, early 19th century

Sites disappear; others are created. That nasty little railway station, devoid of taste and style, becomes an element of beauty in the landscape which at first it made ugly.

RÉMY DE GOURMONT, *Promenades philosophiques*, 1905

Nothing is so conditional, let us say *circumscribed*, as our feeling for the beautiful. Anyone who tried to divorce it from man's pleasure in himself would find the ground give way beneath him. The 'beautiful in itself' is not even a concept, merely a phrase.

NIETZSCHE, *Twilight of the Idols*, 1889

Exuberance is beauty.
> BLAKE, *The Marriage of Heaven and Hell*, 1790–3

Reckoned physiologically, everything ugly weakens and afflicts man. It recalls decay, danger, impotence; he actually suffers a loss of energy in its presence.
> NIETZSCHE, *Twilight of the Idols*, 1889

There is no excellent beauty that hath not some strangeness in the proportion.
> SIR FRANCIS BACON, 'Of Beauty', *Essays*, 1597–1625

An imperial crown cannot be one continued diamond; the gems must be held together by some less valuable matter.
> DR JOHNSON, 'Dryden', *Lives of the Poets*, 1779–81

Continuous eloquence is tedious.
> PASCAL, *Pensées*, 1670

Even imperfection itself may have its ideal or perfect state.
> THOMAS DE QUINCEY, 'On Murder Considered as one of the Fine Arts', 1827

In everything, no matter what it may be, uniformity is undesirable. Leaving something incomplete makes it interesting, and gives one the feeling that there is room for growth.
> YOSHIDA KENKO, *Essays in Idleness*, c.1340

The beautiful souls are they that are universal, open, and ready for all things.
> MONTAIGNE, 'Of presumption', *Essays*, 1580–8

Great & Small

❀

Who knows whether the best of men be known? or whether there be not more remarkable persons forgot, than any that stand remembered in the known account of time?

SIR THOMAS BROWNE, Urn Burial, 1658

To achieve great things we must live as though we were never going to die.

VAUVENARGUES, Reflections and Maxims, 1746

Greatness is usually the result of a natural equilibrium among opposite qualities.

DIDEROT, Rameau's Nephew, 1761

The best people usually owe their excellence to a combination of qualities which might have been supposed incompatible.

BERTRAND RUSSELL, Sceptical Essays, 1928

I have known *strong* minds, with imposing, undoubting, Cobbett-like manners; but I have never met a *great* mind of this sort. The truth is, a great mind must be androgynous.

COLERIDGE, Table Talk, 1832

There are some minds which, although of a superior order, are underrated through want of a recognized standard by which to measure them. They are like a precious metal for which there is no test.

JOUBERT, Pensées, 1842

The highest preeminence in any one study commonly arises from the concentration of the attention and the faculties on that one study. He who expects from a great name in politics, in philosophy, in art, equal greatness in other things, is little versed in human nature.

HAZLITT, Characteristics, 1823

Great discoverers are not necessarily great men. Who changed the
world more than Columbus? What was he? An adventurer. He had
character, it is true, but he was not a great man.

FREUD, cit. Ernest Jones, *Life and Work of Sigmund Freud*, 1953–7

It is not the clear-sighted who rule the world. Great achievements
are accomplished in a blessed, warm mental fog.

JOSEPH CONRAD, *Victory*, 1915

Just as the meanest and most vicious deeds require spirit and talent,
so even the greatest deeds require a certain insensitiveness which on
other occasions is called stupidity.

LICHTENBERG, *Aphorisms*, 1764–99

Mountains appear more lofty, the nearer they are approached, but
great men resemble them not in this particular.

LADY BLESSINGTON, 'Night Thought Book', 1834

In great affairs men show themselves as they wish to be seen, in small
things they show themselves as they are.

CHAMFORT, *Maximes et pensées*, 1805

Greatness of soul is never apparent, for it conceals itself; a little
originality is usually all that shows. Greatness of soul is more frequent than one would suppose.

STENDHAL, *Love*, 1822

Noble patterns must be fetched here and there from single persons,
rather than whole nations, and from all nations, rather than any
one.

SIR THOMAS BROWNE, *Christian Morals*, mid 17th century

If you're strong enough, there *are* no precedents.

SCOTT FITZGERALD, *The Crack-Up*, 1945

It is as easy for the strong man to be strong, as it is for the weak to be
weak.

EMERSON, 'Self-Reliance', *Essays*, First Series, 1841

It sometimes happens that he who would not hurt a fly will hurt a nation.

SIR HENRY TAYLOR, *The Statesman*, 1836

He who is not afraid to suffer is strong. He who is not afraid to die is stronger. Strongest of all is he who is not afraid to cause suffering and death.

COMTESSE DIANE, *Maximes de la vie*, 1908

The effects of weakness are inconceivable, and more prodigious than those of the most violent passions.

CARDINAL DE RETZ, *Memoirs*, 1673–6

You cannot be a hero without being a coward.

BERNARD SHAW, Preface to *John Bull's Other Island*, 1907

The heroic actions are performed by such as are oppressed by the meanness of their lives. As in thickest darkness the stars shine brightest.

THOREAU, *Journal*, 1842

It is more difficult to be an honourable man for a week than to be a hero for fifteen minutes.

JULES RENARD, *Journal*, 1907

It is in private life that we find the great characters. They are too great to get into the public world.

G. K. CHESTERTON, *Charles Dickens*, 1906

Society is a more level surface than we imagine. Wise men or absolute fools are hard to be met with, as there are few giants or dwarfs.

HAZLITT, *Characteristics*, 1823

Great talents and great virtues – if you should have them – will procure you the respect and admiration of mankind, but it is the lesser talents, the *leniores virtutes*, which must procure you their love and affection.

LORD CHESTERFIELD, *Letters*, 1749

Mediocrity is a hand-rail.

MONTESQUIEU, *Mes pensées*, *c.*1722–55

Great success is commoner than great abilities.

VAUVENARGUES, *Reflections and Maxims*, 1746

Great necessity elevates man, petty necessity casts him down.

GOETHE, conversation with Riemer, 1803

Men are seldom more commonplace than on supreme occasions.

SAMUEL BUTLER (II), *Notebooks*, 1912

Commonplace people have an answer for everything and nothing ever surprises them.

DELACROIX, *Journal*, 1852

The hand of one person may express more than the face of another.

NATHANIEL HAWTHORNE, *American Notebooks*, 1841–52

Unless one is a genius, it is best to aim at being intelligible.

ANTHONY HOPE, *The Dolly Dialogues*, 1894

The veriest nobodies in the world are the greatest busybodies.

BENJAMIN WHICHCOTE, *Moral and Religious Aphorisms*, 1703

It takes a nonentity to think of everything.

BALZAC, *Pierre Grassou*, 1839

Cardinal de Retz very sagaciously marked out Cardinal Chigi for a little mind, from the moment he told him he had wrote three years with the same pen, and that it was an excellent good one still.

LORD CHESTERFIELD, *Letters*, 1749

Great men too make mistakes, and many among them do it so often that one is almost tempted to call them little men.

LICHTENBERG, *Aphorisms*, 1764–99

Eminence without merit earns deference without esteem.

CHAMFORT, *Maximes et pensées*, 1805

Insignificant people are a necessary relief in society. Such characters are extremely agreeable, and even favourites, if they appear satisfied with the part they have to perform.

HAZLITT, *Characteristics*, 1823

Some people are like popular songs that you only sing for a short time.

LA ROCHEFOUCAULD, *Maxims*, 1665

No man is a hero to his valet. But that is not because the hero is no hero, but because the valet is a valet.

HEGEL

When I meet those remarkable people whose company is coveted, I often wish they would show off a little more.

DESMOND MacCARTHY, *Experience*, 1935

We should console ourselves for the lack of great talents the same way as we do for the lack of high office; our good nature would unfit us for either of them.

VAUVENARGUES, *Reflections and Maxims*, 1746

A small man's salvation will always be a great salvation and the greatest of all facts *for him*.

WILLIAM JAMES, *The Varieties of Religious Experience*, 1902

He who fails to become a giant need not remain content with being a dwarf.

ERNEST BRAMAH, *Kai Lung Unrolls his Mat*, 1928

In reading the life of any great man, you will always, in the course of his history, chance upon some obscure individual, who, on some particu'ar occasion, was greater than him whose life you are reading.

CHARLES CALEB COLTON, *Lacon*, 1825

Those who despise mankind believe themselves great men.
VAUVENARGUES, *Reflections and Maxims*, 1746

Diogenes I hold to be the most vainglorious man of his time, and more ambitious, in refusing all honours, than Alexander in rejecting none.
SIR THOMAS BROWNE, *Religio Medici*, 1643

The great man is he who has not lost the heart of a child.
MENCIUS (4th century BC)

It is seldom that the great or the wise suspect that they are despised or cheated.
DR JOHNSON, 'Pope', *Lives of the Poets*, 1779–81

The highest point to which a weak but experienced mind can rise is detecting the weaknesses of better men.
LICHTENBERG, *Aphorisms*, 1764–99

Every great man, of whatever kind be his greatness, has among his friends those who officiously or insidiously quicken his attention to offence, heighten his disgust, and stimulate his resentment.
DR JOHNSON, 'Pope', *Lives of the Poets*, 1779–81

Ambition can creep as well as soar.
EDMUND BURKE, *Letters on a Regicide Peace*, 1796–7

Weak people never give way when they ought to.
CARDINAL DE RETZ, *Memoirs*, 1673–6

A wise man is cured of ambition by ambition itself; his aim is so exalted that riches, office, fortune and favour cannot satisfy him.
LA BRUYÈRE, 'Of Personal Merit', *Characters*, 1688

Contemptible things are not always things to be treated with contempt.
CARDINAL DE RETZ, *Memoirs*, 1673–6

The superior man is distressed by his want of ability.
CONFUCIUS, Analects, 6th century BC

Show me a hero and I will write you a tragedy.
SCOTT FITZGERALD, The Crack-Up, 1945

> there is always some
> little thing that is too
> big for us every
> goliath has his david and so on ad infinitum
DON MARQUIS, 'the merry flea'

The things which matter most are readily understood and easy to describe, but when it comes to the minor affairs of life one has to go into a great deal of detail.
BALZAC, Le Curé de Tours, 1832

It is the nature of all greatness not to be exact.
EDMUND BURKE, speech on American Taxation, 1774

Great minds tend toward banality.
ANDRÉ GIDE, Pretexts, 1903

Great men are but life-sized. Most of them, indeed, are rather short.
MAX BEERBOHM, And Even Now, 1921

History & the
Passing Generations

●

Each generation imagines itself to be more intelligent than the one that went before it, and wiser than the one that comes after it.

GEORGE ORWELL, review of 'A Coat of Many Colours', 1945

Men are more like the times they live in than they are like their fathers.

ALI IBN-ABI-TALIB, *Sentences*, 7th century

The century is advanced, but every individual begins afresh.

GOETHE, *Maxims and Reflections*, early 19th century

Ask counsel of the Ancients, what is best; but of the Moderns, what is fittest.

THOMAS FULLER (II), *Introductio ad Prudentiam*, 1731

A man is wise with the wisdom of his time only, and ignorant with its ignorance. Observe how the greatest minds yield in some degree to the superstitions of their age.

THOREAU, *Journal*, 1853

The greatest of men are always linked to their age by some weakness or other.

GOETHE, *Maxims and Reflections*, early 19th century

Resist your time – take a foothold outside it.

LORD ACTON, MSS notes, Cambridge, late 19th century

The people who live in a Golden Age usually go around complaining how yellow everything looks.

RANDALL JARRELL, *A Sad Heart at the Supermarket*, 1965

Better not to have glory in times and countries where few people know what glory is. It will very soon fade.

PRINCE DE LIGNE, *Mes écarts*, 1796

A generation is a drama with four or five thousand outstanding characters.

BALZAC

The one thing that does not change is that at any and every time it appears that there have been 'great changes'.

MARCEL PROUST, *Remembrance of Things Past* (*Within a Budding Grove*, 1919)

Our ignorance of history makes us libel our own times. People have always been like this.

FLAUBERT

Each generation believes on the one hand that the ancients were better than the moderns; and on the other that the human race is continually progressing and improving.

LEOPARDI, 'Sayings of Filippo Ottonieri', *Essays and Dialogues*, 1824–32

Antiquity is full of eulogies of another more remote antiquity.

VOLTAIRE, *Philosophical Dictionary*, 1764

Do not seek to follow in the footsteps of the men of old; seek what they sought.

MATSUO BASHO, 'The Rustic Gate', late 17th century

Use the memory of thy predecessor fairly, and tenderly; for if thou dost not, it is a debt will sure be paid, when thou art gone.

SIR FRANCIS BACON, 'Of Great Place', *Essays*, 1597–1625

They that say the world grows worse and worse are very much mistaken, for Adam who had but one commandment to keep broke that, and Cain slew his brother Abel when there was but two of them to share the whole world.

SAMUEL BUTLER (I), *Prose Observations*, 1660–80

By despising all that has preceded us, we teach others to despise ourselves.

HAZLITT, 'On Reading Old Books', 1821

Each generation criticizes the unconscious assumptions made by its parent. It may assent to them, but it brings them out in the open.

A. N. WHITEHEAD, *Science and the Modern World*, 1925

The certainties of one age are the problems of the next.

R. H. TAWNEY, *Religion and the Rise of Capitalism*, 1926

Every generation revolts against its fathers and makes friends with its grandfathers.

LEWIS MUMFORD, *The Brown Decades*, 1931

The novelties of one generation are only the resuscitated fashions of the generation before last.

BERNARD SHAW, Preface to *Three Plays for Puritans*, 1900

Makes of men date, like makes of cars.

ELIZABETH BOWEN, *The Death of the Heart*, 1938

Nothing is so old as a dilapidated charm.

EMILY DICKINSON, notebook, *c.*1880

The man who sees two or three generations is like someone who sits in a conjurer's booth at a fair, and sees the tricks two or three times. They are meant to be seen only once.

SCHOPENHAUER, 'On the Doctrine of the Suffering of the World', *Parerga and Paralipomena*, 1851

And now the artificial ruins were gradually becoming natural ones. Ruins to the second power.

LICHTENBERG, *Aphorisms*, 1764–99

He that will not apply new remedies must expect new evils; for time is the great innovator.

SIR FRANCIS BACON, 'Of Innovations', *Essays*, 1597–1625

In these new towns, one can find the old houses only in people.
                    ELIAS CANETTI, *The Human Province*, 1978

Among the dead there are those who still have to be killed.
                    FERNAND DESNOYERS, article, 1858

When man has wiped the slate clean and tries to write his own
message, the past which lives in him and has moulded him will bring
back the very things he has tried to obliterate.
                    SIR LEWIS NAMIER, *Avenues of History*, 1952

It is horrible to see everything that one detested in the past coming
back wearing the colours of the future.
                    JEAN ROSTAND, *Carnet d'un biologiste*

Posterity is as likely to be wrong as anybody else.
                    HEYWOOD BROUN, *Sitting on the World*, 1924

One would expect people to remember the past and to imagine the
future. But in fact, when discoursing or writing about history, they
imagine it in terms of their own experience, and when trying to
gauge the future they cite supposed analogies from the past: till, by a
double process of repetition, they imagine the past and remember
the future.
                    SIR LEWIS NAMIER, *Conflicts*, 1942

The obscurest epoch is today.
                    ROBERT LOUIS STEVENSON, *Across the Plains*, 1892

Th' further ye get away fr'm anny peeryod th' betther ye can write
about it. Ye are not subjict to interruptions by people that were
there.
                    FINLEY PETER DUNNE, *Mr. Dooley on Making a Will*, 1919

It is impossible to write ancient history because we do not have
enough sources, and impossible to write modern history because we
have far too many.
                    CHARLES PÉGUY, *Clio*, 1909–12

Facts relating to the past, when they are collected without art, are compilations; and compilations, no doubt, may be useful; but they are no more History than butter, eggs, salt and herbs are an omelette.

LYTTON STRACHEY, *Portraits in Miniature*, 1931

History books begin and end, but the events they describe do not.

R. G. COLLINGWOOD, *An Autobiography*, 1939

Political history is far too criminal and pathological to be a fit subject of study for the young. Children should acquire their heroes and villains from fiction.

W. H. AUDEN, *A Certain World*, 1971

The tree of humanity forgets the labour of the silent gardeners who sheltered it from the cold, watered it in time of drought, shielded it against wild animals; but it preserves faithfully the names mercilessly cut into its bark.

HEINE, *The Romantic School*, 1833

Imagination itself can scarcely feign any calamity so great that it has not been realized in the past or present history of the human race, or may not be realized in the future.

LEOPARDI, 'Sayings of Filippo Ottonieri', *Essays and Dialogues*, 1824–32

Everything which could possibly enter into the most disordered of imaginations might well be said of the history of the world.

DOSTOEVSKY, *Notes from the Underground*, 1864

Reading is the greatest of all joys, but there is more anger than joy in reading history. But, after all, there is pleasure in such anger.

CHANG CH'AO, *Sweet Dream Shadows*, mid 17th century

It is pleasant to be transferred from an office where one is afraid of a sergeant-major into an office where one can intimidate generals, and perhaps this is why History is so attractive to the more timid amongst us.

E. M. FORSTER, 'The Consolations of the Past', *Abinger Harvest*, 1936

Just as philosophy is the study of other people's misconceptions, so history is the study of other people's mistakes.

PHILIP GUEDALLA, Supers and Supermen, 1920

What is amusing now had to be taken in desperate earnest once.

VIRGINIA WOOLF, A Room of One's Own, 1929

How fond men are of justice when it comes to judging the crimes of former generations.

ARMAND SALACROU, Boulevard Durand, 1961

We are not to measure the feelings of one age by those of another. Had Walton lived in our day, he would have been the first to cry out against the cruelty of angling.

HAZLITT, Characteristics, 1823

We cannot reform our forefathers.

GEORGE ELIOT, Adam Bede, 1859

Throughout history the world has been laid waste to ensure the triumph of conceptions that are now as dead as the men that died for them.

HENRY DE MONTHERLANT, Notebooks, 1930–44

Reflect on things past, as wars, negotiations, factions, and the like; we enter so little into those interests, that we wonder how men could possibly be so busy, and concerned for things so transitory: Look on the present times, we find the same humour, yet wonder not at all.

SWIFT, Thoughts on Various Subjects, 1711

Countless things that humanity acquired in earlier stages, but so feebly and embryonically that no one could perceive this acquisition, suddenly emerge into the light much later – perhaps after centuries; meanwhile they have become strong and ripe.

NIETZSCHE, The Gay Science, 1882–7

Homer's Epos has not ceased to be true; yet it is no longer our Epos, but shines in the distance, if clearer and clearer, yet also smaller and smaller, like a receding Star.

CARLYLE, Sartor Resartus, 1833

There is no way of telling what may yet become part of history. Perhaps the past is still essentially undiscovered! So many retroactive forces are still needed!

NIETZSCHE, *The Gay Science*, 1882–7

History is a drama without a denouement; every decision glides over into a resumption of the plot.

PIETER GEYL, *Encounters in History*, 1963

In Sickness & In Health

●

Is not disease the rule of existence? There is not a lily pad floating on the river but has been riddled by insects. Almost every shrub and tree has its gall, oftentimes esteemed its chief ornament and scarcely to be distinguished from the fruit. If misery loves company, misery has company enough. Now, at midsummer, find me a perfect leaf or fruit.

THOREAU, *Journal*, 1851

Health is infinite and expansive in mode, and reaches out to be filled with the fullness of the world; whereas disease is finite and reductive in mode, and endeavours to reduce the world to itself.

OLIVER SACKS, *Awakenings*, 1973

How sickness enlarges the dimensions of a man's self to himself.

CHARLES LAMB, 'The Convalescent', *Last Essays of Elia*, 1833

Diseases have a character of their own, but they also partake of our character; we have a character of our own, but we also partake of the world's character.

OLIVER SACKS, *Awakenings*, 1973

It is happy enough that the same vices which impair one's fortune frequently ruin our constitution, that the one may not survive the other.

WILLIAM SHENSTONE, *Essays on Men and Manners*, 1764

In the case of illness, one's confinement, one's hopes and one's fears, what one hears, or believes, one's physician, *his* behaviour, are all coalesced in a single picture or drama.

OLIVER SACKS, *Awakenings*, 1973

Optimistic lies have such immense therapeutic value that a doctor who cannot tell them convincingly has mistaken his profession.

BERNARD SHAW, Preface to *Misalliance*, 1914

It takes a wise doctor to know when not to prescribe.

GRACIÁN, *The Art of Worldly Wisdom*, 1647

Formerly, when religion was strong and science weak, men mistook magic for medicine; now, when science is strong and religion weak, men mistake medicine for magic.

THOMAS SZASZ, *The Second Sin*, 1974

I wondher why ye can always read a doctor's bill an' ye niver can read his purscription.

FINLEY PETER DUNNE, *Mr. Dooley Says*, 1910

Before undergoing a surgical operation arrange your temporal affairs. You may live.

AMBROSE BIERCE, *The Devil's Dictionary*, 1906

To safeguard one's health at the cost of too strict a diet is a tiresome illness indeed.

LA ROCHEFOUCAULD, *Maxims*, 1665

A man who is 'of sound mind' is one who keeps the inner madman under lock and key.

VALÉRY, *Mauvaises pensées et autres*, 1942

For the mental patient's family and society, mental illness is a 'problem'; for the patient himself it is a 'solution'.

THOMAS SZASZ, *The Second Sin*, 1974

Absence of psychoneurotic illness may be health, but it is not life.

D. W. WINNICOTT, *Playing and Reality*, 1971

Doubt is to certainty as neurosis is to psychosis. The neurotic is in doubt and has fears about persons and things; the psychotic has convictions and makes claims about them. In short, the neurotic has problems, the psychotic has solutions.

THOMAS SZASZ, *The Second Sin*, 1974

Free association: the term a psychoanalyst uses to register his approval of the patient who talks about what the analyst wants him to talk about.

THOMAS SZASZ, *The Second Sin*, 1974

Neurosis seems to be a human privilege.

FREUD, *Moses and Monotheism*, 1939

Tout psychologizer, c'est tout pardonner.

ANON.

Kinship is healing; we are physicians to each other.

OLIVER SACKS, *Awakenings*, 1973

We are all ill; but even a universal sickness implies an idea of health.

LIONEL TRILLING, *The Liberal Imagination*, 1950

Pleasures & Penalties

Nothing can exceed the vanity of our existence but the folly of our pursuits.

OLIVER GOLDSMITH, *The Good-Natured Man*, 1768

Nature has made us frivolous to console us for our miseries.

VOLTAIRE, *Philosophical Dictionary*, 1764

One prospect lost, another still we gain;
And not a vanity is given in vain.

POPE, *An Essay on Man*, 1733

He that shuns trifles must shun the world.

GEORGE CHAPMAN, 'Epistle Dedicatory', *Hero and Leander*, 1598

As if the world were not vain enough of itself, we derive our delights from those things that are vainer than it: as plays, masques, romances, pictures, new fashions, excess etc. For as we were begotten with a caprice, so we endeavour to live up to it.

SAMUEL BUTLER (I), *Prose Observations*, 1660–80

Without its parasites – thieves, singers, dancers, mystics, poets, philosophers, businessmen – humanity would be a community of animals, or not even a community, but a species: the earth would lack salt.

VALÉRY, *Tel Quel*, 1941–3

Overwork, *n.* A dangerous disorder affecting high public functionaries who want to go fishing.

AMBROSE BIERCE, *The Devil's Dictionary*, 1906

Pastime, like wine, is poison in the morning.

THOMAS FULLER (I), *The Holy State and the Profane State*, 1642

Man rejoices in an incomparable faculty for presently mutilating and disfiguring any plaything that has helped to create for him the illusion of leisure.

HENRY JAMES, 'The Future of the Novel', 1899

If you are losing your leisure, look out! You may be losing your soul.

LOGAN PEARSALL SMITH, *Afterthoughts*, 1931

Most men pursue pleasure with such breathless haste that they hurry past it.

KIERKEGAARD, *Either/Or*, 1843

The follies which a man regrets most are those which he didn't commit when he had the opportunity.

HELEN ROWLAND, *Reflections of a Bachelor Girl*, 1903

The finest amusements are the most pointless ones.

JACQUES CHARDONNE (1884–1968), *Propos comme ça*

Nothing would be more tiresome than eating and drinking if God had not made them a pleasure as well as a necessity.

VOLTAIRE, *Dialogues philosophiques*, 18th century

A kiss is but a modified bite, and a fond mother, when she says her babe is 'almost good enough to eat', merely shows that she is herself only a trifle too good to eat it.

AMBROSE BIERCE, *Tangential Views*

There is no love sincerer than the love of food.

BERNARD SHAW, *Man and Superman*, 1903

What is a roofless cathedral compared to a well-built pie?

WILLIAM MAGINN, *Maxims of Sir Morgan O'Doherty, Bart.*, 1849

Enough is as good as a meal.

attrib. OSCAR WILDE

Gluttony is an emotional escape, a sign that something is eating us.

PETER DE VRIES, *Comfort Me With Apples*, 1956

If only it were as easy to banish hunger by rubbing the belly as it is to masturbate.

DIOGENES THE CYNIC (4th century BC), cit. Diogenes Laertius, *Lives and Opinions of Eminent Philosophers*

You should punish your appetites rather than allow yourself to be punished by them.

EPICTETUS, *Fragments*, 1st century

It is the unbroken testimony of all history that alcoholic liquors have been used by the strongest, wisest, handsomest, and in every way best races of all times.

GEORGE SAINTSBURY, *Notes on a Cellar-Book*, 1920

If we heard it said of Orientals that they habitually drank a liquor which went to their heads, deprived them of reason and made them vomit, we should say: 'How very barbarous!'

LA BRUYÈRE, 'Of Opinions', *Characters*, 1688

Sobriety diminishes, discriminates, and says no; drunkenness expands, unites, and says yes. Not through mere perversity do men run after it.

WILLIAM JAMES, *Varieties of Religious Experience*, 1902

A man who exposes himself when he is intoxicated has not the art of getting drunk.

DR JOHNSON in Boswell's *Life of Johnson*, 1779

Some people tell you you should not drink claret after strawberries. They are wrong.

WILLIAM MAGINN, *The Maxims of Sir Morgan O'Doherty, Bart.*, 1849

The believing we do something when we do nothing is the first illusion of tobacco.

EMERSON, *Journals*, 1859

Opiate, *n*. An unlocked door in the prison of Identity. It leads into the jail yard.

AMBROSE BIERCE, *The Devil's Dictionary*, 1906

Nothing brings a man sooner into fashion and renders him of greater importance than gambling; it is almost as good as getting drunk.

LA BRUYÈRE, 'Of Fashion', *Characters*, 1688

Always make water when you can.

DUKE OF WELLINGTON

What uses up a life is not so much its great tragedies as its small annoyances and the recurrent waste of time. It is not our enemies who wear us down, but rather our friends, or those half-friends who keep on wanting to meet us, although we have no corresponding desire to meet them.

HENRY DE MONTHERLANT, *Notebooks*, 1930–44

One of the pleasures of reading old letters is the knowledge that they need no answer.

BYRON

The best time to frame an answer to the letters of a friend, is the moment you receive them. Then the warmth of friendship, and the intelligence received, most forcibly co-operate.

WILLIAM SHENSTONE, *Essays on Men and Manners*, 1764

A man in a hurry of business of any sort is expected and ought to be expected to look to everything – his mind is in a whirl, and what matters it – what whirl? But to require a letter of a man lost in idleness is the utmost cruelty.

KEATS, letter, 1819

If it is a wrong number you will be sorry you have been troubled.

BEACHCOMBER, *Gallimaufry*, 1936

I sometimes say to myself: 'Life is too short to be worth troubling about.' Yet if a bore calls on me, prevents me from going out or

attending to my affairs, I lose patience and cannot endure it for half
an hour.

> VAUVENARGUES, *Reflections and Maxims*, 1746

One can be bored until boredom becomes a mystical experience.

> LOGAN PEARSALL SMITH, *Afterthoughts*, 1931

The effect of boredom on a large scale in history is underestimated. It
is a main cause of revolutions, and would soon bring to an end all the
static Utopias and the farmyard civilization of the Fabians.

> W. R. INGE, *The End of an Age*, 1948

Most sorts of diversion in men, children, and other animals, are an
imitation of fighting.

> SWIFT, *Thoughts on Various Subjects*, 1711

A man would have but few spectators, if he offered to show for
three-pence how he could thrust a red-hot iron into a barrel of
gunpowder, and it should not take fire.

> SWIFT, *Thoughts on Various Subjects*, 1711

There are charms made only for distant admiration. No spectacle is
nobler than a blaze.

> DR JOHNSON, 'Waller', *Lives of the Poets*, 1783

About the peculiar charm of white paper, bound into a book. Paper
which hasn't yet lost its virginity and still shines in the colour of
innocence is always better than after it has been used.

> LICHTENBERG, *Aphorisms*, 1764–99

Pleasures to those that have no inclination to them are more uneasy
than labour and pains, and so are all glories to those that are not
vainglorious.

> SAMUEL BUTLER (I), *Prose Observations*, 1660–80

As charms are nonsense, nonsense is a charm.

> BENJAMIN FRANKLIN, *Poor Richard's Almanack*, 1734

The Family

●

I hate babies. They're so human – they remind one of monkeys.

SAKI, *The Watched Pot*, 1924

Defenceless as babies are, they have mothers at their command, families to protect the mothers, societies to support the structure of families, and traditions to give a cultural continuity to systems of tending and training.

ERIK ERIKSON, *Insight and Responsibility*, 1966

What the mother sings to the cradle goes all the way down to the coffin.

HENRY WARD BEECHER, *Proverbs from Plymouth Pulpit*, 1887

The precursor of the mirror is the mother's face.

D. W. WINNICOTT, *Playing and Reality*, 1971

Nothing has a stronger influence psychologically on their environment, and especially on their children, than the unlived life of the parents.

JUNG, 'Paracelsus', 1934

A man who has been the indisputable favourite of his mother keeps for life the feeling of a conqueror, that confidence of success that often induces real success.

FREUD, cit. Ernest Jones, *The Life and Work of Sigmund Freud*, 1953–7

What was silent in the father speaks in the son; and often I found the son the unveiled secret of the father.

NIETZSCHE. *Thus Spake Zarathustra*. 188?–?

The imitativeness of our early years makes us acquire the passions of
our parents, even when these passions poison our lives.

STENDHAL, *Love*, 1822

Tristan and Isolde were unloved only children.

W. H. AUDEN, cit. Stravinsky and Craft, *Memories and
Commentaries*, 1959

We find delight in the beauty and happiness of children that makes
the heart too big for the body.

EMERSON, 'Illusions', *The Conduct of Life*, 1860

It is not just Mowgli who was raised by a couple of wolves; any child
is raised by a couple of grown-ups. Father and Mother may be nearer
and dearer than anyone will ever be again – still, they are members of
a different species.

RANDALL JARRELL, *The Third Book of Criticism*, 1969

We can't form our children on our own concepts; we must take them
and love them as God gives them to us.

GOETHE, *Hermann and Dorothea*, 1797

Allow children to be happy in their own way, for what better way
will they ever find?

DR JOHNSON, letter, 1780

> In the policeman's arms
> The lost child points
> Towards the sweet-shop.

ANON., Japanese, modern (trans. Geoffrey Bownas and
Anthony Thwaite)

We can keep from a child all knowledge of earlier myths, but we
cannot take from him the need for mythology.

JUNG, *Symbols of Transformation*, 1912

It is, in some ways, but a pedestrian fancy that the child exhibits. It is
the grown people who make the nursery stories; all the children do is
jealously to preserve the text.

ROBERT LOUIS STEVENSON, *Virginibus Puerisque*, 1881

Something you consider bad may bring out your child's talents;
something you consider good may stifle them.

CHATEAUBRIAND, *Mémoires d'Outre-Tombe*, 1849–50

Don't limit a child to your own learning, for he was born in another
time.

RABBINIC SAYING

Every adult, whether he is a follower or a leader, a member of a mass
or an élite, was once a child. He was once small. A sense of smallness
forms a substratum of his mind, ineradicably. His triumphs will be
measured against this smallness, his defeats will substantiate it.

ERIK ERIKSON, *Childhood and Society*, 1950

A toy car is a projection of a real car, made small enough for a child's
hand and imagination to grasp.
    A real car is a projection of a toy car, made large enough for an
adult's hand and imagination to grasp.

MICHAEL FRAYN, *Constructions*, 1974

It is only rarely that one can see in a little boy the promise of a man,
but one can almost always see in a little girl the threat of a woman.

ALEXANDRE DUMAS *fils* (1824–95)

Permissiveness is the principle of treating children as if they were
adults; and the tactic of making sure they never reach that stage.

THOMAS SZASZ, *The Second Sin*, 1974

It is wise to remember that rebellion belongs to the freedom you
have given your child by bringing him or her up in such a way that
he or she exists in his or her own right. In some instances it could be
said: 'You sowed a baby and you reaped a bomb.' In fact this is
always true, but it does not always look like it.

D. W. WINNICOTT, *Playing and Reality*, 1971

Greatness of name, in the father, ofttimes helps not forth, but
overwhelms the son: they stand too near one another. The shadow
kills the growth.

BEN JONSON, *Timber; or Discoveries*, 1640

There is no more sombre enemy of good art than the pram in the hall.

CYRIL CONNOLLY, *Enemies of Promise*, 1938

A father is a banker provided by nature.

ANON., French

The affection of a father and a son are different: the father loves the person of the son, and the son loves the memory of his father.

ANON., *Characters and Observations*, early 18th century

Nobody, who has not been in the interior of a family, can say what the difficulties of any individual of that family may be.

JANE AUSTEN, *Emma*, 1816

Young & Old

●

Why in our youth does the life we still have before us look so immeasurably long? Because we have to find room for the boundless hopes with which we cram it.

SCHOPENHAUER, 'On the Different Periods of Life', *Parerga and Paralipomena*, 1851

During the first period of a man's life the greatest danger is: *not to take the risk*.

KIERKEGAARD, *Journal*, 1850

It is better to waste one's youth than to do nothing with it at all.

GEORGES COURTELINE, *La philosophie de Georges Courteline*, 1917

When one considers how much the energy of young men needs to explode, one is not surprised that they decide for this cause or that without being at all subtle or choosy. What attracts them is the sight of the zeal that surrounds a cause.

NIETZSCHE, *The Gay Science*, 1882–7

Ask the young: they know everything!

JOUBERT, *Pensées*, 1842

Young men for some time have an idea that such a thing as happiness is to be had and therefore are extremely impatient under any unpleasant restraining – in time, however, of such stuff is the world about them, they know better and instead of striving from Uneasiness greet it as an habitual sensation.

KEATS, letter, 1818

One stops being a child when one realizes that telling one's trouble does not make it better.

CESARE PAVESE, *This Business of Living: Diaries 1935–50*

Conscious futility is something only for the young. One cannot go on 'despairing of life' into a ripe old age.

> GEORGE ORWELL, review of 'Four Quartets', 1942

Especially in youth, the goal of our happiness is fixed in the form of a few pictures that hover before us and often persist for half our lives and sometimes till the very end. They are really taunting ghosts; for when we have acquired them, they fade away into nothing.

> SCHOPENHAUER, 'Counsels and Maxims', *Parerga and Paralipomena*, 1851

If youth is a fault, it is one which is soon corrected.

> GOETHE, *Maxims and Aphorisms*, early 19th century

When a well-educated young man first enters society he is liable to commit many errors which the world terms childish, simply because he has not yet learned how childish grown men really are.

> LEOPARDI, *Pensieri*, 1834–7

One should never make one's *début* with a scandal. One should reserve that to give an interest to one's old age.

> OSCAR WILDE, *The Picture of Dorian Gray*, 1891

A child becomes an adult when he realizes he has a right not only to be right but also to be wrong.

> THOMAS SZASZ, *The Second Sin*, 1974

Men are but children of a larger growth.

> DRYDEN, *All for Love*, 1678

Alas! it is not the child, but the boy that generally survives in the man.

> SIR ARTHUR HELPS, *Thoughts in the Cloister and the Crowd*, 1835

It costs a great deal to be reasonable; it costs youth.

> MADAME DE LA FAYETTE (1634–93)

It is fitting that we should hold the young in awe. How do we know that generations to come will not be the equal of the present? Only when a man reaches the age of forty or fifty without distinguishing himself in any way can one say, I suppose, that he does not deserve to be held in awe.

CONFUCIUS, *Analects*, 5th century BC

Youth lasts much longer than young people think.

COMTESSE DIANE, *Maximes de la vie*, 1908

Whoever in middle age attempts to realize the hopes and wishes of his early youth, invariably deceives himself. Each ten years of a man's life has its own fortunes, its own hopes, its own desires.

GOETHE, *Elective Affinities*, 1809

To grow mature is to separate more distinctly, to connect more closely.

HUGO VON HOFMANNSTHAL, *The Book of Friends*, 1922

As we grow older we grow both more foolish and wiser at the same time.

LA ROCHEFOUCAULD, *Maxims*, 1665

Manny a man that cudden't direct ye to th' drug store on th' corner whin he was thirty will get a rispictful hearing whin age has further impaired his mind.

FINLEY PETER DUNNE, *Mr. Dooley on Making a Will*, 1919

Young men think old men are fools; but old men *know* young men are fools.

GEORGE CHAPMAN, *All Fools*, 1605

'Heartless Cynics,' the young men shout,
Blind to the world of Fact without;
'Silly Dreamers,' the old men grin,
Deaf to the world of Purpose within.

W. H. AUDEN, *New Year Letter*, notes, 1941

As a man's desires grow cooler, he becomes better equipped to deal with other men or to succeed in society. Nature, with her usual benevolence, has ordained that men shall not learn to live until they lose the motives for living.

LEOPARDI, *Pensieri*, 1834–7

When we are sighing for the loss of our past youth, which will return no more, let us reflect that decrepitude will come, when we shall regret the mature age we have reached and do not sufficiently value.

LA BRUYÈRE, 'Of Mankind', *Characters*, 1688

At fifty you begin to be tired of the world, and at sixty the world is tired of you.

COUNT OXENSTIERNA, *Reflections and Maxims*, mid 17th century

We are afraid of the old age which we may never attain.

LA BRUYÈRE, 'Of Mankind', *Characters*, 1688

Old age is the most unexpected of all the things that happen to a man.

TROTSKY, *Diary in Exile*, 1935

It is so comic to hear oneself called old, even at ninety I suppose!

ALICE JAMES, letter, 1889

Those who in their youth did not live in self-harmony, and who did not gain the true treasures of life, are later like long-legged old herons standing sadly by a lake without fish.

The Dhammapada, probably 3rd century BC

Every old man complains of the growing depravity of the world, of the petulance and insolence of the rising generation.

DR JOHNSON, *The Rambler*, 1750–2

The denunciation of the young is a necessary part of the hygiene of older people, and greatly assists the circulation of the blood.

LOGAN PEARSALL SMITH, *Last Words*, 1933

Whoever saw old age that did not applaud the past and condemn the present time, laying the fault of his misery and discontent upon the world and the manners of men?

MONTAIGNE, 'Of judging the death of another', *Essays*, 1580–8

Some old men by continually praising the time of their youth would almost persuade us that there were no fools in those days; but unluckily they are left themselves for examples.

POPE, *Thoughts on Various Subjects*, 1727

If it is the devil that tempts the young to enjoy themselves, is it not, perhaps, the same personage that persuades the old to condemn their enjoyment? And is not condemnation perhaps merely the form of excitement appropriate to old age?

BERTRAND RUSSELL, *Human Society in Ethics and Politics*, 1954

Thought of an ageing man: that, if he but lived to see it, the rising generation could throw a revealing light upon him.

HUGO VON HOFMANNSTHAL, *The Book of Friends*, 1922

The fundamental difference between youth and age will always be that the former has in prospect life, the latter death.

SCHOPENHAUER, 'On the Different Periods of Life', *Parerga and Paralipomena*, 1851

In age we talk much because we have seen much, and soon after shall cease talking for ever.

JOSEPH HALL, *Occasional Meditations*, 1630

Old men think themselves cunning.

THOMAS FULLER (II), *Gnomologia*, 1732

We ought not to heap reproaches on old age, seeing that we all hope to reach it.

BION, 3rd century BC, cit. Diogenes Laertius, *Lives and Opinions of Eminent Philosophers*

There is more felicity on the far side of baldness than young men can possibly imagine.

LOGAN PEARSALL SMITH, *Last Words*, 1933

He cannot bear old men's jokes. That is not new. But now he begins
to think of them himself.

MAX FRISCH, *Sketchbook 1966–71*

Rotten speeches are worst in withered age, when men run after that
sin in their words which flieth from them in deed.

THOMAS FULLER (I), *The Holy State and the Profane State*, 1642

Childishness follows us all the days of our life. If anybody seems
wise it is only because his follies are in keeping with his age and
circumstances.

LA ROCHEFOUCAULD, *Maxims*, 1665

Caesar was too old, it seems to me, to go off and amuse himself
conquering the world. Such a pastime was all right for Augustus and
Alexander; they were young men, not easily held in check, but
Caesar ought to have been more mature.

PASCAL, *Pensées*, 1670

It does not become an old man to run after the fashion of the
moment, either in thought or in dress. But he should know where he
is, and what the others are aiming at.

GOETHE, *Maxims and Reflections*, early 19th century

The fault of not perceiving betimes and of not being sensible of the
feebleness and extreme alteration that age naturally brings upon
both body and mind has lost the reputation of most of the great men
in the world.

MONTAIGNE, 'Of the affection of fathers to their children',
Essays, 1580–8

The tragedy of old age is not that one is old, but that one is young.

OSCAR WILDE, *The Picture of Dorian Gray*, 1891

We grow with years more fragile in body, but morally stouter, and
can throw off the chill of a bad conscience almost at once.

LOGAN PEARSALL SMITH, *Afterthoughts*, 1931

Shame on the soul, to falter on the road of life while the body still perseveres.

> MARCUS AURELIUS, *Meditations*, 2nd century

The older we grow, the greater become the ordeals.

> GOETHE, *Maxims and Reflections*, early 19th century

Old age has the last word: the purely naturalistic look at life, however enthusiastically it may begin, is sure to end in sadness.

> WILLIAM JAMES, *The Varieties of Religious Experience*, 1902

The tears of old people are as terrible as those of children are natural.

> BALZAC, *Ursule Mirouet*, 1841

There are so many sorts of defects in old age, so much imbecility, and it is so liable to contempt, that the best acquisition a man can make is the kindness and affection of his own family; command and fear are no longer his weapons.

> MONTAIGNE, 'Of the affection of fathers to their children', *Essays*, 1580–8

It is reasonable to rejoice, as the day declines, to find that it has been spent with the approbation of mankind.

> DR JOHNSON, letter, 1783

Few envy the consideration enjoyed by the oldest inhabitant.

> EMERSON, 'Old Age', *Society and Solitude*, 1870

The injunction to respect age stems from periods when long lives were exceptional.

> MAX FRISCH, *Sketchbook 1966–71*

In childhood life is like a theatrical décor seen from a distance, in old age it looks like the same décor seen at very close quarters.

> SCHOPENHAUER, 'On the Different Periods of Life', *Parerga and Paralipomena*, 1851

Human beings cling to their delicious tyrannies and to their exquisite nonsense, till death stares them in the face.

SYDNEY SMITH

If a man is old only in years then he is indeed old in vain.

The Dhammapada, probably 3rd century BC

Who could imagine that Diogenes in his younger days should be a falsifier of money who in the after-course of his life was so great a contemner of metal, as to laugh at all that loved it? But men are not the same in all divisions of their ages.

SIR THOMAS BROWNE, *Commonplace Book*, mid 17th century

He is the happiest man who can trace an unbroken connection between the end of his life and the beginning.

GOETHE, *Maxims and Reflections*, early 19th century

A man must have grown old and lived long in order to see how short life is.

SCHOPENHAUER, 'On the Different Periods of Life', *Parerga and Paralipomena*, 1851

Do not try to live for ever. You will not succeed.

BERNARD SHAW, Preface to *The Doctors' Dilemma*, 1911

Time & Transience

●

Come-and-go pervades everything of which we have knowledge, and though great things go more slowly, they are built up of small ones and must fare as that which makes them.

SAMUEL BUTLER (II), *Notebooks*, 1912

The monarch to whom it is said that he is a god has always been reminded by his own heart that he shall die like a man.

DR JOHNSON, sermon, 1752

For mortals, mortal things. And all things leave us. Or if they do not, then we leave them.

LUCIAN (*c.*115–180), *The Greek Anthology* (trans. Edwin Morgan)

Man, whatever he may think, is a very limited being; the world is a narrow circle drawn about him; the horizon limits our immediate view; immortality means a century or two.

HAZLITT, 'On Old English Writers and Speakers', 1825

This mortal life is a little thing, lived in a little corner of the earth; and little, too, is the longest fame to come – dependent as it is on a succession of fast-perishing little men who have no knowledge even of their own selves, much less of one dead and gone.

MARCUS AURELIUS, *Meditations*, 2nd century

Where are you dying tonight?

EVELYN WAUGH, *Diaries*, 1961

Everything we love, no doubt, will pass away, perhaps tomorrow, perhaps thousands of years hence. Neither it nor our love for it is any the less valuable for that reason.

JOHN PASSMORE, *The Perfectibility of Man*, 1970

Providence gives us the same reply as the soldier who was begged by a prisoner to spare his life: 'Impossible – though you can ask me for anything else.'

XIMÉNÈS DOUDAN, *Pensées et fragments*, 1880

He that runs against Time has an antagonist not subject to casualties.

DR JOHNSON, 'Pope', *Lives of the Poets*, 1779–81

A mortal should think mortal thoughts, not immortal thoughts.

EPICHARMUS OF SYRACUSE (6th–5th century BC)

If man were never to fade away like the dews of Adashino, never to vanish like the smoke over Toribeyama, but lingered on forever in the world, how things would lose their power to move us! The most precious thing in life is its uncertainty.

YOSHIDA KENKO, *Essays in Idleness*, c.1340

> Man is in love and loves what vanishes,
> What more is there to say?

W. B. YEATS, 'Nineteen Hundred and Nineteen', *The Tower*, 1928

In every parting there is an image of death.

GEORGE ELIOT, *Scenes of Clerical Life*, 1858

I can generally bear the separation, but I don't like the leave-taking.

SAMUEL BUTLER (II), *Notebooks*, 1912

You cannot step twice into the same river, for other waters are continually flowing in.

HERACLITUS, *Fragments*, c.500 BC

Don't wait for the Last Judgement. It takes place every day.

ALBERT CAMUS, Jean-Baptiste Clamance in *The Fall*, 1956

All of us are creatures of a day; the rememberer and the remembered alike.

MARCUS AURELIUS, *Meditations*, 2nd century

The present moment is a powerful goddess.

GOETHE, *Tasso*, 1790

The most insignificant present has over the most insignificant past the advantage of *reality*.

SCHOPENHAUER, 'On the Doctrine of the Vanity of Existence', *Parerga and Paralipomena*, 1851

It is plain enough that all that is immediately present to a man is what is in his mind in the present instant. His whole life is in the present. But when he asks what is the content of the present instant, his question always comes too late.

C. S. PEIRCE, *Collected Papers*, I, late 19th–early 20th century

We cannot put off living until we are ready. The most salient characteristic of life is its coerciveness: it is always urgent, 'here and now' without any possible postponement. Life is fired at us point blank.

JOSÉ ORTEGA Y GASSET, *The Mission of the University*, 1944

Very few men, properly speaking, live at present; but few are providing to live another time.

SWIFT, *Thoughts on Various Subjects*, 1711

There is no glory so bright but the veil of business can hide it effectually. With most men life is postponed to some trivial business and so therefore is heaven. Men think foolishly they may abuse and misspend life as they please and when they get to heaven turn over a new leaf.

THOREAU, *Journal*, 1851

If you imagine that once you have accomplished your ambitions you will have time to turn to the Way, you will discover that your ambitions never come to an end.

YOSHIDA KENKO, *Essays in Idleness*, c.1340

When told of a man who had acquired great wealth, a sage replied, 'Has he also acquired the days in which to spend it?'

SOLOMON IBN GABIROL, *The Choice of Pearls*, c.1050

Time ought, above all other kinds of property, to be free from invasion; and yet there is no man who does not claim the power of wasting that time which is the right of others.

DR JOHNSON, *The Idler*, 1758

Some people can stay longer in an hour than others can in a week.

attrib. WILLIAM DEAN HOWELLS

The less one has to do the less time one finds to do it in.

LORD CHESTERFIELD, *Letters*

Many who find the day too long, think life too short.

CHARLES CALEB COLTON, *Lacon*, 1825

The years teach us much which the days never knew.

EMERSON, 'Experience', *Essays*, Second Series, 1844

The grand truisms of life only life itself is said to bring to life.

EDWARD FITZGERALD, *Polonius*, 1852

Nothing ever becomes real till it is experienced – even a proverb is no proverb to you till your life has illustrated it.

KEATS, letter, 1819

Habit is overcome by habit.

THOMAS À KEMPIS, *The Imitation of Christ*, c.1420

There are things one does not say for a long time, but, once they are said, one never stops repeating them.

BENJAMIN CONSTANT, *Adolphe*, 1815

Time makes more converts than reason.

TOM PAINE, *Common Sense*, 1776

One of the great misfortunes of mankind is that even his good qualities are sometimes useless to him, and that the art of employing and well directing them is often the latest fruit of his experience.

CHAMFORT, *Maximes et pensées*, 1805

Time is the old justice that examines all offenders.

> SHAKESPEARE, *As You Like It*, 1599–1600

What is unimportant is always being added to; for through frequent repetition many things that at first seem to us important gradually become unimportant.

> SCHOPENHAUER, 'On the Different Periods of Life', *Parerga and Paralipomena*, 1851

Time is a great teacher, but unfortunately it kills all its pupils.

> BERLIOZ, *Almanach des lettres françaises*

The career of every individual man or woman is essentially non-progressive.

> ALDOUS HUXLEY, *Themes and Variations*, 1950

What man strives to preserve, in preserving himself, is something which he has never been at any particular moment.

> SANTAYANA, *The Life of Reason*, 1905–6

Nothing is worth more than this day.

> GOETHE, *Maxims and Reflections*, early 19th century

Observations & Oddities

●

One should always be a little improbable.

OSCAR WILDE, 'Phrases and Philosophies for the Use of the Young', 1894

The formula 'Two and two make five' is not without its attractions.

DOSTOEVSKY, *Notes from the Underground*, 1864

When you have a taste for exceptional people you always end up meeting them everywhere.

PIERRE MAC ORLAN, *Le bal du pont du Nord*, 1946

Every man is bound to leave a story better than he found it.

MRS HUMPHRY WARD, *Robert Elsmere*, 1888

One is telling a story about old times when someone breaks in with a little detail that he happens to know, implying that one's own version is inaccurate – disgusting behaviour!

The Pillow Book of Sei Shonagon, 10th century

All the news that fits we print.

ANON., composing room, *New York Times*

One always has the air of someone who is lying when one speaks to a policeman.

CHARLES-LOUIS PHILIPPE (1874–1909), *Les chroniques du canard sauvage*

Worrying is the most natural and spontaneous of all human functions. It is time to acknowledge this, perhaps even to learn to do it better.

LEWIS THOMAS, *The Medusa and the Snail*, 1979

Impatient people always arrive too late.

>   JEAN DUTOURD, *Le fond et la forme*, 1958

> So obsessive a ritualist
> a pleasant surprise
> makes him cross.
>
>   W. H. AUDEN, 'Profile', *City Without Walls*, 1969

Before doing someone a favour, make sure that he isn't a madman.

>   EUGÈNE LABICHE, *Le voyage de M. Perrichon*, 1860

It is easier to get an actor to be a cowboy than to get a cowboy to be
an actor.

>   attrib. JOHN FORD (1895–1973)

The children of other nations always seem precocious. That's
because the strange manners of their elders have caught our attention
and the children echo those manners enough to seem like their
parents.

>   SCOTT FITZGERALD, *The Crack-Up*, 1945

When I give a hundred-franc bill, I give the dirtiest one.

>   JULES RENARD, *Journal*, 1898

An actress without talent, forty years old, ate a partridge for dinner,
and I felt sorry for the partridge, for it occurred to me that in its life it
had been more talented, more sensible, and more honest than the
actress.

>   CHEKHOV, *Notebooks*, 1892–1904

The most powerful soporific is sleep itself.

>   MARCEL PROUST, *Remembrance of Things Past* (*Cities of the
>   Plain*, 1921–2)

The reason the Romans built their great paved highways was
because they had such inconvenient footwear.

>   MONTESQUIEU, *Mes pensées*, c.1722–55

Plato banished poets out of his Republic, and yet forgot that that very commonwealth was merely poetical.

> SAMUEL BUTLER (I), *Prose Observations*, 1660–80

Among our peers of the realm, those that have honours entailed on their posterity are called Lords Temporal, that is for the time being; and those that have it only for their lives Lords Spiritual in opposition to the other.

> SAMUEL BUTLER (I), *Prose Observations*, 1660–80

'Tis strange that the Lacedaemonians who were so thrifty of their words should call themselves by so long a name.

> SAMUEL BUTLER (I), *Prose Observations*, 1660–80

Pomskizillious: 'The Coast Scenery may truly be called pomskizillious and gromphibberous, being as no words can describe its magnificence.'

> EDWARD LEAR, *Mr Lear's Wurbl Inwentions: a little dictionary*

Fact is richer than diction.

> J. L. AUSTIN, 'A Plea for Excuses', *Philosophical Papers*, 1961

Drouth is stronger than faction.

> JAMES JOYCE, *Finnegans Wake*, 1939

He who drinks a tumbler of London water has literally in his stomach more animated beings than there are men, women and children on the face of the globe.

> SYDNEY SMITH, letter, 1834

I see several animals that live so entire and perfect a life, some without sight, others without hearing: who knows whether to us also one, two, or three, or many other senses, may not be wanting?

> MONTAIGNE, 'Apology for Raimond de Sebonde', *Essays*, 1580–8

Fish die belly-upward and rise to the surface; it is their way of falling.

> ANDRÉ GIDE, *Journals*, 1930

Why has not Man a microscopic eye?
For this plain reason, Man is not a Fly.

POPE, *Essay on Man*, 1733

Why has not man a collar and a log?
For this plain reason – man is not a dog.
Why is not man served up with sauce in dish?
For this plain reason – man is not a fish.

SYDNEY SMITH in Lady Holland, *Memoir*, 1855

As the old hermit of Prague, that never saw pen and ink, very wittily
said to a niece of King Gorboduc, 'That that is, is'.

SHAKESPEARE, *Twelfth Night*, *c.*1600

Death

●

The hour which gives us life begins to take it away.
SENECA, *Hercules Furens*, 1st century

Old and young, we are all on our last cruise.
ROBERT LOUIS STEVENSON, *Virginibus Puerisque*, 1881

Death feeds us up, keeps an eye on our weight,
and herds us like pigs through the abattoir gate.
PALLADAS (4th–5th century), *The Greek Anthology* (trans. Tony Harrison)

If some persons died, and others did not die, death would indeed be a terrible affliction.
LA BRUYÈRE, 'Of Mankind', *Characters*, 1688

While I thought that I was learning how to live, I have been learning how to die.
LEONARDO DA VINCI, *Notebooks*, 1508–18

A bearer of news of death appears to himself as very important. His feeling – even against all reason – makes him a messenger from the realm of the dead.
WALTER BENJAMIN, *One-Way Street*, 1925–6

The long habit of living indisposeth us for dying.
SIR THOMAS BROWNE, *Urn Burial*, 1658

I feel so much the *continual* death of everything and everybody, and have so learned to reconcile myself to it, that the final and official end loses most of its impressiveness.
SANTAYANA, *Letters*, 1931

Like a fish that is thrown on dry land, taken from his home in the waters, the mind strives and struggles to get free from the power of Death.

The Dhammapada, probably 3rd century BC

A free man thinks of nothing less than of death, and his wisdom is a meditation not of death but of life.

SPINOZA, *Ethics*, 1677

No man should be afraid to die, who hath understood what it is to live.

THOMAS FULLER (II), *Gnomologia*, 1732

The good man should go on living as long as he ought to, not just as long as he likes.

SENECA, *Epistles*, 1st century

To save a man's life against his will is the same as killing him.

HORACE, *Ars Poetica*, *c*.8 BC

Where it is permissible both to die and not to die, it is an abuse of valour to die.

MENCIUS (4th century BC)

Our repugnance to death increases in proportion to our consciousness of having lived in vain.

HAZLITT, 'On the Love of Life', 1815

A philosophical contempt of life is no guarantee of courage in the face of death.

GUSTAVE VAPEREAU, later 19th century

Just when I seem to be coming out of school – very sorry to have been such a foolish boy, yet having taken a prize or two, and expecting to enter now upon some more serious business than cricket – I am dismissed by the Master I hoped to serve, with a – 'That's all I want of you, sir.'

RUSKIN, *St. Mark's Rest*, 1877–84

It is important what a man still plans at the end. It shows the measure of injustice in his death.

ELIAS CANETTI, *The Human Province*, 1978

How do I know that love of life is not a delusion after all? How do I know but that he who dreads death is not as a child who has lost his way and does not know his way home?

CHUANG-TZU, *On Levelling All Things*, 4th century BC

To the psychotherapist an old man who cannot bid farewell to life appears as feeble and sickly as a young man who is unable to embrace it.

JUNG, *Modern Man in Search of a Soul*, 1933

It may be said that disease generally begins that equality which death completes.

DR JOHNSON, *The Rambler*, 1750–2

When you are taken unawares by an outbreak of fire or the news of a death, there is in the first mute shock a feeling of guilt, the indistinct reproach: did you really not know of this? Did not the dead person's name, the last time you uttered it, sound differently in your mouth? Do you not see in the flames a sign from yesterday evening, in a language you only now understand?

WALTER BENJAMIN, *One-Way Street*, 1925–6

Death is part of this life and not of the next.

ELIZABETH BIBESCO, *Haven*, 1951

Our life gets as complicated as a comedy as it goes on, but the complications get gradually resolved: see that the curtain comes down on a good denouement.

GRACIÁN, *The Art of Worldly Wisdom*, 1647

A lot of people, on the verge of death, utter famous last words or stiffen into attitudes, as if the final stiffening in three days' time were not enough; they will have ceased to exist three days' hence, yet they still want to arouse admiration and adopt a pose and tell a lie with their last gasp.

HENRY DE MONTHERLANT, 'Explicit Mysterium', 1931

Death must be distinguished from dying, with which it is often confounded.

> SYDNEY SMITH, 'Maxims and Rules of Life', in Lady Holland, *Memoir*, 1855

A man may by custom fortify himself against pain, shame, and suchlike accidents; but as to death, we can experience it but once, and are all apprentices when we come to it.

> MONTAIGNE, 'Use makes perfect', *Essays*, 1580–8

It's not that I'm afraid to die. I just don't want to be there when it happens.

> WOODY ALLEN, *Getting Even*, 1971

What is to be undergone only once we may undergo: what must be comes almost of its own accord.

> CARLYLE, 'On Boswell's *Life of Johnson*', 1832

Strength or weakness at the hour of death depends on the nature of the last illness.

> VAUVENARGUES, *Reflections and Maxims*, 1746

To die is easy when we are in perfect health. On a fine spring morning, out of doors, on the downs, mind and body sound and exhilarated, it would be nothing to lie down on the turf and pass away.

> MARK RUTHERFORD, *More Pages from a Journal*, 1910

A man's dying is more the survivors' affair than his own.

> THOMAS MANN, *The Magic Mountain*, 1924

If a person very close to us is dying, there is something in the months to come that we dimly apprehend – much as we should have liked to share it with him – could only happen through his absence. We greet him at last in a language that he no longer understands.

> WALTER BENJAMIN, *One-Way Street*, 1925–6

Why do dying people never shed tears?

> MAX FRISCH, *Sketchbook 1966–71*

I cannot say, strictly speaking, that I *die*, since – dying a violent death or not – I am conscious of only part of the event. And a great share of the terror which I experience at the idea of death derives perhaps from this: bewilderment at remaining suspended in the middle of a seizure whose outcome I can never know.

MICHEL LEIRIS, *L'Age d'Homme*, 1946

Until death, it is all life.

CERVANTES, *Don Quixote*, 1605–15

The last act is bloody, however fine the rest of the play. They throw earth over your head and it is finished for ever.

PASCAL, *Pensées*, 1670

Worldly faces never look so worldly as at a funeral.

GEORGE ELIOT, *Scenes of Clerical Life*, 1858

At the funerals of our relations we do our best to put on long faces, but at the luncheon afterwards our hilarity breaks out. For it is he who has died and not ourselves.

GERALD BRENAN, *Thoughts in a Dry Season*, 1978

All I desire for my own burial is not to be buried alive.

LORD CHESTERFIELD, *Letters*, 1769

Extinction, *n*. The raw material out of which theology created the future state.

AMBROSE BIERCE, *The Devil's Dictionary*, 1906

Although contemporary events obscure past events in a living man's life, yet as soon as he is dead, and his whole life is a matter of history, one action stands out as conspicuously as another.

COLERIDGE, *Table Talk*, 1830

Moderate lamentation is the right of the dead, excessive grief the enemy to the living.

SHAKESPEARE, *All's Well That Ends Well*, 1601–3

What we call mourning for our dead is perhaps not so much grief at not being able to call them back as it is grief at not being able to want to do so.

THOMAS MANN, *The Magic Mountain*, 1924

The deep pain that is felt at the death of every friendly soul arises from the feeling that there is in every individual something which is inexpressible, peculiar to him alone, and is, therefore, absolutely and *irretrievably* lost.

SCHOPENHAUER, 'Psychological Remarks', *Parerga and Paralipomena*, 1851

People do not die for us immediately, but remain bathed in a sort of *aura* of life which bears no relation to true immortality but through which they continue to occupy our thoughts in the same way as when they were alive. It is as though they were travelling abroad.

MARCEL PROUST, *Remembrance of Things Past* (*The Fugitive*, 1925)

There's one thing that keeps surprising you about stormy old friends after they die – their silence.

BEN HECHT, *Letters from Bohemia*, 1964

The dead are often just as living to us as the living are, only we cannot get them to believe it. They can come to us, but till we die we cannot go to them. To be dead is to be unable to understand that one is alive.

SAMUEL BUTLER (II), *Notebooks*, 1912

The dead don't die. They look on and help.

D. H. LAWRENCE, letter, 1923

A grave is a tranquillizing object.

WORDSWORTH, *Essay upon Epitaphs*, 1810

The strong walled houses of the dead are the ones to have outlived the centuries, not the houses of the living: not the inns of the living, but the dwellings of permanence.

MIGUEL DE UNAMUNO, *The Tragic Sense of Life*, 1913

Oh well, no matter what happens, there's always death.

NAPOLEON, 1817

We do not know what thoughts stirred in the mind of the last of the mastodons, but we can take it that they were nothing very remarkable. It is hardly likely that the last man will have the mind of a Goethe. He will die, and that will be the last stage of human progress.

ANATOLE FRANCE, *Under the Rose*, 1925

The Afterlife

We feel and know that we are eternal.

SPINOZA, Ethics, 1677

Is there another life? Shall I awake and find all this a dream? There must be, we cannot be created for this sort of suffering.

KEATS, letter, 1820

We sometimes congratulate ourselves at the moment of waking from a troubled dream; it may be so the moment after death.

NATHANIEL HAWTHORNE, American Notebooks, 1835–7

Nothing is eternal, alas, except eternity.

PAUL FORT, Ballades françaises, 1922–58

Christ's death has impressed the world more than His resurrection.

VALÉRY, Mauvaises pensées et autres, 1942

Expect no greater happiness in Eternity, than to rejoice in God.

BENJAMIN WHICHCOTE, Moral and Religious Aphorisms, 1703

God will often say to us: 'You are not in Heaven for fun!'

JULES RENARD, Journal, 1906

Hell is the most dreadful of inventions, and it is hard to understand how one can expect any good of people after this invention. Will they not *always* have to invent hells?

ELIAS CANETTI, The Human Province, 1978

The most frightful idea that has ever corroded human nature – the idea of eternal punishment.

JOHN MORLEY, 'Vauvenargues', Miscellanies, 1886

I can believe anything, but the justice of this world does not give me a very reassuring idea of the justice in the next. I am very much afraid that God will go on blundering: he will receive the wicked in Paradise and hurl the good into Hell.

JULES RENARD, *Journal*, 1906

The other world will be admirable for congruities.

BENJAMIN WHICHCOTE, *Moral and Religious Aphorisms*, 1703

It is possible that God may not be altogether pleased when He sees pious people firmly persuaded that there is a future life. Perhaps, in His fatherly kindness, He wants to give us a surprise.

HEINE, *Thoughts and Fancies*

What is vanity but the longing to survive?

MIGUEL DE UNAMUNO, *The Tragic Sense of Life*, 1913

Wouldn't you think a man a prize fool if he burst into tears because he didn't live a thousand years ago? A man is as much a fool for shedding tears because he isn't going to be alive a thousand years from now.

SENECA, *Epistles*, 1st century

The fact of having been born is a bad augury for immortality.

SANTAYANA, *The Life of Reason*, 1905–6

Do not the indiscretions which occur only after a person's life on earth is ended prove that nobody really believes in a future life?

MARCEL PROUST, *Remembrance of Things Past* (*The Fugitive*, 1925)

After your death you will be what you were before your birth.

SCHOPENHAUER, 'On the Doctrine of the Indestructibility of Our True Nature', *Parerga and Paralipomena*, 1851

God is growing bitter, He envies man his mortality.

JACQUES RIGAUT, *Pensées*, *c.*1920

Aphorists & Aphorisms

II

The great writers of aphorisms read as if they had all known each other well.

ELIAS CANETTI, The Human Province, 1978

Pointed axioms and acute replies fly loose about the world, and are assigned successively to those whom it may be the fashion to celebrate.

DR JOHNSON, 'Waller', Lives of the Poets, 1779–81

Genuine bons mots surprise those from whose lips they fall, no less than they do those who listen to them.

JOUBERT, Pensées, 1842

Whatever sentence will bear to be read twice, we may be sure was thought twice.

THOREAU, Journal, 1842

Wit is like science, not of particulars but universals; for as arguments drawn from particulars signify little to universal nature, which is the proper object of science, so wit that is raised upon any one particular person goes no further unless it be from thence extended to all human nature.

SAMUEL BUTLER (I), Prose Observations, 1660–80

Few maxims are true in every respect.

VAUVENARGUES, Reflections and Maxims, 1746

> For wit and judgment often are at strife,
> Tho' meant each other's aid, like man and wife.

POPE, Essay on Criticism, 1711

Paradoxes are useful to attract attention to ideas.

BISHOP CREIGHTON in L. Creighton, Life of Mandell Creighton, 1904

The platitude turned on its head is still a platitude.

> NORMAN MAILER, *Advertisements for Myself*, 1961

Our live experiences, fixed in aphorisms, stiffen into cold epigram. Our heart's blood, as we write with it, turns to mere dull ink.

> F. H. BRADLEY, *Aphorisms*, 1930

This delivering of knowledge in distinct and disjointed aphorisms doth leave the wit of man more free to turn and toss, and to make use of that which is so delivered to more several purposes and applications.

> SIR FRANCIS BACON, *Novum Organum*, 1620

Solomon made a book of proverbs, but a book of proverbs never made a Solomon.

> ANON.

Constant popping off of proverbs will make thee a byword thyself.

> THOMAS FULLER (II), *Introductio ad Prudentiam*, 1731

All the good maxims already exist in the world; we just fail to apply them.

> PASCAL, *Pensées*, 1670

What the first philosopher taught the last will have to repeat.

> THOREAU, *Journal*, 1840

Acknowledgements

●

The editor and publishers gratefully acknowledge permission to reproduce copyright material in this book:

S. J. Andreski: from *Social Sciences as Sorcery*. Copyright © 1972 by Stanislav Andreski. Reprinted by permission of André Deutsch Ltd.

W. H. Auden: from *The Dyer's Hand and Other Essays*, copyright © 1962 by W. H. Auden. From *City Without Walls and Other Poems*, copyright © 1969 by W. H. Auden. From *Collected Poems*, edited by Edward Mendelson; 'Tristan and Isolde were unloved only children' (source unidentified). All reprinted by permission of Faber & Faber Ltd., and Random House, Inc. From *A Certain World*, copyright © 1970 by W. H. Auden. A William Cole Book. Reprinted by permission of Faber & Faber Ltd., and Viking Penguin Inc.

J. L. Austin: from 'Truth' and from 'Ifs and Cans' from *Philosophical Papers*, 3/e 1979 edited by J. O. Urmson and G. J. Warnock, copyright © OUP 1961, 1970, 1979. Reprinted by permission of Oxford University Press. From 'Pretending' and 'A Plea for Excuses', also in *Philosophical Papers*. Reprinted by permission of the Aristotelian Society.

Charles Baudelaire: from *My Heart Laid Bare and Other Prose Writings* (Weidenfeld, 1950), trans. Norman Cameron.

Max Beerbohm: from *Zuleika Dobson*. Copyright 1911 by Dodd, Mead & Co., copyright renewed 1938 by Max Beerbohm. Reprinted by permission of Wm. Heinemann Ltd. and Dodd, Mead & Co. From *Yet Again, And Even Now*, and *Music Halls of My Youth*. Reprinted by permission of Mrs Eva Reichmann.

Saul Bellow: from *Herzog*. Reprinted by permission of A. M. Heath & Co. Ltd., for the author, Weidenfeld & Nicolson and Viking Press, New York.

Walter Benjamin: from *One-Way Street and Other Writings*, trans. Edmund Jephcott and Kingsley Shorter. 'One-Way Street' also appears as an essay in *Reflections* by Walter Benjamin, trans. Edmund Jephcott, published exclusively in the United States and Canada by Harcourt Brace Jovanovich Inc. By permission of the English publisher, New Left Books, and of Harcourt Brace Jovanovich Inc.

Bernard Berenson: from *The Bernard Berenson Treasury*, edited by Hanna Kiel. Copyright © 1962 by Simon & Schuster, Inc. Reprinted by permission of Simon & Schuster.

Elizabeth Bibesco: from *Haven* (James Barrie, 1951).

Elizabeth Bowen: from *The House in Paris* and *The Death of the Heart*. Copyright 1935 and renewed 1963 by Elizabeth Bowen, copyright 1938 and renewed 1966 by Elizabeth D. C. Cameron. Reprinted by permission of the Estate of Elizabeth Bowen, Jonathan Cape Ltd., and Alfred A. Knopf, Inc.

Gerald Brenan: from *Thoughts in a Dry Season* (1978). Reprinted by permission of Cambridge University Press.

Albert Camus: from *The Fall*, trans. Justin O'Brien; and from *Carnets 1942–51*, trans. P. Thody. Reprinted by permission of Hamish Hamilton Ltd.

Elias Canetti: from *The Human Province*, trans. Joachim Neugroschl. English translation copyright © 1978 by The Seabury Press, Inc. Reprinted by permission of the Continuum Publishing Company.

G. K. Chesterton: from *The Wisdom of Father Brown* and *The Innocence of Father Brown*. Reprinted by permission of Dodd, Mead & Co.

Jean Cocteau: from *Opium* (1957) and *Cocteau's World* (1972), trans. Margaret Crosland. Reprinted by permission of Peter Owen Ltd., London.

Ivy Compton-Burnett: from *Manservant and Maidservant, A God and his Gifts, The Mighty and their Fall*, and *Mother and Son*. Reprinted by permission of Victor Gollancz Ltd., and by Curtis Brown Ltd., on behalf of the Estate of Ivy Compton-Burnett.

Confucius: from *The Analects*, edited and translated by D. C. Lau (Penguin Classics, 1979). Copyright © D. C. Lau, 1979. Reprinted by permission of Penguin Books Ltd.

Cyrol Connolly: from *The Unquiet Grave* (Hamish Hamilton, 1945). Reprinted by permission of Deborah Rogers Ltd. From *Enemies of Promise*. Reprinted by permission of the author's estate and the Hogarth Press.

Benjamin Constant: from *Adolphe*, translated by Carl Wildman. Reprinted by permission of New American Library Inc.

Eugène Delacroix: from *The Journal of Eugène Delacroix*, trans. Lucy Norton (1951). Reprinted by permission of Phaidon Press Ltd.

Peter De Vries: from *Let Me Count the Ways*. Copyright © 1965 by Peter De Vries; from *The Tents of Wickedness*, copyright 1950 by Peter De Vries, and from *Comfort Me With Apples*, copyright 1952, 1953 © 1956 by Peter De Vries. Reprinted by permission of Laurence Pollinger Ltd., and of Little, Brown & Co.

Dhammapada, translated from the Pali by Juan Mascaro (Penguin Classics, 1973). Copyright © Juan Mascaro, 1973. Reprinted by permission of Penguin Books Ltd.

Diderot: from *Rameau's Nephew and other works*, trans. Jacques Barzun and Ralph H. Bowen. Copyright © 1956 by Jacques Barzun and Ralph H. Bowen. Reprinted by permission of Doubleday & Co., Inc.

Norman Douglas: from *An Almanac* (Chatto, 1945). Reprinted by permission of The Society of Authors as the literary representatives of the Estate of Norman Douglas.

T. S. Eliot: from *The Family Reunion*, and extract from 'Philip Massinger' from *Selected Essays*; copyright 1932, 1936, 1950 by Harcourt Brace Jovanovich, Inc., copyright 1939, 1960, 1964 by T. S. Eliot, copyright 1967, 1968 by Esme Valerie Eliot. From *The Sacred Wood* (1920). Reprinted by permission of Faber & Faber Ltd., and Harcourt Brace Jovanovich Inc.

Erik Erikson: from *Childhood and Society*. Reprinted by permission of The Hogarth Press Ltd., and W. W. Norton Inc. From *Insight and Responsibility*. Reprinted by permission of Faber & Faber Ltd., and W. W. Norton Inc.

Gavin Ewart: from *The Collected Ewart* (1980). Reprinted by permission of Century Hutchinson Ltd.

Leslie Farber: from *The Ways of the Will* (1966). Reprinted by permission of Constable & Co. Ltd., and Basic Books, New York.

F. Scott Fitzgerald: from *The Crack-up*, copyright 1945 by New Directions Publishing Corporation. Reprinted by permission of The Bodley Head Ltd. and New Directions Publ. Corp.

E. M. Forster: from *Two Cheers for Democracy*, and *Abinger Harvest*. Reprinted by permission of King's College, Cambridge, and The Society of Authors as the literary representatives of the E. M. Forster Estate.

Michael Frayn: from *Constructions* (Wildwood House, 1974). Reprinted by permission of Elaine Greene Ltd.

Sigmund Freud: Reprinted by permission of the Sigmund Freud Copyrights, The Institute of Psycho-Analysis and The Hogarth Press from the *Standard Edition of the Complete Psychological Works of Sigmund Freud*, translated and edited by James Strachey: *The Future of an Illusion*. By permission of Liveright Publishing Corporation as the American publisher. *New Introductory Lectures on Psychoanalysis*. By permission of W. W. Norton & Company, Inc. Copyright © 1965, 1964 by James Strachey. *Moses and Monotheism*, trans. Katherine Jones, Hogarth 1951/Alfred A. Knopf, Inc. 1955. By permission of Alfred A. Knopf, Inc. From Ernest Jones, *The Life and Work of Sigmund Freud*, 3 vols, 1953-7 (Hogarth) © 1963 by Ernest Jones, and published in the USA by Basic Books, Inc.

Max Frisch: from *Sketchbook 1966-1971*, trans. Geoffrey Skelton, © 1974 by Max Frisch and Geoffrey Skelton. Reprinted by permission of Associated Book Publishers Ltd, and Harcourt Brace Jovanovich Inc.

André Gide: from *Pretexts*, trans. Justin O'Brien, © Editions Gallimard et Mecure de France. Reprinted by permission of Georges Borchardt, Inc. and Editions Gallimard. From *Journals*, translated by Justin O'Brien, copyright 1951 by Alfred A. Knopf, Inc. Reprinted by permission of Secker & Warburg Ltd., and Alfred A. Knopf, Inc.

E. H. Gombrich: from *Art and Illusion* (1960). Reprinted by permission of Phaidon Press Ltd.

D. W. Harding: from *Experience Into Words*. Reprinted by permission of Chatto and Windus Ltd.

Thomas Hardy: in Florence Hardy, *The Life of Thomas Hardy* (1928/30). Reprinted by permission of Macmillan, London and Basingstoke.

Hermann Hesse: from *Reflections*, selected by Volker Michaels, trans. Ralph Mannheim. Translation copyright © 1974 by Farrar Straus & Giroux, Inc. Reprinted by permission of the Estate of Hermann Hesse, the translator, Jonathan Cape Ltd., and Farrar Straus & Giroux, Inc.

Hugo von Hofmannsthal: from *Selected Prose*, trans. Mary Hottinger, Tania and James Stern, Bollingen Series XXXIII, Vol. I. Copyright 1952, © 1980 renewed by Princeton University Press. Reprinted by permission of Princeton University Press and Routledge & Keegan Paul Ltd.

Aldous Huxley: from *Themes and Variations*, copyright 1943, 1949, 1950 by Aldous Huxley. From 'Adonis and the Alphabet' in *Tomorrow and Tomorrow and Tomorrow*, copyright 1952, 1953, 1955, 1956 by Aldous Huxley. From *Time Must Have a Stop*, copyright 1944 by Aldous Huxley. From *Do What You Will*, copyright 1928, 1929, renewed 1956, 1957 by Aldous Huxley. From *Music at Night*, copyright 1930, 1931, renewed 1958, 1959 by Aldous Huxley.

All reprinted by permission of Mrs Laura Huxley, Chatto & Windus Ltd., and Harper & Row, Publishers, Inc.

Kobayashi Issa: from *The Penguin Book of Japanese Verse*, trans. Geoffrey Bownas and Anthony Thwaite (The Penguin Poets, 1964) pp. 122, 124. Copyright © Geoffrey Bownas and Anthony Thwaite, 1964. Reprinted by permission of Penguin Books Ltd.

Randall Jarrell: from *The Third Book of Criticism*, copyright © 1965 by Mrs Randall Jarrell. Reprinted by permission of Faber & Faber Ltd., and Farrar Straus & Giroux, Inc. From *Poetry and the Age*. Reprinted by permission of Faber & Faber Ltd., and Mrs Randall Jarrell. From *Kipling, Auden & Co.* (originally included in *A Sad Heart at the Supermarket*) by Randall Jarrell, copyright © 1958, 1980 by Mrs Randall Jarrell. Copyright © 1958 by The Curtis Publishing Co. Reprinted by permission of Carcanet Press and Farrar Straus & Giroux, Inc.

James Joyce: from *Ulysses*, copyright 1914, 1918 by Margaret Caroline Anderson and renewed 1942, 1946 by Nora Joseph Joyce. Reprinted by permission of The Bodley Head, Random House, Inc., and The Society of Authors. From *Finnegans Wake*, copyright 1939 by James Joyce, copyright renewed 1967 by George Joyce and Lucia Joyce. Reprinted by permission of The Society of Authors, and Viking Penguin Inc.

C. J. Jung: from *Psychological Reflections: A New Anthology of His Writings, 1905–1961*, ed. Jolande Jacobi and R. F. C. Hull, Bollingen Series XXXI. Copyright 1953 by Princeton University Press, new edition © 1970 by Princeton University Press. Reprinted by permission of Princeton University Press and Routledge & Kegan Paul Ltd.

Franz Kafka: from *The Great Wall of China* (1933), trans. Edwin & Willa Muir. Copyright 1936, 1937 by Heinr. Mercy Sohn, Prague, copyright © 1946, 1974 by Schocken Books, Inc.; from *Shorter Works*, Vol. I, (1973), trans. Malcolm Pasley. Reprinted by permission of Secker & Warburg Ltd., and Schocken Books, Inc.

Yoshida Kenko: from *Essays in Idleness*, translated by Donald Keene (1967). Reprinted by permission of Columbia University Press.

John Maynard Keynes: from *Essays in Persuasion* (1933), © The Royal Economic Society 1972. From *General Theory of Employment, Interest and Money* (1936), © The Royal Economic Society 1973. Reprinted by permission of the Royal Economic Society, and Macmillan, London and Basingstoke.

Kierkegaard: from *A Selection from the Journals of Sören Kierkegaard*, translated and edited by Alexander Dru (1938). Reprinted by permission of Oxford University Press.

La Bruyère: from *Characters*, trans. Henri van Laun and revised by Denys C. Potts, copyright © OUP 1963. Reprinted by permission of Oxford University Press.

La Rochefoucauld: from *Maxims*, trans. Leonard Tancock (Penguin Classics, 1959). Copyright © Leonard Tancock, 1959. Reprinted by permission of Penguin Books Ltd.

Stanislaw Lec: from *Unkempt Thoughts*, trans. J. Galazka (St Martin's Press, 1962). Reprinted by permission of the translator.

Lichtenberg: from *The Lichtenberg Reader*, edited and translated by Franz Mautner and Henry Hatfield. Copyright © 1959 by Franz H. Mautner and

Henry Hatfield. Reprinted by permission of Beacon Press. From *A Doctrine of Scattered Occasions*, trans. J. P. Stern, reconstructed from Lichtenberg's *Aphorisms and Reflections* by J. P. Stern (1963). Reprinted by permission of Professor J. P. Stern.

Desmond MacCarthy: from *Criticism* (Putnam 1932).

Mary McCarthy: from *On the Contrary* (Heinemann, 1962). Reprinted by permission of A. M. Heath & Co. Ltd., for the author.

Norman Mailer: from *Advertisements for Myself* and *The Presidential Papers*. Reprinted by permission of André Deutsch Ltd.

Thomas Mann: from *The Magic Mountain*, trans. H. T. Lowe-Porter, copyright 1927 and renewed 1955 by Alfred A. Knopf, Inc., copyright 1952 by Thomas Mann. Reprinted by permission of Martin Secker & Warburg Ltd., and Alfred A. Knopf Inc.

Marcus Aurelius: from *Meditations*, trans. Maxwell Staniforth (Penguin Classics, 1964). Copyright © Maxwell Staniforth, 1964. Reprinted by permission of Penguin Books Ltd.

Don Marquis: 'Archy on this and that' and 'The Merry Flea' from *The Lives and Times of Archy and Mehitabel* by Don Marquis, copyright 1927, 1930 by Doubleday & Co., Inc., copyright 1916, 1917, 1918, 1919, 1921, 1922 by Sun Printing & Publishing Association, copyright 1922, 1923, 1924, 1925 by New York Tribune, Inc., copyright 1925, 1926, 1933 by P. F. Collier and Son Company. Reprinted by permission of Faber & Faber Ltd., and Doubleday & Co., Inc.

W. Somerset Maugham: from *Cakes and Ale* and from *The Moon and Sixpence*. Reprinted by permission of the Estate of the late W. Somerset Maugham, A. P. Watt Ltd., and Doubleday & Co., Inc.

Guy de Maupassant: from *Pierre et Jean*, trans. Leonard Tancock (Penguin Classics, 1979). Introduction and translation copyright © Leonard Tancock, 1979. Reprinted by permission of Penguin Books Ltd.

Mencius: translated by D. C. Lau (Penguin Classics, 1970). Copyright © D. C. Lau, 1970. Reprinted by permission of Penguin Books Ltd.

H. L. Mencken: from *Minority Report: H. L. Mencken's Notebooks*, and *A Book of Burlesques*, copyright © 1956 by Alfred A. Knopf, Inc., and copyright 1916 by Alfred A. Knopf, Inc., and renewed 1944 by H. L. Mencken. Reprinted by permission of the publisher.

Montesquieu: from *Persian Letters*, trans. C. J. Betts (Penguin Classics, 1973). Copyright © C. J. Betts, 1973. Reprinted by permission of Penguin Books Ltd.

Henry de Montherlant: from *Selected Essays*, trans. J. G. Weightman (Weidenfeld, 1960).

Marianne Moore: from 'Spenser's Ireland', copyright 1941, and renewed 1969 by Marianne Moore; from 'Snakes, Mongooses, Snake-charmers and the like', copyright 1935 by Marianne Moore renewed 1963 by Marianne Moore and T. S. Eliot; in *Collected Poems of Marianne Moore* (Macmillan, New York, 1951) and also in *The Complete Poems of Marianne Moore* (Faber), and *Selected Poems of Marianne Moore* (Faber, n/e 1969). Reprinted by permission of Macmillan Publishing Co., Inc., and of Faber & Faber Ltd.

Sir Lewis Namier: from *Vanished Supremacies* (1958) and from *Personalities and Powers* (1955). Reprinted by permission of Hamish Hamilton Ltd.

372 ACKNOWLEDGEMENTS

Nietzsche: from *The Gay Science*, translated, with commentary, by Walter Kaufmann, © 1974 by Random House, Inc. Reprinted by permission of the publisher. From *Twilight of the Idols/The Anti-Christ*, trans. R. J. Hollingdale (Penguin Classics, 1968), © R. J. Hollingdale, 1968. Reprinted by permission of Penguin Books Ltd. From *A Nietzsche Reader* trans. R. J. Hollingdale (1977/1978). Reprinted by permission of Penguin Books Ltd.

George Orwell: from *Collected Essays, Journalism and Letters* (Secker 1968/ Harcourt Brace Jovanovich 1971). Reprinted by permission of A. M. Heath & Co., Ltd., on behalf of the Estate of the late Sonia Brownell Orwell and the American publisher.

Pascal: from *Pensées*, trans. A. J. Krailsheimer (Penguin Classics, 1966). Copyright © A. J. Krailsheimer, 1966. Reprinted by permission of Penguin Books Ltd.

John Passmore: from *The Perfectibility of Man* (1970). Reprinted by permission of Gerald Duckworth & Co., Ltd.

Cesare Pavese: from *This Business of Living: Diaries 1935–50*, trans. A. E. Murch. Reprinted by permission of Peter Owen Ltd., London.

C. S. Peirce: from *Collected Papers of Charles Sanders Peirce*, 6 vols, ed. Charles Hartshorne and Paul Weiss. Reprinted by permission of Harvard University Press.

Peter Porter: from *The Last of England*, © Oxford University Press 1970. Reprinted by permission of Oxford University Press.

V. S. Pritchett: from *The Myth Makers*, copyright © 1979 by V. S. Pritchett. Reprinted by permission of Chatto & Windus Ltd., for the author, and of Random House Inc.

Marcel Proust: from *Remembrance of Things Past*, trans. Scott Moncrieff and revised by Terence Kilmartin. Translation copyright © 1981 by Random House, Inc., and Chatto & Windus. Reprinted by permission of Chatto & Windus Ltd., and Random House, Inc.

Publilius Syrus: from Publilius Syrus, *Minor Latin Poets*, trans. J. Wight Duff, 1934, Reprinted by permission of the Loeb Classical Library (Harvard University: William Heinemann).

Jules Renard: from *The Journals of Jules Renard*, trans. Louise Bogan and Elizabeth Roget (1964). Original French edition, *Journal de Jules Renard*, copyright Editions Gallimard 1935. Reprinted by permission of George Braziller, Inc., and Editions Gallimard, Paris.

Harold Rosenberg: from *Discovering the Present: Three Decades in Art, Culture and Politics*, copyright © 1973 by Harold Rosenberg. Reprinted by permission of The University of Chicago Press.

Franz Rosenzweig: from *Franz Rosenzweig: His Life and Work*, trans. Nahum H. Glatzer (1953). Copyright © 1953, 1961 by Schocken Books, Inc. Reprinted by permission of the publisher.

Bertrand Russell: from *Unpopular Essays*. Reprinted by permission of George Allen & Unwin Ltd., and Simon & Schuster Inc. From *Sceptical Essays* and *Human Society in Ethics and Politics*. Reprinted by permission of George Allen & Unwin Ltd. From *Education*. Reprinted by permission of George Allen & Unwin Ltd., and Liveright Publishing Corp.

Oliver Sacks: from *Awakenings* (1973). Reprinted by permission of Gerald Duckworth & Co., Ltd.

George Santayana: from *The Life of Reason*, ed. Daniel M. Cory, copyright 1953 Daniel M. Cory, copyright renewed 1981 Margot Cory. From *Scepticism and Animal Faith*. Reprinted by permission of Constable & Co., Ltd., and Charles Scribner's Sons. From *Letters* by permission of Mrs M. Cory. From *Winds of Doctrine* by permission of J. M. Dent & Sons Ltd.

Schopenhauer: from *Parerga and Paralipomena*, trans. E. F. J. Payne, © OUP 1974. Reprinted by permission of Oxford University Press.

Seneca: from *Letters from a Stoic*, trans. Robin Campbell (Penguin Classics, 1969). Copyright © Robin Campbell, 1969. Reprinted by permission of Penguin Books Ltd.

George Bernard Shaw: extracts reprinted by permission of The Society of Authors on behalf of the Bernard Shaw Estate.

Sir Charles Sherrington: from *Man On His Nature* (1940). Reprinted by permission of Cambridge University Press.

Andrei Sinyavsky: from *A Voice From the Chorus*, trans. Max Hayward and Kyril Fitzlyon (1976). Reprinted by permission of William Collins, Sons & Co. Ltd.

Logan Pearsall Smith: from *All Trivia* (1933). Reprinted by permission of Constable & Co. Ltd.

Stevie Smith: from *The Collected Poems of Stevie Smith* (Allen Lane). Reprinted by permission of James MacGibbon, Literary Executor.

Wallace Stevens: from *Opus Posthumous*, copyright © 1957 by Elsie Stevens and Holly Stevens. Reprinted by permission of Faber & Faber Ltd., and Alfred A. Knopf, Inc.

Thomas Szasz: from *The Second Sin*. Copyright © 1973 by Thomas Szasz. Reprinted by permission of Doubleday & Co., Inc., and Faber & Faber Ltd.

Rabindranath Tagore: from *Stray Birds*, copyright 1916 by Macmillan Co., Inc., renewed 1944 by Rabindranath Tagore. Reprinted by permission of Macmillan, London, and Macmillan Publ. Co., Inc., New York.

Lewis Thomas: from *The Medusa and the Snail: More Notes of a Biology Watcher*, copyright © 1979 by Lewis Thomas. Most of the essays in this book originally appeared in the *New England Journal of Medicine*. Reprinted by permission of Viking Penguin, Inc., and Penguin Books Ltd.

James Thurber: from *Fables For Our Time*. Copr. 1940 James Thurber, © 1968 Helen Thurber. Published by Harper & Row. From *Thurber Country*. Copr. © 1953 James Thurber. Copr. © 1981 Helen Thurber and Rosemary Thurber. Published by Simon & Schuster, Inc. Reprinted by permission of Mrs James Thurber.

Lionel Trilling: from *The Liberal Imagination*, copyright 1950 Lionel Trilling; copyright renewed Diana Trilling and James Trilling. Reprinted by permission of Charles Scribner's Sons. From 'Freud: Within and Beyond Culture' in *Beyond Culture*, copyright © 1955 by Lionel Trilling. Reprinted by permission of Harcourt Brace Jovanovich, Inc.

Miguel de Unamuno: from *The Tragic Sense of Life in Men and Nations*, trans. Anthony Kerrigan, Vol. 4 of *Selected Works of Miguel de Unamuno*, Bollingen Series LXXXV, copyright © 1972 by Princeton University Press. Reprinted by permission of Princeton University Press and Routledge & Kegan Paul Ltd.

Paul Valéry: from *Analects*, trans. Stuart Gilbert, Vol. 14 of *The Collected Works in English*, Bollingen Series XLV, copyright © 1970 by Princeton University Press. Reprinted by permission of Princeton University Press and Routledge & Kegan Paul Ltd.

D. W. Winnicott: from *Playing and Reality* (1971). Reprinted by permission of Tavistock Publications.

Virginia Woolf: from *The Common Reader*, Vol. I and *A Room of One's Own*; copyright 1925, 1929 by Harcourt Brace Jovanovich, Inc., renewed 1953, 1957 by Leonard Woolf. Reprinted by permission of the Author's Literary Estate, The Hogarth Press Ltd., and Harcourt Brace Jovanovich, Inc.

W. B. Yeats: from 'A Prayer for My Daughter', copyright 1924 by Macmillan Publishing Company, renewed 1952 by Bertha Georgie Yeats and from 'Nineteen Hundred and Nineteen', copyright 1928 by Macmillan Publishing Company, renewed 1956 by Georgie Yeats, both from *Collected Poems* of William Butler Yeats; from *Autobiography*, © 1916, 1936 by Macmillan Publishing Company, renewed 1944, 1964 by Bertha Georgie Yeats and from 'Anima Hominis' in *Mythologies*, copyright 1959 by Mrs W. B. Yeats. Reprinted by permission of A. P. Watt Ltd., on behalf of M. B. Yeats, Anne Yeats and Macmillan, London Ltd., and by permission of Macmillan Publishing Company.

While every effort has been made to secure permission, we may have failed in a few cases to trace the copyright holder. We apologize for any apparent negligence.

Index

Acton, John Dalberg, 1st Baron, 116, 182, 319
Adams, Henry, 85, 107
Addison, Joseph, 75
Adler, Alfred, 256
Adler, Renata, 106
Agathon, 297
Alain (Emile Chartier), 109, 255
Alcott, Louisa May, 99
Ali ibn-Abi-Talib, 136, 319
Allen, Woody, 358
Amiel, Henri Frédéric, 36, 71, 81, 122, 291, 309
Anacharsis, 94
Andreski, Stanislav, 93, 230
Anon., 95, 182, 216, 231, 286, 328, 335, 337, 351, 365; see also *Characters and Observations*
Antimedon, 106
Antisthenes, 137
Antrim, Minna, 271
Archidamus, 124
Aristotle, 39, 41
Arnold, Matthew, 116
Auden, W. H., 68, 73, 123, 130, 180, 285, 309, 323, 335, 340, 352
Austen, Jane, 147, 272, 337
Austin, J. L., 227, 235, 255, 256, 281, 283, 302, 353
Aymé, Marcel, 48, 105
Ayton, Sir Robert, 21

Bacon, Sir Francis, 2, 9, 22, 60, 61, 93, 100, 115, 120, 126, 131, 133, 136, 142, 143, 206, 221, 226, 235, 249, 264, 267, 271, 285, 311, 320, 321, 365
Bagehot, Walter, 15, 27, 53, 77, 101, 104, 119, 240, 246, 253, 264, 289, 293
Balzac, Honoré de, 96, 118, 204, 206, 292, 315, 318, 320, 344
Baring, Maurice, 293
Barthes, Roland, 154
Basho, Matsuo, 320

Baudelaire, Charles, 13, 23, 90, 98, 154, 281
Bauer, Gérard, 54
Beachcomber (J. B. Morton), 111, 332
Beaumarchais, Pierre de, 129, 149
Beausacq, Marie de, see Diane, Comtesse
Becque, Henry, 118
Beecher, Henry Ward, 334
Beerbohm, Sir Max, 38, 143, 208, 210, 264, 269, 284, 318
Bellow, Saul, 21, 104, 238, 258
Benjamin, Walter, 6, 108, 112, 155, 156, 205, 273, 286, 306, 355, 357, 358
Bennett, Arnold, 173, 203, 309
Bentham, Jeremy, 110
Ben Zoma, 267
Berenson, Bernard, 33, 81, 173, 256, 278
Berkeley, George, Bishop, 129, 172, 198, 199, 227
Berlioz, Hector, 350
Bernard, Tristan, 184, 251, 302
Betjeman, Sir John, 113
Bibesco, Elizabeth, Princess, 39, 59, 72, 84, 104, 134, 135, 163, 190, 251, 357
Bierce, Ambrose, 10, 88, 97, 103, 107, 108, 109, 124, 216, 262, 283, 327, 329, 330, 332, 359
Billings, Josh, 228
Bion, 342
Blake, William, 7, 8, 17, 18, 23, 33, 35, 43, 51, 135, 227, 237, 238, 240, 243, 245, 268, 286, 294, 295, 308, 311
Blessington, Marguerite, Countess of, 85, 313
Bogan, Louise, 299
Boileau-Despréaux, Nicolas, 243
Bolingbroke, Henry St John, 1st Viscount, 31
Borges, Jorge Luis, 292
Bourget, Paul, 171
Bourne, Randolph, 249
Bowen, Elizabeth, 45, 69, 81, 140, 164, 321

Bradley, F. H., 1, 23, 44, 56, 67, 72, 84, 89, 168, 193, 198, 365
Bramah, Ernest, 48, 147, 235, 316
Brant, Sebastian, 225
Brasillach, Robert, 114
Brenan, Gerald, 16, 33, 58, 78, 101, 197, 246, 298, 359
Broadhurst, 202
Brontë, Emily, 112
Broun, Heywood, 322
Browne, Sir Thomas, 9, 11, 55, 56, 65, 71, 126, 170, 174, 179, 195, 226, 263, 270, 274, 285, 312, 313, 317, 345, 355
Büchner, Georg, 69
Buffon, Georges-Louis, Comte de, 290
Bulwer-Lytton, Edward, 1st Baron Lytton, 93, 135, 196, 209
Bunam of Pzysha, Rabbi, 176
Burke, Edmund, 104, 115, 117, 120, 121, 122, 124, 133, 137, 222, 247, 304, 317, 318
Burton, Robert, 247
Bussy-Rabutin, Roger de, 154
Butler, Samuel (1612–80), 1, 34, 88, 91, 93, 96, 101, 111, 161, 173, 177, 179, 186, 190, 219, 229, 235, 265, 269, 306, 307, 320, 329, 333, 353, 364
Butler, Samuel (1835–1902), 7, 11, 12, 16, 23, 32, 47, 82, 98, 148, 192, 195, 218, 224, 237, 252, 254, 315, 346, 347, 360
Byron, George Gordon, 6th Baron, 148, 151, 165, 241, 332

Caillavet, Gaston, see Flers, Robert de and Gaston Caillavet
Callimachus, 159, 286
Calvino, Italo, 57
Camus, Albert, 78, 121, 148, 181, 199, 262, 347
Canetti, Elias, 6, 12, 28, 39, 46, 67, 124, 197, 204, 209, 231, 232, 273, 274, 282, 290, 322, 357, 362, 364
Capus, Alfred, 109, 244
Carlyle, Thomas, 45, 79, 94, 96, 116, 255, 280, 281, 286, 324, 358
Carroll, Lewis, 287
Carus, C. G., 237
Cervantes, Miguel de, 13, 51, 71, 105, 106, 206, 265, 279, 359
Chamfort, Sébastien Nicolas Roche, 14, 38, 43, 81, 82, 83, 87, 134, 139, 148,

150, 152, 154, 179, 187, 193, 198, 199, 205, 209, 234, 241, 242, 243, 245, 247, 276, 313, 316, 349
Chamson, André, 274
Chang Ch'ao, 160, 309, 310, 323
Chapman, George, 329, 340
Chapman, John Jay, 305
Characters and Observations (Anon.), 40, 63, 90, 94, 101, 102, 103, 106, 137, 139, 144, 149, 152, 155, 181, 184, 185, 199, 201, 202, 203, 210, 214, 216, 221, 240, 257, 260, 265, 337
Chardonne, Jacques, 330
Chateaubriand, François René de, Vicomte de, 83, 152, 188, 336
Chekhov, Anton, 3, 30, 107, 147, 172, 176, 269, 295, 306, 352
Chesterfield, Philip Dormer Stanhope, 4th Earl of, 30, 34, 60, 61, 63, 73, 81, 88, 129, 130, 147, 185, 195, 211, 212, 213, 223, 224, 226, 314, 315, 349, 359
Chesterton, G. K., 3, 8, 14, 17, 21, 49, 65, 71, 78, 80, 81, 103, 104, 109, 115, 142, 167, 174, 177, 180, 220, 223, 236, 237, 238, 254, 258, 282, 287, 288, 293, 298, 301, 310, 314
Chincholles, Charles, 119
Chofetz Chaim, The, 185
Chuang-tzu, 240, 263, 357
Churchill, Charles, 251
Churchill, Sir Winston, 268
Cicero, 181
Clare, John, 9, 176
Clement of Alexandria, St, 39
Clough, Arthur Hugh, 12, 26, 148, 177
Cocteau, Jean, 47, 48, 161, 225, 294, 298, 299, 300
Coleridge, Samuel Taylor, 6, 56, 73, 74, 202, 302, 312, 359
Collingwood, R. G., 323
Collins, John Churton, 90, 93, 94, 134, 175, 190, 192, 210, 214, 246
Colton, Charles Caleb, 22, 89, 122, 127, 131, 160, 180, 244, 271, 316, 349
Compton-Burnett, Dame Ivy, 131, 146, 225, 294
Confucius, 71, 174, 202, 221, 250, 318, 340
Congreve, William, 160
Connolly, Cyril, 24, 46, 148, 150, 163, 214, 255, 287, 337

Conrad; Joseph, 37, 40, 96, 180, 214, 272, 313
Constant, Benjamin, 38, 68, 156, 349
Courteline, Georges, 164, 195, 338
Cowley, Hannah, 61
Crabbe, George, 289
Craigie, Pearl, see Hobbes, J. O.
Creighton, Mandell, Bishop, 365
Croisset, Francis de, see Flers, Robert de and Francis de Croisset
Cromwell, Oliver, 126

Darling, Mr Justice (Sir Charles John), 93, 110, 120, 209, 218, 219, 264
Deffand, Marie, Marquise du, 151
Delacroix, Eugène, 121, 136, 138, 241, 292, 299, 315
Democritus of Abdera, 35, 139, 167, 174, 208, 233
De Morgan, Augustus, 254
De Quincey, Thomas, 311
Descartes, René, 247
Desnoyers, Fernand, 322
De Vries, Peter, 52, 186, 288, 331
Dhammapada, The, 169, 179, 207, 341, 345, 356
Diane, Comtesse (Marie de Beausacq), 16, 61, 94, 157, 195, 215, 292, 314, 340
Dickens, Charles, 66, 183, 187
Dickinson, Emily, 13, 20, 26, 144, 171, 223, 321
Diderot, Denis, 11, 14, 15, 25, 31, 163, 186, 212, 219, 312
Diogenes (the Cynic), 331
Disraeli, Benjamin (1st Earl of Beaconsfield), 62, 85, 93, 115, 149, 166, 208, 250
D'Israeli, Isaac, 268
Donne, John, 6, 18, 62, 94, 105, 130, 142, 189, 190, 236
Dostoevsky, Fedor, 23, 24, 323, 351
Doudan, Ximenès, 290, 347
Douglas, Norman, 65, 110, 112, 145, 246, 248, 249
Drummond, William, 254
Dryden, John, 261, 276, 307, 339
Du Deffand, Marquise, see Deffand, Marie, Marquise du
Duhamel, Georges, 12, 112
Dumas, Alexandre, fils, 14, 150, 245, 336

Dunne, Finley Peter, 102, 125, 144, 259, 269, 322, 327, 340
Dutourd, Jean, 352

Ebner-Eschenbach, Maria von, 61, 108
Ecclesiasticus (Ben Sirach), 169, 242
Eckhart, Meister, 5
Eliot, George, 38, 42, 62, 72, 98, 102, 138, 140, 149, 185, 204, 324, 347, 359
Eliot, T. S., 47, 292, 295
Emerson, Ralph Waldo, 3, 4, 11, 16, 30, 33, 34, 41, 63, 71, 75, 80, 84, 110, 112, 153, 185, 194, 211, 216, 242, 265, 266, 268, 269, 299, 308, 313, 331, 335, 344, 349
Enright, D. J., 299
Epicharmus of Syracuse, 347
Epictetus, 12, 73, 184, 205, 331
Epicurus, 134
Erikson, Erik, 37, 334, 336
Euripides, 131, 134
Ewart, Gavin, 130, 160, 182

Fabre d'Olivet, Antoine, 21
Farber, Leslie, 36, 143, 158, 189
Farquhar, George, 150
Ferguson, Adam, 25, 133
Firbank, Ronald, 31
Fitzgerald, Edward, 261
Fitzgerald, F. Scott, 45, 74, 113, 160, 204, 313, 318, 349, 352
Flaubert, Gustave, 242, 300, 301, 303, 310, 320
Flers, Robert de and Francis de Croisset, 104, 221
Flers, Robert de and Gaston Caillavet, 151
Ford, John, 352
Forneret, Xavier, 218, 274
Forster, E. M., 129, 305, 308, 323
Fort, Paul, 362
France, Anatole, 11, 12, 17, 20, 34, 35, 55, 107, 110, 162, 163, 186, 199, 241, 246, 253, 361
Franklin, Benjamin, 15, 166, 227, 242, 333
Frayn, Michael, 48, 117, 119, 132, 143, 161, 187, 235, 336
Freud, Sigmund, 6, 16, 22, 79, 227, 239, 263, 313, 328, 334
Frisch, Max, 343, 344, 358
Frost, Robert, 46, 295

Fuller, Thomas (1608–61), 40, 42, 74, 86, 99, 105, 151, 222, 241, 242, 259, 270, 272, 329, 343

Fuller, Thomas (1654–1734), 22, 70, 75, 82, 97, 109, 136, 137, 145, 153, 168, 179, 185, 188, 189, 194, 196, 204, 205, 206, 207, 245, 264, 278, 319, 342, 356, 365

Gay, John, 168, 242

Genlis, Stéphanie Félicité Brulart de Sillery, Comtesse de, 92

George, Daniel, 118

Geyl, Pieter, 325

Gibbon, Edward, 27

Gide, André, 1, 18, 65, 292, 298, 318, 353

Gissing, George, 101, 250

Glanvill, Joseph, 230

Goethe, Johann Wolfgang von, 3, 5, 7, 22, 29, 36, 46, 47, 48, 50, 55, 64, 79, 81, 91, 99, 140, 184, 199, 205, 226, 254, 260, 262, 271, 287, 290, 291, 294, 300, 304, 306, 310, 315, 319, 335, 339, 340, 343, 344, 345, 348, 350

Goldsmith, Oliver, 156, 292, 329

Gombrich, E. H., 225, 231, 300

Goncourt, Edmond and Jules de, 50, 243, 288

Gorgias of Leontini, 278

Gourmont, Rémy de, 15, 43, 63, 111, 299, 310

Gracián, Baltasar, 1, 58, 87, 91, 92, 94, 98, 127, 128, 131, 132, 138, 141, 169, 179, 205, 209, 210, 212, 218, 247, 249, 250, 273, 278, 327, 357

Grand, James, 145, 309

Gregory of Nyssa, St, 229

Greville, Richard Fulke, 198, 244, 247

Guedalla, Philip, 286, 308, 324

Guinon, Albert, 77, 208, 261, 306

Guitry, Sacha, 63, 151, 225, 277

Gyp (Sybil Gabrielle de Mirabeau, Comtesse de Martel de Janville), 79

Haldane, J. B. S., 3

Halifax, George Savile, 1st Marquess of, 41, 61, 64, 77, 82, 83, 87, 90, 95, 107, 109, 116, 126, 127, 128, 137, 140, 141, 143, 175, 186, 194, 199, 203, 205, 207, 211, 215, 219, 243, 244, 245, 247, 258, 260, 264, 267, 274, 285

Hall, Joseph, Bishop, 342

Hammarskjöld, Dag, 165

Harding, D. W., 212, 297

Hardy, Thomas, 10, 21, 30, 39, 115, 155, 170, 210, 214, 297, 303, 307

Hare, Augustus, 222, 282

Hare, Julius, 59, 95, 207, 243

Harris, Joel Chandler, 263

Hawthorne, Nathaniel, 18, 143, 159, 183, 280, 315, 362

Haydon, Benjamin Robert, 2

Hazlitt, William, 35, 36, 38, 39, 42, 50, 52, 67, 68, 70, 82, 123, 127, 129, 141, 142, 143, 182, 187, 188, 193, 196, 197, 206, 208, 213, 214, 222, 223, 246, 259, 260, 268, 271, 276, 278, 281, 283, 309, 310, 312, 314, 316, 321, 324, 346, 356

Hecht, Ben, 360

Hegel, Georg Wilhelm Friedrich, 316

Heine, Heinrich, 4, 15, 171, 285, 301, 323, 363

Helps, Sir Arthur, 67, 70, 85, 89, 94, 141, 218, 222, 245, 295, 339

Helvétius, Claude-Adrien, 189

Heraclitus, 28, 37, 44, 110, 347

Herbert, George, 145, 168

Herford, Oliver, 287

Hesiod, 142

Hesse, Hermann, 48, 166, 168, 245

Hobbes, John Oliver (Pearl Craigie), 91, 169

Hobbes, Thomas, 25, 39, 113, 143, 168, 203, 257, 271, 276, 278, 283

Hoffer, Eric, 78, 117, 202

Hofmannsthal, Hugo von, 52, 66, 119, 134, 136, 158, 211, 230, 265, 301, 340, 342

Holmes, Oliver Wendell, sen., 28, 47, 230, 248

Holmes, Oliver Wendell, jun., 231

Hooker, Richard, 120, 300

Hope, Anthony, 315

Hopkins, Gerard Manley, 12, 54

Horace, 75, 282, 356

Houellé, 155

Howe, E. W., 201

Howells, William Dean, 349

Hubbard, Frank McKinney ('Kin'), 7, 102, 300

Hugo, Victor, 128, 133, 170, 193

Hulme, T. E., 280

Hume, David, 34, 42, 60, 71, 74, 84, 113,

115, 119, 142, 144, 169, 178, 179, 233, 236

Huxley, Aldous, 26, 56, 117, 119, 130, 232, 280, 293, 309, 350

Huxley, Thomas Henry, 7, 58, 235, 254, 270

Ibn Gabirol, Solomon, 210, 212, 216, 240, 305, 348

Inge, W. R., Dean, 18, 63, 122, 141, 166, 256, 333

Issa, Kobayashi, 8, 25

Jackson, Holbrook, 287

James, Alice, 172, 341

James, Henry, 295, 305, 306, 330

James, William, 4, 27, 28, 31, 42, 64, 72, 166, 168, 176, 183, 229, 238, 240, 248, 284, 306, 316, 331, 344

Jarrell, Randall, 105, 288, 291, 305, 307, 308, 319, 335

Jerome, Jerome K., 62, 102, 173

Johnson, Samuel, 33, 34, 37, 39, 40, 44, 58, 59, 62, 65, 70, 74, 80, 85, 88, 96, 97, 99, 104, 106, 108, 110, 111, 113, 117, 122, 124, 127, 128, 130, 133, 142, 147, 148, 160, 167, 168, 169, 176, 178, 182, 191, 192, 193, 194, 196, 197, 200, 201, 203, 204, 208, 212, 217, 219, 221, 222, 224, 225, 226, 229, 245, 246, 250, 251, 256, 261, 263, 264, 275, 277, 282, 283, 293, 306, 307, 311, 317, 331, 333, 335, 341, 344, 346, 347, 349, 357, 364

Jonson, Ben, 70, 86, 137, 157, 177, 233, 243, 256, 257, 260, 278, 280, 282, 308, 336

Joubert, Joseph, 88, 111, 120, 126, 194, 228, 232–3, 255, 261, 267, 270, 283, 286, 292, 303, 312, 338, 364

Jowett, Benjamin, 100

Joyce, James, 278, 353

Jung, Carl Gustav, 19, 48, 51, 56, 68, 71, 83, 182, 196, 256, 297, 334, 335, 357

Kafka, Franz, 14, 36, 44, 58, 83, 99, 138, 181

Keats, John, 22, 45, 58, 98, 138, 170, 179, 200, 234, 298, 332, 338, 349, 362

Kenko, Yoshida, see Yoshida Kenko

Keynes, John Maynard, Baron, 108, 109, 116

Kierkegaard, Sören, 18, 135, 254, 256, 330, 338

Kingsmill, Hugh, 123

Kipling, Rudyard, 146

Koretser Rabbi, The, 12, 177

Kraus, Karl, 124, 146, 152, 162, 265, 290

Labiche, Eugène, 224, 352

La Bruyère, Jean de, 16, 17, 34, 40, 73, 85, 87, 88, 89, 90, 91, 101, 105, 106, 107, 108, 121, 127, 128, 130, 131, 135, 142, 153, 155, 158, 159, 163, 164, 168, 183, 186, 188, 190, 213, 215, 242, 244, 272, 309, 317, 331, 332, 341, 355

La Fayette, Marie Madeleine Motier, Comtesse de, 339

La Grange, A. E. Lelièvre, Marquis de, 73, 74

Lamartine, Alphonse de, 35, 117

Lamb, Charles, 169, 194, 241, 246, 294, 326

Landor, Walter Savage, 24, 122, 277, 298

Landowska, Wanda, 296

Langland, William, 203

La Rochefoucauld, François, Duc de, 20, 38, 51, 54, 59, 60, 67, 73, 88, 90, 99, 103, 114, 133, 134, 142, 144, 149, 157, 162, 165, 173, 178, 181, 187, 189, 192, 202, 206, 209, 213, 220, 240, 241, 244, 248, 261, 316, 327, 340, 343

La Sablière, Marguerite de, 38

Lawrence, D. H., 4, 5, 21, 36, 50, 51, 82, 160, 198, 241, 263, 265, 299, 360

Lear, Edward, 353

Le Bon, Gustave, 196

Lec, Stanislaw, 78, 112, 121, 260, 262

Leiris, Michel, 359

Leonardo da Vinci, 355

Leopardi, Giacomo, Count, 60, 82, 84, 87, 97, 142, 172, 180, 188, 234, 264, 320, 323, 339, 341

Leverson, Ada, 159

Lewis, C. S., 275

Lichtenberg, Georg Christoph, 4, 6, 10, 13, 20, 22, 23, 29, 31, 52, 60, 77, 78, 98, 141, 148, 175, 192, 228, 232, 234, 235, 237, 243, 245, 250, 259, 262, 266, 268, 281, 284, 285, 287, 291, 295, 313, 315, 317, 321, 333

Ligne, Charles-Joseph, Prince de, 2, 81, 192, 208, 320

Livy, 127

Lowell, James Russell, 58

Lucian, 346

Luther, Martin, 11

Macaulay, Dame Rose, 23, 274
Macaulay, Thomas Babington, Baron, 228, 295
MacCarthy, Sir Desmond, 307, 308, 316
McCarthy, Mary, 44, 84, 188, 230
Macdonald, Dwight, 113
Machiavelli, Niccolò, 94, 97, 122, 124
Mac Orlan, Pierre, 351
Maginn, William, 135, 330, 331
Mailer, Norman, 32, 112, 288, 365
Maistre, Joseph de, 53
Malesherbes, Chrétien de, 1
Mallet, Robert, 55, 68, 152, 154
Mandeville, Bernard, 17
Mann, Thomas, 358, 360
Manning, Henry Edward, Cardinal, 305
Marcus Aurelius, 3, 7, 8, 27, 42, 66, 72, 85, 136, 139, 145, 173, 174, 175, 190, 194, 195, 206, 219, 344, 346, 347
Marguerite de Valois, 278
Marivaux, Pierre de, 159, 170
Marquis, Don, 103, 224, 271, 318
Martin Du Gard, Maurice, 248
Masters, Edgar Lee, 32
Maugham, W. Somerset, 79, 220
Maupassant, Guy de, 30, 49, 291
Maurois, André, 277
Melbourne, William Lamb, 2nd Viscount, 285
Melville, Herman, 107, 230
Mencius, 171, 191, 317, 356
Mencken, H. L., 16, 96, 134, 150, 191, 198, 234
Mendel of Kotzk, 12
Meredith, George, 150, 273
Mill, John Stuart, 118, 121, 235, 253, 257, 258
Molière, Jean Baptiste Poquelin de, 178
Montague, C. E., 124
Montaigne, Michel de, 11, 13, 24, 37, 41, 51, 54, 67, 69, 103, 123, 161, 162, 170, 172, 174, 191, 201, 222, 249, 253, 254, 265, 267, 280, 285, 309, 311, 342, 343, 344, 353, 358
Montesquieu, Charles, Baron de, 16, 92, 110, 117, 122, 169, 173, 185, 187, 205, 248, 269, 276, 289, 315, 352
Montherlant, Henry de, 14, 35, 47, 54, 55, 153, 156, 157, 161, 185, 234, 239, 301, 324, 332, 357

Moore, Marianne, 196, 197
Morgenstern, Christian, 289
Morley, John, Viscount, 175, 250, 259, 362
Morton, J. B., see Beachcomber
Mumford, Lewis, 321
Munro, H. H., see Saki
Musil, Robert, 58

Nachman of Bratislav, 292
Namier, Sir Lewis, 16, 113, 116, 119, 236, 322
Napoleon I (Bonaparte), 11, 91, 121, 122, 124, 202, 361
Newman, John Henry, Cardinal, 13, 140, 220, 258
Nicole, Pierre, 225
Nietzsche, Friedrich Wilhelm, 1, 17, 18, 20, 34, 37, 45, 54, 56, 64, 66, 69, 73, 74, 75, 76, 110, 112, 119, 124, 128, 137, 141, 144, 145, 173, 202, 210, 220, 223, 226, 230, 234, 236, 237, 238, 251, 253, 255, 258, 259, 261, 268, 270, 273, 282, 297, 302, 307, 310, 311, 324, 325, 334, 338
Nodier, Charles, 70
Norris, John, 232
Novalis (Baron Friedrich von Hardenberg), 259, 297

Ortega y Gasset, José, 121, 348
Orwell, George, 104, 122, 123, 124, 125, 132, 197, 250, 255, 279, 286, 308, 319, 339
Ouida (Louise de la Ramée), 144
Ovid, 157, 159, 163, 189
Oxenstierna, Axel, Count, 341

Paine, Tom, 349
Paley, William, 232
Palladas, 102, 223, 355
Pascal, Blaise, 11, 20, 24, 25, 26, 27, 44, 52, 86, 99, 139, 169, 171, 172, 191, 193, 229, 238, 247, 251, 260, 276, 290, 311, 343, 359, 365
Passmore, John, 118, 178, 346
Pasteur, Louis, 204
Patmore, Coventry, 159
Pavese, Cesare, 19, 41, 48, 49, 55, 65, 68, 69, 79, 138, 148, 155, 164, 213, 272, 338
Peacock, Thomas Love, 102, 147

Péguy, Charles, 322
Peirce, Charles Sanders, 3, 4, 6, 225, 229, 236, 237, 239, 248, 348
Penn, William, 16, 262
Petit, Henri, 105
Philippe, Charles-Louis, 351
Pigott, Charles, 120
Pinero, Sir Arthur Wing, 95
Pliny the Elder, 5, 10
Pliny the Younger, 183
Poe, Edgar Allan, 298
Pope, Alexander, 26, 31, 39, 42, 102, 104, 159, 187, 215, 233, 249, 251, 268, 329, 342, 353, 364
Porter, Peter, 50, 102, 273
Potts, Paul, 77
Pound, Ezra, 287
Powell, Anthony, 65
Préault, Auguste, 83
Priestley, Joseph, 270
Pritchett, Sir Victor S., 57, 296
Protagoras of Abdera, 20
Proust, Marcel, 45, 55, 57, 59, 92, 98, 154, 156, 157, 158, 162, 163, 164, 192, 219, 222, 227, 230, 249, 258, 260, 272, 284, 297, 299, 303, 320, 352, 360, 363
Publilius Syrus, 31, 42, 170, 180, 214
Pushkin, Alexander, 242, 281, 298

Rabbinic sayings, 28, 336
Rabelais, François, 279
Raleigh, Sir Walter (1861–1922), 269
Renard, Jules, 10, 63, 79, 80, 99, 107, 108, 192, 212, 233, 273, 274, 277, 289, 293, 302, 309, 314, 352, 362, 363
Repplier, Agnes, 276
Retz, Jean François Paul de Gondi, Cardinal de, 30, 92, 115, 131, 186, 314, 317
Reverdy, Pierre, 61
Richter, Jean Paul, 276
Ricks, Christopher, 215
Rigaut, Jacques, 363
Rilke, Rainer Maria, 241, 273
Rivarol, Antoine de, 26, 189, 277, 307, 310
Rojas, Fernando de, 246
Rosenberg, Harold, 52, 232, 291, 294, 303, 305
Rosenzweig, Franz, 12, 15, 45
Rostand, Jean, 2, 69, 70, 89, 90, 113, 137, 143, 149, 150, 164, 183, 189, 192, 223, 233, 257, 295, 305, 322
Rourke, Constance, 279
Rousseau, Jean-Jacques, 238
Roux, Joseph, 1
Rowland, Helen, 147, 151, 159, 330
Rozanov, V. V., 19, 303
Ruskin, John, 108, 302, 356
Russell, Bertrand, 4, 23, 86, 119, 195, 200, 253, 257, 260, 312, 342
Rutherford, Mark (William Hale White), 4, 31, 33, 79, 97, 140, 166, 176, 251, 261, 358

Sacks, Oliver, 326, 328
Sa'di, 42
Saint-Evremond, Charles de, 164
Sainte-Beuve, Charles-Augustin, 37, 87
Saintsbury, George, 331
Saki (H. H. Munro), 120, 146, 193, 268, 334
Salacrou, Armand, 324
Sand, George, 30, 228
Santayana, George, 10, 29, 49, 64, 72, 97, 253, 259, 350, 355, 363
Schopenhauer, Arthur, 5, 14, 21, 29, 35, 40, 44, 48, 51, 54, 59, 77, 82, 86, 123, 136, 139, 140, 160, 179, 190, 203, 209, 210, 211, 212, 215, 221, 224, 231, 243, 248, 250, 251, 268, 272, 288, 289, 321, 338, 339, 342, 344, 345, 348, 350, 360, 363
Schumann, Robert, 296
Scudéry, Madeleine de, 153, 154, 158
Scott, Sir Walter, 75
Sei Shonagon, 138, 351
Selden, John, 17, 18, 62, 91, 101, 126, 147, 196, 206, 264, 265, 280
Senal, Jean, 171
Seneca, 13, 33, 43, 80, 109, 112, 131, 172, 187, 195, 216, 253, 355, 356, 363
Sévigné, Marie de Rabutin-Chantal, Marquise de, 134, 136
Shaftesbury, Anthony Ashley Cooper, 3rd Earl of, 76, 277
Shakespeare, William, 63, 89, 128, 160, 170, 244, 279, 300, 350, 354, 359
Shaw, George Bernard, 55, 93, 109, 111, 120, 123, 125, 145, 167, 177, 188, 190, 197, 210, 217, 257, 279, 314, 321, 327, 330, 345
Shelley, Mary, 146

Shenstone, William, 43, 76, 101, 198, 278, 291, 293, 298, 326, 332
Sheridan, Richard Brinsley, 2, 308
Sherrington, Sir Charles, 5, 6, 7, 8, 28, 50, 170, 171, 174, 178, 237
Shestov, Leo, 11, 63, 76, 257, 258, 259
Shih-T'ao, 296
Shmelke of Nickelsburg, Rabbi, 199
Siegfried, André, 202
Simeon ben Eleazar, Rabbi, 135
Simonides, 144
Sinyavsky, Andrey, 30, 273
Smith, Adam, 95, 103
Smith, Logan Pearsall, 79, 87, 92, 98, 263, 293, 330, 333, 341, 342, 343
Smith, Stevie, 30, 198
Smith, Sydney, 8, 75, 86, 109, 111, 133, 145, 167, 194, 197, 199, 240, 262, 289, 345, 353, 354, 358
Solon, 172
Sophocles, 40
South, Robert, 283
Spence, Joseph, 167
Spinoza, Baruch (or Benedict), 24, 33, 40, 75, 78, 89, 267, 300, 356, 362
Spooner, William Archibald, 269
Staël, Madame de, 276
Stein, Gertrude, 2
Stendhal (Marie-Henri Beyle), 78, 87, 111, 126, 155, 158, 163, 278, 313, 335
Stephens, James, 229
Sterne, Laurence, 249
Stevens, Wallace, 294, 299, 306
Stevenson, Robert Louis, 33, 46, 47, 60, 146, 169, 198, 222, 223, 229, 243, 322, 335, 355
Strachey, Lytton, 323
Stravinsky, Igor, 296
Svevo, Italo, 29, 182
Swift, Jonathan, 29, 61, 80, 89, 92, 107, 123, 130, 149, 180, 201, 214, 218, 219, 238, 249, 279, 290, 291, 324, 333, 348
Szasz, Thomas, 58, 77, 88, 150, 161, 228, 327, 328, 336, 339

Tacitus, 180, 205
Tagore, Sir Rabindranath, 13, 23, 57, 61, 99, 175, 180, 197, 227, 228
Talleyrand-Périgord, Charles Maurice, Prince de, 135
Talmud, The, 13, 172
Tasso, Torquato, 153

Tawney, R. H., 110, 321
Taylor, Sir Henry, 57, 61, 84, 93, 97, 129, 131, 141, 209, 216, 314
Terence, 157
Theophrastus, 153
Thomas à Kempis, 13, 175, 349
Thomas, Dylan, 71
Thomas, Lewis, 80, 231, 351
Thoreau, Henry David, 1, 2, 15, 21, 45, 47, 50, 52, 59, 69, 80, 129, 133, 164, 177, 193, 211, 241, 252, 280, 282, 290, 292, 294, 295, 300, 310, 314, 319, 326, 348, 364, 365
Thurber, James, 118, 149
Tillotson, John, 10
Tocqueville, Alexis de, 116, 118
Tolstoy, Leo, 111
Tournier, Achille, 118, 151
Traherne, Thomas, 250
Trilling, Lionel, 118, 207, 233, 302, 328
Trollope, Anthony, 26, 215
Trotsky, Leon, 341
'Tut-tut, Mr', 90, 92, 188, 246, 248
Twain, Mark, 22, 25, 65, 135, 149, 184, 191, 201, 211, 218, 221, 225, 279, 280

Unamuno, Miguel de, 7, 14, 259, 360, 363
Updike, John, 161

Valéry, Paul, 15, 19, 29, 36, 56, 57, 73, 75, 116, 126, 138, 146, 155, 168, 175, 177, 181, 204, 232, 274, 291, 327, 329, 362
Vanbrugh, Sir John, 162, 164
Vapereau, Gustave, 356
Vauvenargues, Luc de Clapiers, Marquis de, 1, 24, 31, 40, 43, 46, 56, 60, 62, 64, 65, 69, 74, 75, 77, 88, 96, 97, 99, 115, 118, 127, 128, 132, 135, 138, 162, 166, 167, 177, 181, 182, 185, 191, 192, 194, 210, 215, 218, 228, 230, 231, 244, 264, 267, 312, 315, 316, 317, 333, 358, 364
Veblen, Thorstein, 112
Vigny, Alfred de, 155
Voltaire, François Marie Arouet de, 11, 25, 26, 64, 117, 134, 139, 171, 183, 190, 201, 204, 208, 223, 296, 320, 329, 330

Ward, Mrs Humphry, 351
Waugh, Evelyn, 346

Weinreich, Max, 346
Wellington, Arthur Wellesley, 1st Duke of, 332
Wells, H. G., 91
West, Dame Rebecca, 123
Whateley, Richard, Archbishop, 25, 57
Whichcote, Benjamin, 28, 62, 129, 275, 315, 362, 363
Whistler, James McNeill, 297
Whitehead, Alfred North, 5, 321
Wilde, Oscar, 20, 52, 57, 60, 65, 111, 150, 151, 153, 163, 184, 190, 251, 269, 283, 287, 330, 339, 343, 351
Wilson, Thomas, Bishop, 167, 184
Winnicott, D. W., 29, 327, 334, 336

Woolf, Virginia, 28, 51, 72, 146, 301, 324
Wordsworth, William, 41, 42, 175, 181, 255, 301, 360
Wycherley, William, 158

Xenophanes, 10

Yeats, W. B., 14, 57, 68, 117, 290, 347
Yoshida Kenko, 35, 167, 220, 283, 311, 347, 348

Zeno of Citium, 166
Zohar, The, 41, 157, 201